JEANNE CRUMLEY

Carl A. Rudisill Library

WITHDRAWN
L. R. COLLEGE LIBRARY

A

SEVENTEENTH-CENTURY ORGAN LITERATURE

WITHDRAWN
L. R. COLLEGE LIBRARY

ORGAN LITERATURE OF THE SEVENTEENTH CENTURY

A STUDY OF ITS STYLES

BY

JOHN R. SHANNON

AT THE SUNBURY

RALEIGH

1978

CARL A. RUDISILL LIBRARY
LENOIR-RHYNE UNIVERSITY

Copyright © 1978 by The Sunbury Press.

All rights reserved. This book may not be reproduced in whole or in part (except for reviewers for the public press) without written permission from the publisher.

Library of Congress Cataloging in Publication Data

Shannon, John R.
Organ literature of the seventeenth century.

"A selected bibliography of editions of seventeenth-century organ literature": p.

Includes bibliographical references and index.

1. Organ music — History and criticism.
2. Music — History and criticism — 17th century.

I. Title.
ML604.S5 786.8'09'032 78-1581
ISBN O-915548-06-2

ML
604
.S5
1978

$74.99

Printed for The Sunbury by Bynum Printing Company, Raleigh

June 2011

CARL A. RUDISILL LIBRARY
LENOIR-RHYNE UNIVERSITY

TO

Fenner Douglass

whose support in ways both tangible and intangible,
both as a teacher and as a friend,
has been for this study and my work infinitely valuable.

Permissions to Reprint

The author would like to thank the many publishers who granted permission for the quotation of musical examples. He would particularly like to thank The American Institute of Musicology and its director, Dr. Armen Carapetyan, for the many citations from the *Corpus of Early Keyboard Music.* Certain publishers requested that specific information relative to republication of materials be cited. These are listed below cued to the numbering of the musical examples:

I - 1, 2, 3: Copyright © 1959 by B. Schott's Söhne. Used by permission. All rights reserved.

I - 18, 19: Copyright © by G. Ricordi and Company, Milan. By kind permission of G. Ricordi and Company, S.P.A.

III - 3, 4, 5, 6, 12, 14, 21, 29, 30: Copyright 1967 by B. Schott's Söhne. Used by permission. All rights reserved.

III - 11, 17, 24, 27: Copyright © 1969 by B. Schott's Söhne. Used by permission. All rights reserved.

III-12, III-14, III-21, and II -30: Copyright © 1967 by B. Schott's Söhne. Used by permission. All rights reserved.

III-29: Copyright © 1967 by B. Schott's Söhne. Used by permission. All rights reserved.

III - 19: Permission to reprint, Broude Brothers, Limited.

IV - 8, 9, 15: Permission to reprint, Novello and Co., Limited.

IV - 17, 18, 19: Copyright © 1958, 1972 by Schott and Company, Ltd. Used by permission. All rights reserved.

V-18: Permission to reprint, Associated Music Publishers.

VI-52: Copyright © 1939 by Henry Litolff's Verlag. Reprint permission granted by the publisher.

VII - 26, 28, 29: Copyright © 1973 by Henry Litolff's Verlag. Reprint permission granted by the publisher.

VII-35: Copyright © 1951 by C. F. Peters. Reprint permission granted by the publisher.

Table of Contents

CONTENTS

CONTENTS

CONTENTS

PREFACE

During the last decade there has been a sudden blossoming of interest in many facets of early music. The seed of this interest has been with us for many years, but its ripening in the general musical culture is a very recent event. In the past, interest in works written before Bach had occurred largely on the periphery of the musical world. Occasionally concert performers cast condescending glances at this great wealth of music. A singer might have opened a recital with a heavily romanticized rendition of a Caccini aria, a pianist might have done the ultimate injustice to an *ordre* of Couperin by removing it from the harpsichord; and even the great works of Bach and Handel, which had become a part of the general musical tradition, have been commonly performed in such distorted versions that their real musical meaning could hardly surface. That Baroque music could survive the application of the heavy forces of late Romantic musical practice is a tribute to the vitality of the music itself.

Recently these attitudes have been rapidly changing. Performers, both at the professional and amateur levels, are playing old music to larger and larger audiences. In the colleges and universities the study of this music has passed from the music history classroom and the musicology seminar to live performances particularly by the many *collegia musica* which have recently been founded on many campuses. The conflict, which many of us had felt in the past, between the musicologist and the performer, is now dying. Neither side in this needless battle has been free of guilt. Often in rendering their finds to the larger musical world, the musicologists insisted on editorial practices that made the music hardly more intelligible than it had been in its original state. Clefs which were no longer in general musical use and mensural values which distorted for modern eyes the true movement of the music made the score a hindrance to those it was intended to serve. On the other hand, the failure of the performer lay in his unwillingness to modify his conceptions of performance in light of information provided him by the musicologist. That a real divorce rather than a secure marriage existed between the two sides lay in the widely held notion that musicology belonged in the university, performance in the conservatory. At a recent national meeting of the American Musicological Society some of the most exciting events were sessions chaired by performers of old music and concerts by a number of university *collegia.* Truly an old order is changing for the better.

The many studies of old instruments, the restoration of extant ones, and the production of new instruments based on our new-found knowledge of the past are also most encouraging. The study of performance practices has provided the interested musician a wealth of material to aid him in performing the music as its composers intended. At one time a performance which sought a firm foundation in historical procedures would have been lampooned as affected, lifeless, and unmusical. Now such performances are being recognized for the integrity they represent, and performances without such considerations are subject to legitimate criticism.

There now exists a need, particularly at the undergraduate level of instruction, to provide guidelines for the study of music of the past. Much material is obviously available to the student who has the disposition to seek it out himself. However, in many schools the library resources he may find are limited, and without guideance he may find the search difficult. It is as such a guide to the organ literature of the seventeenth century that this volume is written. This book will trace the gradual development of keyboard styles as they appear, somewhat haltingly, in the early sixteenth century until they mature as the full-grown national styles of the late seventeenth century. The study will aim to define as clearly as possible the various elements of these styles as they relate particularly to organ literature, the ways these elements came into being, the ways they interlock to form distinctively national styles, and the ways these national styles embrace one another.

The reader should be equally aware of the areas of study this book does not discuss. The area of performance practices is avoided almost completely, and no mention is made of the disposition of old organs, except in the case of France, where such an omission would threaten the understanding of her national style. Many studies of both areas are readily available, and to have approached them here would have been unnecessary and would have compromised the general intent of the work. Some composers, such as Michael Praetorius and Christian Erbach, who would certainly merit discussion in a comprehensive study, are intentionally omitted because their work largely reflects the accomplishments of others. One paramount consideration in selection of the material to be covered has been the availability of performance scores of the music itself. In almost all cases material which is easily obtainable has been selected for discussion. Fortunately, so much literature for the organ from this century is now in print that an accurate picture can be drawn largely from these sources alone. Only rarely has material which remains in manuscript been mentioned here and then only for a special purpose.

For a more comprehensive study of the general keyboard literature of the seventeenth century the student is directed to Willi Apel's monumental work, *The History of Keyboard Music to 1700.*[1] I would be less than honest if I did not acknowledge in the beginning my debt to this volume in particular and to Apel's many other studies of early keyboard music. His general editorship of the *Corpus of Early Keyboard Music*[2] has provided many sources of lesser known literature upon which this book relies. It would be practically impossible to undertake any work in the field of seventeenth-century keyboard literature without borrowing in some ways from its most distinguished scholar. I hope such borrowings in the present volume, some certainly unconscious and others as carefully cited as possible, will stand in the tradition of the parody masses of the Renaissance. For a young composer to draw from an esteemed elder was taken as a honor to him and not as a theft from him.

The absence of a general bibliography in a work of this type needs some explanation. In writing the book, I have relied so com-

[1] Willi Apel, *The History of Keyboard Music to 1700*, translated and revised by Hans Tischler, Bloomington: The University of Indiana Press, 1972. (The work originally appeared in German. Tischler's work is more than a translation. Particularly important updating of the bibliographical sources was made.) Hereafter this work is cited as *Apel K.*

[2] Willi Apel, general editor, *The Corpus of Early Keyboard Music,* The American Institute of Musicology, presently 39 volumes and others are in progress. Hereafter the series is cited as *CEKM.*

pletely upon the musical scores themselves, that few citations from other materials were necessary. These have been made in appropriate references in the text itself. Again it would be impossible to improve upon the bibliographical work contained in *The History of Keyboard Music,* and the student is directed there for further material on nearly every subject in the field. I hope, however, that the annotated bibliography of performing editions which concludes this volume will be a ready help to the student in acquiring his own library of this literature.

I must express my thanks to the libraries of the University of North Carolina at Chapel Hill and Oberlin College for assistance in many ways in the research for this book. The Faculty Research Committee of Sweet Briar College and the Maurice L. Mednick Memorial Fund provided much-needed financial assistance at several points in the study. The College also provided a sabbatical leave which enabled me to begin this work. I am indebted to Dr. William S. Newman of the University of North Carolina faculty and to my colleagues, Mr. Allen Huszti and Dr. Jane Perry Camp, for their kindness in reading portions of the manuscript and providing valuable suggestions. My students, particularly Miss Sara Ruhle and Miss Clarissa Nielsen, also have been very helpful in their careful and critical proofing of various drafts. Miss Carol Newman undertook the difficult task of preparing the musical examples. Finally I heartily thank Richard Parsons of the Sunbury Press for his interest and support in this project. One wishes that more members of the publishing trade would evidence such concern for areas of scholarship which from the economic point of view are less than enticing.

John R. Shannon
Sweet Briar College
October 1976.

Introduction

The study of music of the seventeenth century has generally labored under a series of difficulties which should be clearly defined before we begin. The first of these is the concept that the music of the period is transitional in nature; that it lies between the matured styles of the sixteenth and eighteenth centuries; and that, as such, the music has little vitality of its own. The music of the century has been often studied less for its intrinsic merit than for the light that it might shed on the style of the late Baroque. The century has been regarded as a period in which composers felt the decay of their immediate heritage, on the one hand, and sought, on the other hand, to replace this heritage with a largely experimental music. This view derives from an evolutionary view of music, which sees the efforts of one generation become the basis for the work of the next. Implicit in this view, however, is a perhaps subconscious value judgment that automatically assigns greater value to works created by composers operating in a matured style and regards periods in which composers seek varied, perhaps highly individual answers to musical questions as periods of lesser artistic merit. Despite the lip-service paid so frequently to Monteverdi, Schütz, Frescobaldi, Buxtehude, and others, it is a fact that these composers carry the rather patronizing label of pre-Bach composers. Their individual genius is too rarely attested to, and their creations are so often viewed with eyes for things to come.

To some degree this evolutionary approach to music of the seventeenth century is partially explained by the zeal with which some writers have proposed to defend the integrity of the concept of the Baroque. Keller expresses this view concisely when he states, "When we examine the history of music we find that in it, too, the Baroque is more homogeneous and self-contained than any other musical period. The thorough-bass period coincides amazingly with the limits of the Baroque."[1] Given this bias it is easy to espouse a

[1] Hermann Keller, *The Organ Works of Bach,* trans. Helen Hewitt, New York: C. F. Peters, 1967, 11.

view of the period which would see Baroque music grow from the tentative, tottering steps of early seventeenth-century composers to the massive self-assured strides of Bach and Handel. In fact the matter of the homogeneity of the Baroque is open to challenge, and it is certainly easier to view Bach and Handel as essentially eighteenth-century composers than late-blooming seventeenth-century ones.

Another impediment to this study is the lack of one clear international musical language spoken by even a majority of seventeenth-century composers. It would be fair to assert that in this century there are distinct national musical languages with many cognate relationships existing among them. In both the sixteenth and eighteenth centuries, on the other hand, one finds universal musical languages with very discernable musical dialects within each. Moreover, the lack of one accepted international language in the seventeenth century did lead, on the part of some composers, to highly individual modes of expression. The work of Frescobaldi is a case in point. Much of his music is so intensely personal that it bears little similarity to that of his predecessors, contemporaries, or followers. Moreover, the multiplicity of possible styles can lead a composer to change rapidly from one musical frame of reference to another even within the same composition. For instance, it is possible to trace within a single chorale fantasia of a North-German composer distinct borrowings from English, Dutch, Italian, South-German and Middle-German traditions. While the diversity can be very baffling for the uninitiated, it is certainly one of the great strengths of the music of the century. The very variety, which no doubt poses a hindrance to the beginner, provides endless fascination after one has mastered the many linguistic distinctions.

A final difficulty in understanding seventeenth-century music is related to a basic difference which exists between seventeenth- and eighteenth-century concepts of formal organization. The eighteenth-century composer had available to him the expanded implications of tonal harmony allowing modulation to closely related keys. The resulting freedom allowed him to construct individual movements of some length without sacrifice of interest or the risk of tonal boredom. In a very real sense the history of the eighteenth-century form is involved with these implications of tonality. Lacking the tonal means whereby a single thematic idea could be presented and extensively developed without tiring the ear, the seventeenth-century composer tended to rely on a technique of sectional composition. In an initial section his ideas could be presented; to a limited degree amplified; and then contrasted with other sections differing in mood, meter, and even thematic material. While we are all conditioned to the organizations of the eighteenth-century composer, the subtleties of seventeenth-century formal patterns can easily escape us. Few of us have difficulties in appreciating the complex working-out of a single theme in a Bach fugue. The equally fascinating means by which Buxtehude contrasts one short section with its neighbors is more easily missed. Traditional views of form have centered on the relatively static concepts of late eighteenth-century music. These views contrast strikingly with the dynamic and even rhapsodic concepts of formal order held by many of the great composers of the seventeenth century. A real impediment to the appreciation of this music exists when the student seeks to find what is not there, and fails to appreciate the less tangible, but very real, structural relationships which do exist. The predominant concern given to formal and structural problems in this volume reflects the author's view of their importance in understanding the music itself. It is, however, not the eighteenth century concept of formal design superimposed upon musical material, but formal design as it emerges from grappling with the problems of keyboard expression within the context of a nascent tonality. Since early seventeenth-century styles are a direct outgrowth of the Renaissance accomplishments in keyboard music, we will begin our study with a survey of organ music in the sixteenth century.

CHAPTER I.

Organ Music in the Late Renaissance

The musical environment in which we have lived since the eighteenth century has left us with a bias in favor of instrumental music. For the most part early musical training has been directed toward keyboard practice; our musical vocabulary is largely instrumentally oriented; and, for the most part, it is difficult to think in terms of a musical practice which could be predominately vocal. Prior to the sixteenth century, instrumental music was a very minor part of the musical scene. Instruments of all kinds were used in the performance of vocal music, but a large body of music designed only for instrumental performance simply does not exist. Although instrumental music in general and keyboard music in particular appears in ever growing amounts throughout the sixteenth century, we must be very aware that such creations constituted a minor portion of the output of the major composers of the century. Of the four great masters of the late sixteenth century, Palestrina, Lassus, Vittoria, and Byrd, only the last left any significant instrumental music; and even with Byrd, keyboard works constitute the smaller part of his output. To the Renaissance musician, music did not stand as an art unto itself; it stood as a servant art to the master of word. The purpose of music lay in its almost mystical ability to illumine and make more vivid the images suggested by text, and it was only with some reservations that composers were willing to admit the validity of "concords of sweet sounds" alone.

Our first task will be to attempt to see how the few Renaissance musicians who undertook significant keyboard music viewed their situation and to see how they gradually wrought from an essentially vocal musical language an instrumental language which could be intelligible and meaningful in its own way. As we do this we will try to define the components of a purely instrumental vocabulary with particular emphasis on those elements which belong intrinsically to the keyboard. We must try to see how those concords of harmony, rhythm, and counterpoint, which were so marvelously expressive in sixteenth-century vocal polyphony, were modified to make them a satisfactory medium for textless music. And we must further define the elements of late Renaissance keyboard music which provide the foundation for the seventeenth-century composer.

I would like to suggest at the beginning some of the prerequisites of a successful keyboard language. In the first place, mere pleasing and harmonious sounds alone are unsatisfactory for any but the shortest of compositions. The ear soon demands some type of higher organization of sound beyond momentory sensuous pleasure; and, if it fails to receive this organization, boredom rapidly sets in. To a large degree, but by no means entirely, texts had served to fulfill this organization in vocal music, and in vocal music the composer could rely far more on the pleasantness of sweet sounds alone. It was necessary to devise more sophisticated structures to answer this need when text was no longer present.

In the second place, the purity which characterized contrapuntal vocal lines in the matured sixteenth-century style did not translate well into a keyboard idiom. It was necessary to modify this contrapuntal idiom so that the subtleties felt in the old could be effected in the new. This is not to suggest a radical departure from the procedures of vocal counterpoint, but to suggest a modification, particularly in use of motive, of the older idiom.

Thirdly, the merger of four elements, when grafted onto the older musical language, would produce the birth of the new one. These elements are: 1) significant motivic development, 2) thematic unity providing a basis for meaningful diversity by means of some type of variation, 3) development of new formal patterns depending upon repetition of previous material either as it first appeared or in variations, and 4) a new tonal vocabulary which allows harmonic progressions to move with an integrity of their own.

And finally we must not lose sight of the factor of keyboard virtuosity. The desire to display those features which were inherent to their instrument first appeared in the works of the sixteenth-century lutenists. The keyboardists were very quick to follow in their steps, and particularly in the Venetian and English schools technical display constitutes a vital part of the musical style. By modern standards we may judge the seemingly endless scales, trills, and turns somewhat boring; but we must remember these elements were new, their novelty immense, and the sixteenth-century listener must have been as fascinated with the playing of Merulo as the nineteenth-century listener was with that of Liszt.

A natural point of departure for the chapter would be the discussion of those forms, the *ricercar* and *canzone,* which depended upon vocal music for a model. We will first discuss these, and then we will turn to works of the toccata-type in which idiomatic keyboard writing plays the greatest part. We will then turn to the more conservative works based on *cantus firmus.* Finally we will devote time to a discussion of unique contributions of Spanish and English composers. Since the *ricercar* and *canzone* are Italian in conception and the toccata reaches its Renaissance height in the works of the Venetian composer, our study of these types will be essentially a study of Italian contributions. We will introduce German and French elements as necessary.

THE RICERCAR

The term *ricercar* appears first in compositions for the lute in which it applies to non-imitative pieces of the toccata class. In its first appearance in works for the keyboard, the *Recerchari, motetti, canzoni, Libro I* (1523) of Marco Antonio di Bologna, the elder Cavazzoni, it likewise applies to such works. Apel has shown[1] that the real meaning of the term is related to its English cognate "research", and that its use designated a composition which functioned as an essay on a musical problem. In other words this genre was one in which various aspects of keyboard writing could be explored, problems in style solved, and experimentation with new ideas or modifications of older ones undertaken. Throughout the Renaissance and the Baroque the form retained this learned seriousness, and it provided for the composer a format in which he could work out a given musical problem to his own satisfaction and to that of other serious musicians. It is often stated that the *ricercar* is the instrumental equivalent of the vocal motet. As Apel shows, this is only partially true. It was most natural that the sixteenth-century composers would apply in their study of new keyboard techniques the pervading imitation characteristic of the most serious vocal form, the motet. This occurs in the first keyboard volume published by the

1 Willi Apel, "The Early Development of the Organ Ricercar," *MD* III (1949), 147.

younger Cavazzoni (1543). However, from this beginning onward the composers modified their imitative technique in imaginative ways to accommodate the needs of their new idiom.

The solution to the problem of form in the motet had been a simple but highly effective one. The text, almost always biblical, frequently derived from the Psalter or the canticles, and generally well known, was divided into short but meaningful literary phrases. Each phrase served as the basis for a short polyphonic treatment, most frequently imitative and based on a single thematic idea. Since the text provided the essential unity, the continual presentation of new musical material presented no real problem. The music could, and in the best of the tradition always did, mirror the nature of the changing text quite exactly. Most texts lacked any repetitive literary patterns and hardly suggested repetitive musical ones in their settings. As unity lay in the literary element, the composer was largely left free of concern for extensive musical unity. Music elevated, intensified, ornamented, and refined the textual element; it did not serve to organize it. Quite simply if all voices were engaged in singing a single text, generally well known to the listeners in any event, the problem of large formal order was immediately solved.

Comprehension of music without text was, as the Renaissance composers seemed to have sensed from the beginning, a different problem altogether. A string of short points of imitation each based on a different thematic idea rapidly confused the listener. Beyond the contrapuntal interest of the moment there was little to make the material meaningful and nothing to provide opportunities for alteration, development, or repetition of material in the course of the composition. The motet structure as it stood needed radical modification if it were to be successful for music without text.

Such radical modification is, in fact, apparent in the four *ricercari* from Girolamo Cavazzoni's *Intavolatura cioe recercari, canzoni, himni, magnificati*[2] published in 1542. These remarkable pieces are no mere textless motets. Instead they show the composer's keen awareness of the problems inherent in adapting the techniques of the motet to keyboard compositions. When one compares these *ricercari* with typical motets of the period, the following striking

---

[2] Girolamo Cavazzoni, *Orgelwerke*, ed. Oscar Mischiati, 2 vols. Mainz: Schott's Söhne, 1961.

differences are apparent: 1) a reduction in the number of thematic elements and an attempt to unify diverse themes by subtle relationships existing among them, 2) much more thorough and lengthy working out of a single theme into a well-defined section often concluding with a decorated cadential passage, 3) the building of sections on motivic development of an idea suggested by one of the themes, and 4) the introduction of sections in contrasting meter based on a rhythmic variation of the initial theme. The means by which Cavazzoni relates one theme to the next is shown below by the three themes from the second *ricercar:*[3]

Mus. ex. I-1.

The thematic material derives from the simple ascending three notes encompassing the interval of a third. Particularly interesting is the development of the quarter-note figure suggested in theme A:

Mus. ex. I-2.
Cavazzoni: *Ricercar Secundo,* measures 45-50.

The last two *ricercari* achieve unification by presenting the theme in

[3] *Ibid.,* I, 6.

different meters. The theme with its variations in the fourth *ricercar* is:[4]

Mus. ex. I-3.

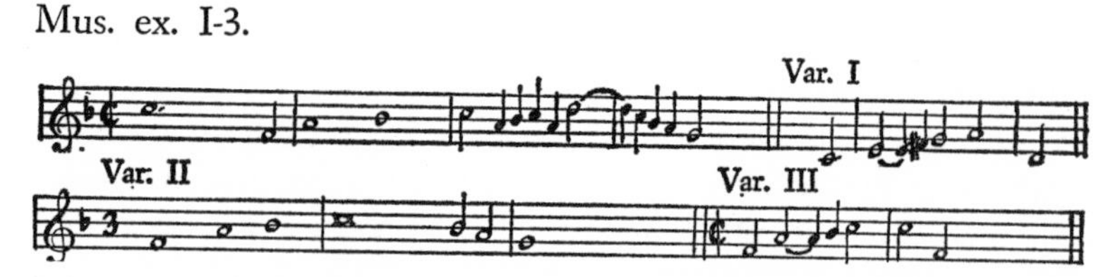

This principle of rhythmic variation of subject material, introduced by Cavazzoni for the first time, becomes very important in the works of both Italian and German composers of the seventeenth century.

The history of Italian organ music in the latter half of the century is centered in Venice with the works of the two Gabrielis, Merulo, Buus, and Padavano. Of these composers Andrea Gabrieli[5] devotes the largest effort to the *ricercar.* Since his keyboard works were published posthumously by his nephew, it is impossible to determine when the *ricercari* were written. Apel has suggested a date of about 1560.[6] The compositions do not appear to be uniform in quality or style, and there may have been a development which is now no longer possible to trace. In some examples Gabrieli seems willing to allow the stereotyped figuration typical of much music of the period to intrude into the serious texture of the *ricercar.* When this happens[7] there is a tendency for the music to degenerate into rather pointless technical display, a tendency we will again encounter in the writing of Merulo. In other examples, however, Gabrieli continues the tradition of Cavazzoni in serious compositions of considerable contrapuntal skill. Gabrieli further reduces the number of thematic elements he employs. Some *ricercari* are built on single themes. Those which are bi-thematic tend to derive their second theme from a bit of contrapuntal material introduced to accompany the initial theme. Gabrieli further refines the sectional structure of the form. Each section develops a specific contrapuntal idea and concludes with a well-articulated cadence very often made florid by

---

[4] *Ibid.,* I, 14; also in *HAM,* I, 121.

[5] Andrea Gabrieli, *Orgel und Klavierwerke,* ed. Pierre Pidoux, 5 vols., Kassel: Baerenreiter, 1952-1970.

[6] *Apel K,* 177.

[7] A good example of such a composition is the *Ricercar in the IXth Tone,* Gabrieli, *op. cit.,* II, 19.

well-controlled written-out ornamentation. Finally Gabrieli introduces into the form the use of devices of "learned counterpoint" such as *stretto,* augmentation, and inversion.

The *Ricercare Secondo Tono*[8] is an excellent example of the quality of Gabrieli's more serious examples. The composition is mono-thematic and is based on a theme which provides an easily recognized rhythmic motive which can function well in *stretto:*

Mus. ex. I-4.
A. Gabrieli: *Ricercare Secondo Tono,* measures 1-3 and 16-18.

Two rather extensive expositions (measures 1-17 and 17-44) develop the theme imitatively. The readily perceivable theme is set in the context of lucid counterpoint, and in the second of these expositions it is developed in *stretto.* The final half of the composition consists of presentations of the theme in double and triple augmentation in the manner of a long-note *cantus firmus.* The theme appears in all voices in each manner. The counterpoint which surrounds it is based upon the thematic material in the original note values:

Mus. ex. I-5.
A. Gabrieli: *Ricercare Secondo Tono,* measures 65-68.

The result is a highly coherent composition, one conceived with the exigencies of keyboard music clearly in mind.

The few published examples of *ricercari* by Giovanni Gabrieli open a new approach to the form. He avoids both the learned seriousness which characterized the better examples of his uncle as

---

[8] *Ibid.,* II, 12.

well as the over-ornateness of the less interesting ones. Instead Giovanni treats the *ricercar* as a format for the development of a single well-defined keyboard motive. His themes, which no longer reflect any vocal antecedents, are distinctly instrumental in shape. They are fashioned of motivic material which will be developed in the course of the composition. Harmony, which in earlier examples had no greater function than in the motet style, now serves as a vehicle within which the instrumental elaboration can take place. This new type of harmonic foundation betokens the function harmony will play in seventeenth-century music. Beyond these unusual features, Giovanni writes in a highly terse style. He seems to sense the limits to which a single motivic idea may be expanded, and he is willing to limit his composition to that length. As a result his works have greater cohesiveness than many examples of his contemporaries.

This trait of cohesiveness is mandatory for a successful instrumental composition. No one feature, at least for modern listeners, limits Renaissance keyboard music as much as the sense of a rambling structure lacking any orientation. Many compositions, of course, were based on well-known vocal models which served to direct and unify the keyboard writing. The modern listener, who lacks these models, easily becomes lost in the wealth of otherwise unorganized ornamentation. Giovanni's accomplishment in these few *ricercari* is most important in that it bypasses the older orientation in favor of one which is decidedly instrumental in outlook. For this he is as strikingly modern in the area of keyboard music as he has been shown to be in the wider arenas of music.

The *Ricercar in the Tenth Tone*[9] serves as an excellent example. The theme and its continuation provide motivic material for the course of the piece:

Mus. ex. I-6.

[9] Giovanni Gabrieli, *Werke fuer Tasteninstrumente,* ed. Bedbrook, Kassel: Baerenreiter, 1957. 7.

For the most part it is the bracketed figure above which Gabrieli chooses to elaborate through extensive sequential passages similar to the following:

Mus. ex. I-7.
G. Gabrieli: *Ricercar in the Tenth Tone,* measures 16-19.

This use of sequential elaboration on a large scale is another very modern aspect of Gabrieli's style. Such development, of course, becomes one of the most important devices enabling Baroque composers to extend their compositions. In his reliance on sequential elaboration Gabrieli has broken with the past tradition which relied on contrapuntal complexity for interest. The equality of voices characteristic of Renaissance polyphony seems deliberately avoided in favor of a structure which allows that voice which at a moment carries motivic material to shine through. Despite the previous skillful efforts of composers to achieve a meaningful keyboard language, these efforts of Gabrieli seem by far the most satisfying. The language being spoken is distinctly instrumental; it is distinctly different from that which grew from the vocal tradition; and it suggests the arrival of an entirely new means of instrumental expression characteristic of the seventeenth century.

As a final example of the Renaissance *ricercar* we should give attention to a large scale work of Hans Leo Hassler. It is obvious that Hassler absorbed the revolutionary keyboard style of his teacher, Giovanni Gabrieli, as he also absorbed his vocal style. The composition in question is the second of three *ricercari* published in the *Denkmäler der Tonkunst in Bayern.*[10] Unfortunately many more examples of Hassler's work remain in manuscript. These no doubt would throw further light on the nature of the form in the late sixteenth century. The composition in question reaches a length of

[10] Hans Leo Hassler, *Ausgewählte Werke,* ed. Ernst Werra, *DTB,* IV, ii, 61.

139 measures without losing cohesiveness or interest. This is achieved by means of a well-defined formal plan which is as follows:

1. Complete exposition of the principal theme (measures 1-40)
2. Complete exposition of a secondary theme (measures 41-62)
3. Development of both themes simultaneously in the manner of what would later be termed a double fugue
4. Coda in triple meter based on the principal theme in variation.

The themes have little in common with the older tradition of the *ricercar:*

Mus. ex. I-8.

Hassler carefully controls the texture in a way which allows principal motivic ideas and their elaboration to become clear. He carefully calculates the entrances of his themes in terms of contrapuntal surroundings, the number of voices present, and the element of range. In his initial lengthy exposition, for example, he never allows all voices to sound simultaneously until they appear together directly prior to the first large cadence. With similar skill he juxtaposes the two themes in the third section so that one is well aware of the integrity of each. This example is an excellent one with which to conclude our study of the Renaissance *ricercar,* for in it are reached the goals which composers seemed to have had for the form since its inception. Here we find a full, comprehensive working out of a limited number of instrumental ideas in a cohesive and organized manner to the end of enjoyment of instrumental music *per se.*

THE CANZONE

Running parallel to the development of the *ricercar* is the development of the lighter *canzone*, a development which was based not on the serious quality of the motet but upon the transparent quality of the *chanson.* It has not been unusual in the history of music for a serious form to be balanced by another less pretentious and more direct. The complex *organa* of the late twelfth century were soon balanced by the lighter motet; *opera buffa* served as a foil for *opera seria;* and in the development of the symphony, the light-hearted *scherzo* balanced the heavier nature of the first two movements.

The French *chanson* provided the instrumental composer with a ready-made model. Its texture was only pseudo-contrapuntal; its harmony was characteristically more functional than that of the motet; and its repetition schemes provided a formal organization which the motet had lacked. The removal of the text from a motet almost always does the work infinite injustice. The removal of the text from a French *chanson,* on the other hand, almost always leaves a musical structure which remains viable. No doubt many *chansons* were typically performed in instrumental versions, and the success of the genre in this manner of performance must have been obvious. It is easy to see how the Italian composers turned so quickly to this popular French device in their search for styles which would be instrumentally successful.

For the sixteenth-century composer the term *canzone* was applied to three related procedures:

1) a relatively exact transcription of a *chanson* which was generally well-known. The technique relies on heavy application of stereotyped ornamentation to the vocal lines;
2) a composition using the motivic materials of a *chanson* and perhaps even extensive literal quotations from it, which, however, transcends the level of a mere transcription and becomes a composition in its own right; and
3) an original composition, based upon no particular vocal model, but employing within the instrumental idiom qualities typical of the form, structure, and texture characteristic of the *chanson.*

The first of these procedures has a long and varied history in the development of keyboard music. A large percentage of the contents of late fifteenth- and early sixteenth-century keyboard tablatures is made up of compositions which are transcriptions of sacred and secular pieces. Many of these tablatures have an expressly pedagogical intent which was to provide the student a manual by which he could learn to improvise his own transcriptions. By the early sixteenth century there had developed an extensive vocabulary of ornamental devices whereby a vocal line could be elaborated at the keyboard. By the mid-sixteenth century this ornamental vocabulary had been so stereotyped that manuals of performance often listed possible elaborations of certain stock musical situations. For instance Diego Ortiz in his *Tratado de glosas* (1553) provides the following *diminutions,* or, as the English called them, divisions, for cadences in the Dorian mode with a final of G.[11] Similar *diminutions* are provided for each cadential situation which a student would encounter.

Mus. ex. I-9.

While Ortiz was concerned primarily with improvisation on the viola da gamba, the same ornamentation was common property of all instrumentalists and even of the singers as well. In German organ writing of the first half of the sixteenth century, particularly in the tablatures of Kotter, Kleber, and Sicher, the standardization of ornamental figurations and the excessive use of them became, on the one hand the most significant feature of the music and, on the

[11] Diego, Ortiz, *Tratado de glosas . . .*, tr. Max Schneider, Kassel: Baerenreiter, 1936, 5.

other hand, its most significant weakness. Some of the more common figurations one encounters are the following:

Mus. ex. I-10.

It is a rare measure in the works of these composers which does not contain at least one of these *formulae*. The following example clearly shows the procedure applied to the opening measures of a vocal model.

Mus. ex. I-11.
Kleber: Transcription of *Zart schöne Frau* with vocal model by Schöfter.[12]

Unfortunately the predilection for ornamented vocal settings which characterized German keyboard music of the period left it an art lacking native inventiveness. The procedure, however, was typical of much keyboard music elsewhere, and no less competent composers than the Venetians rely on this technique in many settings

[12] Hans Loewenfeld, *Leonhard Kleber und sein Orgeltabulaturbuch*, Hilversam: Fritz Knuf, 1968, 47.

of *chansons.* An excellent example readily available for study is Andrea Gabrieli's setting of Crequillon's famous *chanson, Pour ung plaisir.*[13] For the most part the contrapuntal lines of the original are accurately maintained. The harmonic structure is taken over very literally and the texture is only rarely thinned out to allow for the added ornamentation. The process is perfunctory and represents nothing more than the elaboration a skilled improvisator of the period could easily have accomplished.

It is instructive to compare the settings of the same passage by two different composers of the period. The following example represents extracts from a setting by Andrea Gabrieli (1605)[14] and a setting of Sperindio Bertoldo (1591)[15] of a passage from the *chanson, Frisque et gaillard* of *Clemens non Papa.*[16] In both cases the ornamentation is rather stylized and the overall structure of the model remains largely unaltered.

Mus. ex. I-12.

Settings of Clemens non Papa: *Frisque et gaillard* measures 24-30.

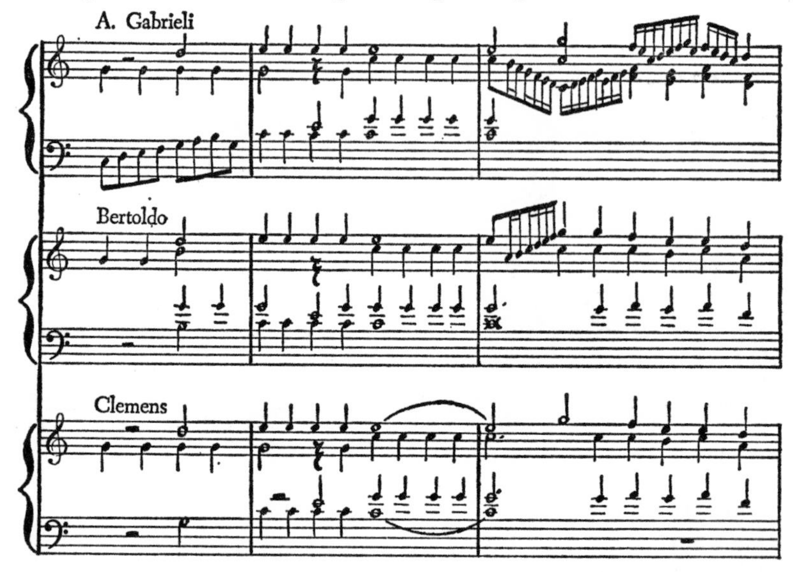

13 Carl Parrish and John Ohl, *Masterpieces of Music before 1750,* New York: W. W. Norton, 1951, 64.

14 Andrea Gabrieli, *op. cit.,* IV, 10.

15 Sperindio Bertoldo, *Compositions for Keyboard,* ed. Speer, *CEKM,* XXXIV, 7.

16 Jacques Clement, *Opera Omnia,* Rome: American Institute of Musicology, 1951-66, X, 37.

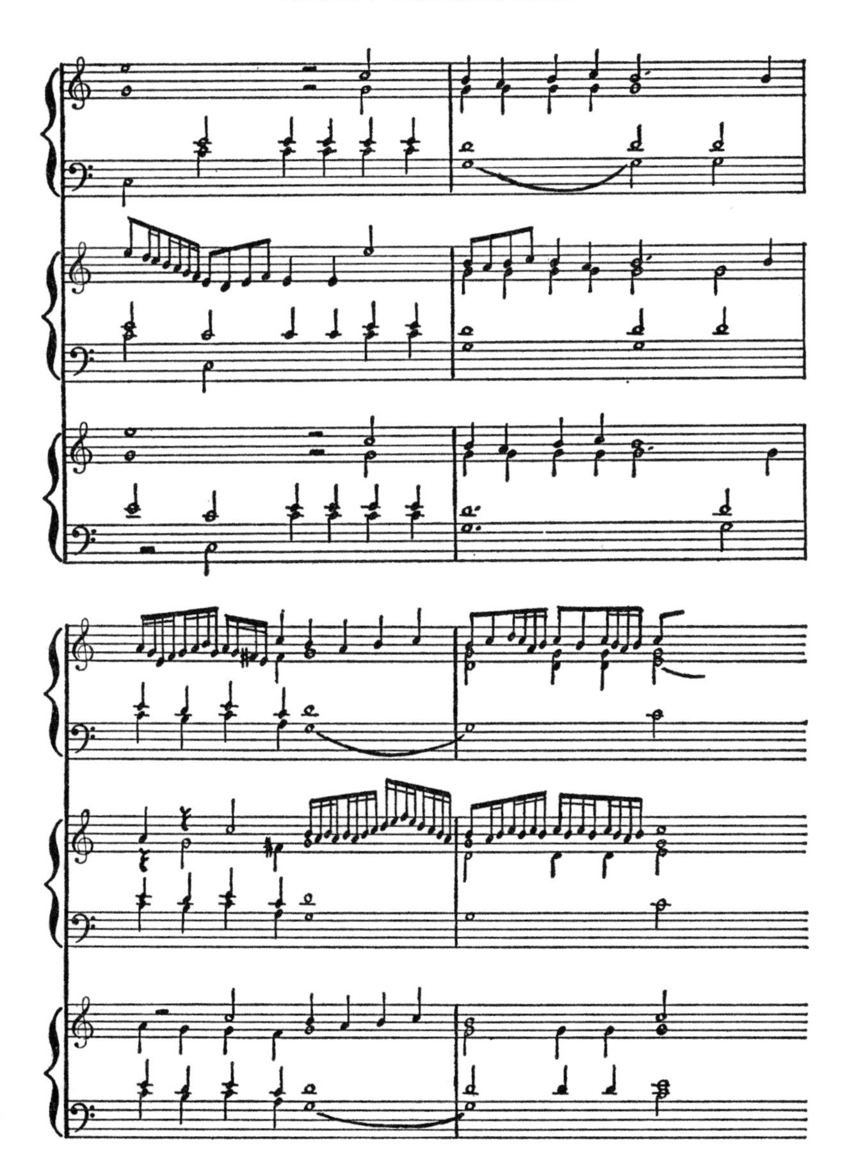

The second type of *canzone* represents the application of the sixteenth-century technique of parody to the French *chanson*. The tradition of basing a composition on a pre-existing model by using its materials in a revised way is as old as the history of contrapuntal music. As the sixteenth century progressed, composers turned more and more in their Mass settings from excerpting a single voice from a motet or *chanson* for use as a *cantus firmus* toward the use of parody wherein the old composition was reworked in the creation of the new. Any element of the model might be retained or altered as the composer saw fit. What resulted was a new composition, one which drew from the past but now had an integrity of its own. It was natural to see the same technique applied in keyboard music to settings of *chansons*.

Of the three procedures outlined above, this one is the rarest, and ready examples of it are somewhat difficult to find. The *Historical Anthology of Music* provides one of the few in the Girolamo Cavazzoni settings of Josquin's highly polyphonic *chanson, Faulte d'argent* also printed in the collection.[17] The keyboard setting is made up, as is the *chanson,* of short points of imitation. Cavazzoni borrows Josquin's themes but develops them largely independently. The five-voice structure of the model is replaced by a four-voice one, and the composer evidences a strong desire, not shared by Josquin in the *chanson,* to cadence each point of imitation rather completely.

In the development of a lively keyboard style, both of these types of *canzoni* had liabilities. The first type had little integrity of its own: It maintained a parasitic existence which depended upon the model for life. While the second type allowed some greater freedom for the composer, the use of borrowed material still imprisoned an imagination which might move toward a freer, more expressive keyboard style. A radical change had to take place in the nature of the *canzone*, a change which would replace the contrapuntal interplay of melodic lines (satisfactory in the vocal idiom) with a more suitable and dynamic keyboard texture. This, as we have already seen in the history of *ricercar,* occurred in the recognition of motivic development.

The third type of *canzone* is a development of the last decade of the sixteenth century, and it provides the basis for the form in the seventeenth century. In this type the vocal antecedents are

[17] Josquin: *HAM,* I, 93; Cavazzoni: *HAM,* I, 121 and Cavazzoni, *op. cit.,* I, 18.

identifiable only in the rather frequent use of the opening rhythm characteristic of the *chanson,* in the repetition schemes, and in the generally light-hearted flavor of these pieces. The characteristics of this type are:

1) short, concise compositions in pseudo-contrapuntal style with a texture similar to that of the *chanson;*
2) opening rhythm characteristic of the *chanson* which is often used for subsequent motivic development;
3) short expositions of well-defined keyboard motives used in lieu of the technique of points of imitation;
4) clearly defined formal organization based on repetition of sections; and
5) the use of sections in triple time and of a more homophonic texture in contrast to the duple sections which are based on motivic development.

Works are found of this type by two composers, Giovanni Paolo Cima, who worked in Milan and published his collection of *ricercari* and *canzoni* in 1606[18] and Giovanni de Macque (1550-1614), who worked in Naples. The first *canzone* in Cima's collection shows features typical of others. The overall form of this composition[19] is ABA, with the A sections built on a motive derived from the initial theme:

The B section is based on the following simple idea and acts as a short contrast to the A sections:

The texture of the piece is made up entirely of motivic development of these two ideas in a clear, concise and terse manner. No longer do we have distinct evidences of a development from the *chanson.*

---

18 Giovanni Paolo Cima, *Partito de ricercare e canzoni alla francese,* ed., Clare Rayner, *CEKM,* XX, 26.
19 *Ibid.,* 26.

The music is now completely within a keyboard idiom and depends for its effectiveness on a structure very similar to that we encountered in the *ricercari* of Giovanni Gabrieli.

Although Macque's *canzoni*[20] are similar, in one of them he introduces a feature we have already encountered in the *ricercari* of Girolamo Cavazzoni, the use of a rhythmic variation of the initial theme in triple meter as the basis for a contrasting section.

Mus. ex. I-13.
Thematic material, Macque: *Canzona alla Francesca III*[21]

This feature will be one adopted by most seventeenth-century composers in their *canzoni* and other sectional compositions.

The history of the *canzone* has moved from a perfunctory transcription of a known *chanson* toward a form in which the vestiges of the old vocal procedures can hardly be seen at all. While there may be some thematic and textural similarities between this last type of *canzone* and the *chanson*, it is in any case an essentially independent form. It is interesting to note that in the tablature of Bernhard Schmidt the Younger (1607) he refers to a set of pieces as "Fugen oder (wie es die Italianer nennen) Canzoni alla Francesce." The groundwork of the seventeenth century fugue has been laid.

FORMS OF THE TOCCATA TYPE

The Renaissance Intonation, Prelude, and Toccata

We have seen that in the search for a meaningful keyboard expression the Italian composers of the Renaissance turned toward vocal music for points of departure. There was, however, a simultaneous development of pieces based on no such models, pieces which derived their inspiration from the desire, which seems native to keyboardists, to demonstrate their expertise in a vocabulary of music native to their instruments. This vocabulary was largely unencumbered with considerations native to other musical styles. Out

20 Charles Guillet, Giovanni (de) Macque, Corolus Luython, *Werken voor Orgel*, ed., Jos. Watelet, *Monumenta musicae Belgicae IV*, Amsterdam: Swets and Zeitlinger, 1968.

21 *Ibid.*, 47.

of it grew the closely related forms of intonation, prelude, toccata, and fantasia. The terms are used rather haphazardly by composers of both the sixteenth and seventeenth centuries, and it is impossible to determine why one should have been selected rather than another.

German tablatures of the late fifteenth and early sixteenth centuries frequently contain short free pieces generally entitled prelude amid the more frequent and valuable compositions based on other material. Both the *Fundamentum organisandi* of Conrad Paumann (1410-1473) and the *Buxheimer Orgelbuch* (ca. 1470) contain such preludes. These are all short and probably served in the function of an intonation, *i.e.* the function of providing the pitch for a subsequent vocal composition. One important characteristic which these show, the juxtaposition of chordal sections with sections based on scales, will appear over and over again in the history of these forms. For the most part these compositions are only of interest in that they demonstrate the concern that composers were beginning to place on compositions without prior material.

Two tablatures in the first half of the sixteenth century provide further evidence of German concern for the free forms. The collection of Hans Kotter (1513) contains nine preludes under various names. Throughout these works the stereotyped *formulae* used by the colorists in their settings of vocal works are exploited. The descending figure  and the cadential turn are particular favorites of Kotter, and he frequently uses such figures in alternation between voices. In the following example the soprano and alto echo the passage just given by the alto and bass. The variation technique, however, is applied in the repetition:

Mus. ex. I-14.
Kotter: *Praeludium in Fa,* measures 19-28.[22]

Less prone to depend upon these stereotyped patterns are the seventeen preludes and fantasias of the Kleber tablature of 1542. An unusual passage of a sequential nature is found in the *Praeambulum in ut manualiter,* measures 14-19.[23]

Mus. ex. I-15.

Another aspect of Kleber's preludes is his occasional use of echo technique, employed throughout most of the *Fantasy in Fa.* Here is a clear antecedent of the echo fantasies of Sweelinck.

Mus. ex. I-16.
Kleber: *Fantasy in Fa,* measures 12-15.[24]

22 Wilhelm Merian, *Der Tanz in den deutschen Tabulaturbüchern,* Leipzig: Breitkopf und Härtel, 1927, 65.

23 Robert Eitner, "Das Buxheimer Orgelbuch," *MfM,* Beilage, XIX (1887) part 2, Anhang, 96.

24 *Ibid.,* 110.

Examples of free forms disappear from German tablatures of the last half of the century, and when they do reappear in the tablature of Bernhard Schmid the Younger in 1607 they are of Italian origin. This suggests that the development of these forms became Italian.

The earliest examples of toccata types in Italy are the two astonishing non-imitative *ricercari* contained in Marc Antonio Cavazzoni's *Recerchari, motetti, canzoni Libro I* published in Venice in 1523.[25] Here we find two free compositions in a well developed style, each exceeding one hundred measures in length. Perhaps there were written precursors of these compositions now lost to us, or more likely the techniques employed in them had been worked out improvisationally for some decades before Cavazzoni chose to compose in the style. These two *ricercari* depend largely upon the juxtaposition of large blocks of chordal or pseudo-contrapuntal texture with lighter textures based on scale passages and ornamental figurations. The composer particularly exploits the higher registers of the keyboard; and in the second *ricercar* he uses the note f''', a note otherwise unused in music of the Italian Renaissance. He also violates such time-honored considerations as parallel perfect consonances and carefully controlled dissonance in his concern for a lively keyboard style.

In many of the toccatas of the sixteenth century we can sense a certain lack of cohesiveness. Formal order was difficult to achieve without the harmonic basis of tonality devised by the seventeenth-century composers. Although this criticism applies to these *ricercari* as much as to other works, Cavazzoni provides at least one passage whose tonal organization is clearcut and remarkably modern in sound. In the following example the passage is organized about a bass descending in fifths:

Mus. ex. I-17.
Cavazzoni: *Ricercar Prime,* measures 100-105.[26]

[25] Knud Jeppesen, *Die Italienische Orgelmusik am Anfang des Cinquecento,* Kopenhagen: J. Jorgensen and Co., 1943.

[26] *Ibid.,* 41.

As we would expect from our study of forms based on vocal models, it is the Venetian composers, in this case Andrea Gabrieli and Merulo, who develop the toccata in Italy in the latter part of the century. These composers make of the toccata a principal form of keyboard expression. We should not lose sight of the fact, which the vocal music shows so well, that the Venetians were very much taken by the opulence of sound itself. Rather than depending upon the perfection of counterpoint typical of the Roman school, the Venetians sought to achieve their ends by the interplay of large masses of choral and instrumental sound. No less important was the dazzling dramatic display which the music must certainly have had in its original setting. Here are elements of technical proficiency and the theatrical which are rarely felt in other Renaissance music. One can see in the keyboard music this same concern for dramatic and technical display apparent in the better known choral music.

The outlines of the Venetian toccata are present in the shorter *intonazione* of Andrea Gabrieli.[27] They rely on a contrast between passages in chordal style, often decorated with some contrapuntal elaboration, and passages built on lengthy scales in one hand with held chords in the other. While to our ears, which are accustomed to later keyboard music, this format may sound a bit naive, it was no doubt highly effective in its original setting. The continuously rolling scales must have amassed considerable amplitude as they echoed in the large recesses of St. Mark's, and the sheer virtuosity demanded of the performer must have been very impressive to ears unaccustomed to anything similar.

In the majority of his toccatas Andrea merely expands the format of the intonation to accommodate a larger piece. In one,[28] however, he interpolates a passage in *ricercar* style as a relief to the seemingly endless scales. Gabrieli seems content to allow his figuration to rely solely on scale passages and stylized written-out ornamentation. Despite the experimentation of the late sixteenth century with harmonic practice, Gabrieli is equally conservative in this area.

Merulo has left two complete books of toccatas (1598 and 1604) plus another set in manuscript.[29] Although he fills many pages

---

[27] A. Gabrieli, *op. cit.*, volume I.

[28] *Toccata del* 6. *Tono, ibid.*, I, 12.

[29] Claudio Merulo, *Toccate per Organo,* 3 vols., ed. Sandro dalla Libera, Milan: Ricordi, 1959.

with continuous scale passages, he rarely allows, as does Andrea, a composition to rely solely on such writing. After the semi-chordal introduction which he uses in common with Gabrieli, Merulo alternates *ricercar*-like passages with sections built on scales. The two most frequent forms are:

1) Chordal introduction, scale section, *ricercar* section, scale section; or
2) Chordal introduction, scale section, *ricercar* section, scale section, *ricercar* section, final scale section.

While his figuration is often as impersonal as that of Gabrieli, Merulo does at other times shape lines in a way that suggests a precedent for the most angular figuration of seventeenth-century composers:

Mus. ex. I-18.
Merulo: *Toccata ottava del 4° tone,* bass, measures 12, 13, and 18.[30]

While Merulo's harmonic practices are generally as conservative as Gabrieli's, one passage from a toccata in manuscript is so suggestive of the seventeenth century that it bears quotation. Although the sound of successive dominant sevenths is rare in this period, even one appearance is an indication of a growing concern for a harmonic structure more functional in nature:

Mus. ex. I-19.
Merulo: *Toccata 8a,* measures 26-27.[31]

It is difficult to ascribe success to the Renaissance toccata. It seems unlikely that modern ears could ever accept the endless monotony of many of these compositions. What the form did establish was a

30 *Ibid.,* I, 12-13.
31 *Ibid.,* III, 27.

level of technical proficiency and a concern for composition without any vocal antecedents. The failure of the sixteenth-century toccata lies for the most part in the directionless quality of Renaissance harmony. What was lacking was a harmonic sense capable of giving an external order to sections based on keyboard figuration. Besides providing this tonal direction, seventeenth-century harmony will provide for the composer suggestions of meaningful shapes for the figuration itself. This harmonic order is perhaps the major accomplishment of instrumental music in the first half of the seventeenth century; and without it, it is unlikely that a vibrant keyboard style would ever have evolved.

There is certain evidence that the composers themselves were becoming more and more aware of the limitations of modal harmonic order. Not only do keyboards exist with split keys allowing different pitches for enharmonic equivalents and thereby allowing the exploitation of multiple key centers; but also a genre of keyboard composition, the *toccata durezza e ligature* (the toccata of dissonances and suspensions), appears as a form for harmonic experimentation. An easily available example by Giovanni Macque[32] employs the same type of abrupt harmonic changes associated with the late Italian madrigal. As Apel has pointed out,[33] Macque's pupils provide the link between the fully developed Renaissance keyboard styles and the highly personal style of Frescobaldi. No doubt experimentation with harmonic sounds *per se,* which was largely avoided in the sacred vocal literature, is an indication that the composers themselves sensed a need for a larger, more definitive tonal order in which their new efforts could come to fruition.

THE CANTUS FIRMUS FORMS

Renaissance organ forms depending upon *cantus firmus* are the organ mass, settings of the Magnificat and other canticles designed for performance in alternation, and settings of Gregorian hymns. As one would expect, the style of these compositions represents the most conservative approach of Renaissance organ music, a style which depends more than others upon that of the sacred vocal polyphony of the period. Since all these forms depend upon exchange between organ verses and the sung chant, any great divergence of

---

[32] *HAM,* I, 200.

[33] See Willi Apel, "Neopolitan Links between Cabezon and Frescobaldi," *MQ,* XXIV (1938), 419.

mood and particularly any extensive technical virtuosity would have been highly inappropriate. Yet despite the resulting conservatism, these forms are the direct precursors of the Baroque organ mass in France, and hence the foundation of that country's unique organ style; and of the Lutheran chorale prelude, the primary foundation for German organ literature.

To a degree a musical function for the organ in the Roman service had to be manufactured. The function of providing musical interludes to cover liturgical action and such accompanying of vocal music as might have been required of the instrument were limited opportunities for the Renaissance player. The practice of substituting organ settings of an appropriate chant in lieu of singing that chant appears in the early part of the fifteenth century. By the mid-sixteenth century an established practice of alternation, phrase by phrase, of the ordinary of the mass between sung chant and organ versicle had developed. Likewise the intonations of the Magnificat, the Te Deum, and alternate verses of Gregorian hymnody were varied by essentially the same procedure. No doubt the practice had its beginnings as much in the desire to elaborate the simple chant without the forces and skill of a polyphonic choir as in the desire of the organists to assert themselves. In any event, two ends were served: The organ found a vital liturgical function and the service could be varied with a minimum expenditure of effort.

The techniques of handling the *cantus firmus* were, of course, worked out in vocal music and then borrowed for instrumental use. These were principally the following:

1) *cantus firmus* in long notes generally in the tenor or bass around which the other voices weave free counterpoint;
2) a soprano melody structured on the notes of the *cantus firmus* but with appropriate ornamental figuration. The melody can become so florid that its origins are obscured.
3) use of the techniques of points of imitation. The themes are derived from the notes of the *cantus.*
4) the use of a technique similar to 1) above with the addition of counterpoint which itself is related to the *cantus;* and
5) combination of methods 1) and 3) wherein short initial imitations suggest the coming entrance of lines of the *cantus.*

These techniques, all of which appear in vocal music of the late fifteenth and sixteenth centuries, are of course identical with techniques used in the treatment of the chant and the chorale in seventeenth-century practice.

Organ movements based on chant had constituted a large part of the contents of the fifteenth-century German tablatures. Many of these tablatures were written as manuals on improvisation on Gregorian melodies. This suggests that it was a common practice to devise such movements without writing them down. That the setting of *cantus firmus* had reached a high level by the early sixteenth century is proven by the publication in 1512 of Arnolt Schlick's *Tabulaturen etlicher Lobgesang und Lidlein.*[34] Here we have a mature approach to the writing of organ music not only from the point of view of compositional technique but also from the conception of the instrument itself. Almost all these compositions are in trio style with the pedal assuming as demanding a part as the manuals.

Schlick treats the *cantus firmus* most of the time in the long-note manner. His elaborating voices, however, have a contrapuntal fluidity transcending much Renaissance keyboard music. While he does make use of stereotyped *formulae*, particularly the turn, these are used in such a natural fashion that they seem to be generic to the melodic lines themselves. Initial imitation plays a part in the opening of several compositions although the imitative theme may not be derivative from the chant which is being set:

Mus. ex. I-20.
Schlick: *Benedictus,* measures 1-5.[35]

In many instances Schlick develops an abstract motive in a truly instrumental fashion in the creation of the elaborating voices:

[34] Arnolt Schlick, *Tabulaturen etlicher Lobgesang und Lidlein uff die Orgeln und Lauten,* ed. Gottlieb Harms, Ugrino: Abt. Verlag, 1924 and 1957.

[35] *Ibid.,* 29.

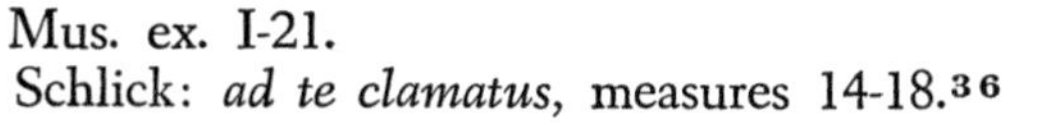
Mus. ex. I-21.
Schlick: *ad te clamatus,* measures 14-18.[36]

Unfortunately the high musical level of Schlick's works does not continue in subsequent German tablatures. Certainly this is true in regard to *cantus firmus* settings which are conspicuously absent from all these manuscripts for the remainder of the century.

The next major collections in the history of this type of music are the two organ books published by Pierre Attaingnant in 1531.[37] Contained in these books are a number of Magnificat settings and two complete organ masses all by anonymous composers. Although the musical style lacks the polish, grace, and genius of Schlick's compositions, the techniques employed are essentially the same. A three-voice texture made up of the voice bearing the *cantus firmus* plus two elaborating ones is the most common. The melody appears in either whole or half-notes with the counterpoint generally moving in eighth-note motion. The elaboration is created almost entirely of stereotyped *formulae* applied with no unusual skill or contrapuntal dexterity. Initial imitation suggested by the melody is used with some frequency, and some verses are made up solely of a short point of imitation. The following example illustrates the imitative technique and the rather stilted and rigid nature of the writing:

Mus. ex. I-22.
Attaignant: *Et ex Patrae,* measures 1-4.[38]

The standard for further examples of *cantus firmus* setting in the sixteenth century is set in the two volumes of organ works of

---

[36] *Ibid.,* 19.

[37] Pierre Attaingnant, *Deux Livres d'Orgue,* ed. Rokseth, *Publications de la Société Française de Musicologie,* Paris: E. Droz, 1925.

[38] *Ibid.,* 13.

Girolamo Cavazzoni. Such pieces constitute the larger part of both of these prints. His first volume contains four hymns and two Magnificat settings; the latter volume is made up entirely of *cantus firmus* compositions: three organ masses, eight hymns, and two Magnificats. Cavazzoni's principal contribution to the *ricercar,* as we have seen, was the application of pervading imitation to the form. It is exactly this procedure which he applies to the forms in question. While we have encountered the use of initial imitations in both the works of Schlick and the compositions published by Attaignant, the technique has by no means conditioned the texture of a significant portion of the music. Cavazzoni's solution to the problem of the short versicle is simply to write a point of imitation based on the appropriate chant material. We have traced the formal difficulties inherent in the use of successive points of imitation in the *ricercar.* In the short versicle such problems were not present. A short point, or possibly two, fitted well the time allotted in the macrorhythm of alternation, and the style was perfectly compatible with the chant which the versicles sought to enhance.

Even in the more extensive hymn settings, which present an entire *cantus firmus,* the melody rarely appears in starkly unadorned long-note values. It will more likely be preceded by an imitative suggestion of its opening notes and it will enter into the texture in as subtle and skillful a way as possible. Once the notes of the *cantus* have been introduced they will be carefully decorated, so that the Gregorian melody stands less as a foundation about which the other parts move than as an active participant in the contrapuntal movement.

Mus. ex. I-23

G. Cavazzoni: *Veni Creator Spiritus,* measures 9-14.[39]

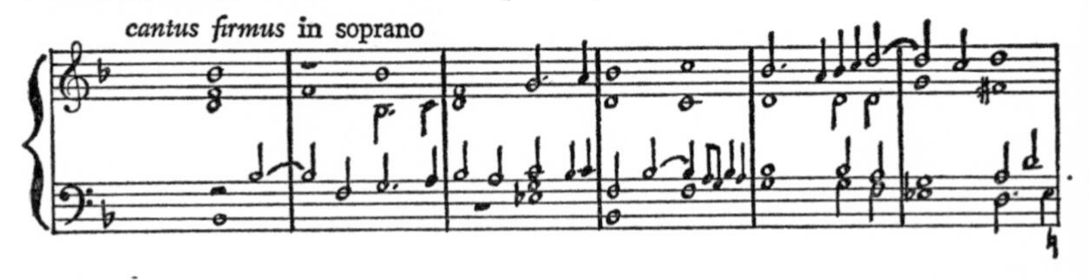

In these hymn settings Girolamo provides a mature format followed in many chorale preludes. In his treatment of the hymn, the

[39] G. Cavazzoni, *op. cit.,* 19.

naturalness of his counterpoint, his subtle addition of ornamentation, the natural application of imitative technique based on the melody itself, and the very high level of musicality, the composer sets a standard for such works for almost a century. Not until the works of Titelouze is he surpassed; and, save for the works of Cabezon, he is unmatched in the Renaissance. Nothing new in technique appears in the setting of *cantus firmus* for the organ until the Protestant organ chorale and the French organ mass of the seventeenth century.

SPANISH KEYBOARD MUSIC OF THE RENAISSANCE

The important collections of Spanish sixteenth-century keyboard music are the *Cifra nueva para tecla, harpa y viheula* (1557), an anthology published by Venegas de Henestrosa,[40] and the *Obras de musica para tecla, arpa y viheula,* the principal source of the music of Cabezon.[41] While the music in these collections is obviously the end product of a long development of Iberian keyboard music, no other printed music survives; and only a few manuscript sources are extant. Reese suggests[42] that the absence of much material may be due to the desire of composers to withhold their works from others, a trend Bermudo was said to have deplored.

Much material in both these collections is based on pre-existing material. Sacred works so based consist of the many versets principally for the Kyrie and Magnificat, hymn settings, and various other settings of chants. The secular forms consist of *glosas* (paraphrases) of *chansons* and *diferencia* (variation sets) on secular songs and dances. As we shall see, the conservative nature of Spanish keyboard music led to a natural predilection for forms based on pre-existing material, forms which lent the composer an opportunity for applying the technique of glossing to his material. The music is not primarily designated for the organ. The term *tecla,* like the

[40] See: Higinio Angles, *La Musica en la Corte de Carlos V, Monumentos de la Musica Espanola,* II, Barcelona: Instituto Espanol de Musicologia, 1944.

[41] Antonio Cabezon, *Obras de musica para tecla, arpa y vihuela, Monumenta de la Musica Española* XXVII, XXVIII, XXIX., ed. Angles, Barcelona: Instituto Español de Musicologia. There is also a new edition: *The Col-*Institute of Medieval Music, 1st vol.: Duos, *Kyries,* Variations and Finales, 1967.

[42] Gustave Reese, *Music in the Renaissance,* 626.

German *Klavier*, merely indicates keyboard. Both titles suggest that the music might be performed on the harp or viheula, although considerable modification of it would, no doubt, be necessary.

No characteristic is more in evidence in these collections than the strong contrapuntal approach to the musical style. The same restrained conservatism which characterizes the sacred works of Victoria and other Spanish vocal composers also characterizes the keyboard music. Ornate display for its own sake is particularly avoided. While the traditional ornamentation of the period is used very frequently, it is always applied with judgment, so that it enhances the contrapuntal lines. Never does one have the feeling that the ornamentation asserts itself at the expense of the polyphonic texture. Many compositions are free of any type of keyboard figuration, and the combination of this purity coupled with the strict texture causes many pieces to resemble scored motets. Even in the variation sets where we might expect this conservatism to be less obvious, the same clarity and purity remain evident. It is certainly no accident that Spanish composers avoided those forms which relied principally on display. Toccatas and kindred forms do not occur in this music. Since the works of the Spanish school center so closely on those of Cabezon the following discussion is based solely on his works.

The most conservative compositions are naturally those with liturgical function. In his *versetti* and settings of the Kyrie, Cabezon employs movements based both on the long-note *cantus firmus* and the point of imitation technique. In most settings of a *cantus firmus* the elaborating counterpoint is itself imitative, although it is rare that Cabezon derives the imitative material from the chant itself. The following example demonstrates both the technique and the austerity of the style of most versets.

Mus. ex. I-24.
Cabezon: *Versos del tono tercero VI,* measures 1-8.[43]

[43] Cabezon — Angles, *op. cit.*, II, 19.

In the larger hymn settings Cabezon adheres to the same conservative approach. The *cantus firmus,* almost always in long-note values, serves as the basis for polyphonic elaboration. The chant is almost always in the tenor or bass voices and was probably performed on the rudimentary pedals found on Spanish organs of the period.

The Spanish equivalent of the *ricercar* is the *tiento.* The form, however, has little of the learned seriousness of its Italian counterpart. Instead, it remains close to the motet style from which it was obviously derived. It relies on careful control of successive points of imitation and on the polished counterpoint we have been discussing. At times there is no overt effort to make the multiple themes relate to one another in any way except by general mood. At other times Cabezon relates his themes to one another by means of subtle musical relationships. The composer is particularly fond of inversion of the initial intervals of a subject in the derivation of a new theme.

Mus. ex. I-25.
Cabezon: *Tiento III primer tono,* thematic material.[44]

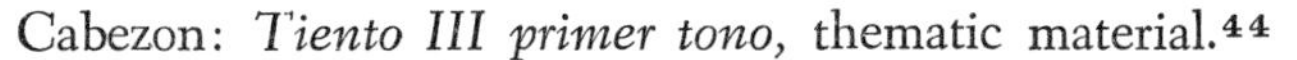

Certainly no greater evidence of the conservative nature of the *tiento* can be found than Cabezon's construction of one on themes from the "Cum sancto spiritu" from Josquin's mass *Beata Virgine.* In the very source of his material Cabezon is asserting his conserva-

---

[44] *Ibid.,* II, 78.

tive outlook, and in constructing a composition carefully attuned to the mood of this material his outlook is further confirmed. The wonder of it all is that the genius of the composer could transform this vocally-oriented idiom in such a way that music of such instrumental vitality could result. The Italian answer in the *ricercar* was to solve instrumental problems by reforming the vocal idiom. The Spanish answer was to write counterpoint of such clarity that, despite the idiom, the music would have instrumental significance. The conservative style of the versets, the hymns, and the *tiento* seems to have had little influence in the subsequent history of organ literature. It is through the *diferencia* that Spanish music had subsequent international influence, particularly as the form influenced English variations.

The writing of sets of variations based on a given melody, *chanson,* or dance does not seem to have been frequently practiced by either Italian or German composers. We have already seen how critical the variation technique was to all keyboard composers of the Renaissance, and it seems strange that a more systematic use of it did not develop outside Spain and England. The Spanish seem to be the first to sense a relationship between the vocabulary of ornamentation, which was common property to all composers, and its systematic exploitation in a chain of variations. No doubt the formalized procedure of *diferencia* grew out of the improvisational tradition described by Ortiz and others. It is only a small step from manuals which discuss how a single line may be infinitely varied to full grown compositions based on sections redoing the same material in one formula after another.

That the variation technique is wedded very closely to that of glossing is proven by an interesting set of eight compositions on *falsobordoni,* simple chordal harmonizations used to accompany psalm intonations.[45] Cabezon follows each harmonization by three variations. In the first the soprano is ornamented; in the second the bass is ornamented; and in the third the two inner voices are simultaneously embellished. Scale passages plus the following ornamental figures constitute the figuration of the elaborating voices:

[45] *Ibid.,* I, 48 following.

Mus. ex. I-26.

That these motives are closely related to the vocal tradition of the century is proven by the fact that in each of them motion in one direction is immediately counterbalanced by motion in the other. The only unusual feature of these pieces is the use of quintuple division of the semi-breves in two variations of the example in tone six.

In the *diferencias* themselves Cabezon is equally conservative. As in the *falsobordoni* he sometimes uses the harmonic structure as a framework for ornamentation. In other sets he simply employs the melody as a *cantus firmus*. In the *Diferencias sobre el "Canto del Cavellero"*[46] he places the melody first in the soprano with slight ornamentation, then in the tenor, next in the alto, and finally in the bass. The other voices form about the *cantus* skillful ornamentations based on a thoroughly disciplined counterpoint. The concern for contrapuntal smoothness in this and other sets of *diferencias* causes Cabezon to bridge with overlapping lines the division between variations.

An inevitable comparison suggests itself between this Spanish form and the variations of the English virginalists, which will concern us next. The basic difference lies in the fact that Spanish variations are based firmly in the tradition of sixteenth-century counterpoint. The elaboration is an outgrowth of this practice and occurs as a result of carefully constructed melodic lines. On the other hand, the revolutionary variations of the virginalists most frequently set this tradition aside in favor of idiomatic keyboard elaboration based on the harmonic material of the theme. It is interesting to observe that the very notation used by the virginalists differs so radically. Spanish tablature is wedded to a fixed number of polyphonic voices, while the staff notation used by the English allows the expression of an expansive style of keyboard writing. It is to the English virginalists that we now turn our attention.

[46] *Ibid.*, III, 60 and *HAM*, I, 145.

THE ENGLISH VIRGINALISTS

Although the manuscript is probably of Italian origin, the Robertsbridge Codex demonstrates the existence of keyboard music in England as early as the fourteenth century. There are, however, no historical ties which bind this work to the vibrant keyboard tradition of the English sixteenth century. Seven compositions from a manuscript in the British Library (Roy. Add. 58) are the earliest known examples of music for the virginal.[47] Two of these pieces, the *Hornpype* of Ashton and *Lady Carey's Dompe* are examples of rudimentary grounds, a form which seems to have attracted English attention.

The principal documents of virginal music are *My Ladye Nevells Book; Benjamin Cosyn's Virginal Book; Will. Forster's Virginal Book; Parthenia, or the Maidenhead of the first Musicke that ever was printed for the Virginalls;* and finally the best known and the most important, *The Fitzwilliam Virginal Book.* A discussion of music for the virginal in a volume on organ music perhaps needs some defense. The keyboard idiom developed by the English composers of the sixteenth century becomes the common property of continental organists in the next century. Without the striking features of virginal figuration, it is difficult to imagine what the nature of seventeenth-century keyboard music might have been. To omit a brief discussion of these works simply because they were intended for a keyboard instrument other than the organ would be to omit a vital chapter in the history of organ style.

One volume of English keyboard music of the sixteenth century, however, was an organ book. The *Mulliner Book,*[48] was compiled by the organist Thomas Mulliner for his own use. It contains motet transcriptions, settings of liturgical *canti firmi*, reductions of English anthems, and various free interludes. Only in the settings of the liturgical melodies do we find much evidence of idiomatic keyboard writing. English composers had an unfortunate habit of selecting lengthy Gregorian melodies and using them intact for a single variation. As a result many of these pieces are unduly long and perhaps a bit dull.

---

[47] See: F. Dawes (ed.), *Schott's Anthology of Early Keyboard Music, English Virginalists,* Vol. I: *Ten Pieces by Hugh Ashton and Others,* Mainz: Schott's Söhne, 1951.

[48] Denis Stevens, (ed.). *The Mulliner Book, Musica Britannica,* I, London: Stainer and Bell Ltd., 1951.

Although there are *ricercari* and other contrapuntal forms in the repertory of the virginalists, the comparative rarity of such forms indicates that the principal concern of the English lay outside the confines of strict counterpoint. The most frequent, successful, and revolutionary works are the sets of variations of secular songs and dances. In the variation form emphasis could be laid on the harmonic resources of the theme. The music could move within a framework based upon the progression of functional harmony and be unified by the vertical element. It was natural that the first consistent efforts to organize a large body of music on a distinctly harmonic basis should have been done in conjunction with the variation form, for here the chordal progressions were stressed by repetition.

It has been suggested that the new concern for harmony may have arisen due to the failure of the lute as a truly polyphonic instrument. The transcription of contrapuntal music for the lute emphasized the vertical element in a way other instrumental transcriptions did not. The lutenists were much more aware of harmonic progressions than were other musicians, for no matter how adept they might have been in transferring complex counterpoint to their in strument, the result would have stressed vertical elements unstressed in the original. Related to the awareness of harmony on the part of the lutenists is also the appearance of sequence as an important instrumental device. As we have seen, sequence occurs occasionally in other sixteenth-century music; but it is rarely used extensively or consistently. In virginal music it becomes a basic element of the idiom.

> There is another element which must not be lost sight of in coming to an understanding of this process of development: the comparative incapacity of the lute — the favourite instrument of the sixteenth century — to adapt itself to imitative playing. Imitation and sequence ended therefore by being hardly distinguishable. Composers for keyboard instruments, being aware how essentially favourable their instruments were for harmonic playing, followed the example of the lutenists and borrowed from them their methods of writing, among which they found sequence as a substitute for imitation.[49]

[49] Charles van den Borren, *The Sources of Keyboard Music in England*, London: Novello, n.d., 89.

Harmonic progressions coupled with sequence most often provided the foundation for the incredible inventiveness in virginal figurations.

The basic difference which exists between English and Continental figuration should be clearly stressed. Continental figuration tended to rely on a fixed number of *formulae* which remained largely unchanged throughout the century. The method and the sensitivity with which various composers applied these motives varied greatly, but the motives remained the same. For the most part the ornamentation was grafted onto an existing musical structure. In other words the figuration tends to be an addition to, rather than a generic part of, the composition in question. Elizabethan figuration is generated by the musical structure itself; indeed, to a very great degree, it is the musical structure itself. In Continental music a composition exists with figuration; in England the figuration is the composition.

The patterns of figuration used by the virginal composers tend to fall into certain classifications.[50] Our method in the following pages will be to demonstrate each type of figuration as it occurs in the monumental set of variations which open the *Fitzwilliam Book.*[51] There seems to be little doubt that the editor of this collection chose Bull's variations on *Walsingham* with the intent of demonstrating the variety of possibilities available to the composer of variations. Not only is it the longest set of variations in the volume, it contains within its measures examples of nearly every type of figuration employed by the virginalists. As such it makes a concise example for our study. The types of figuration are as follows:

1) figuration depending upon the intricacy of contrapuntal writing,
2) stereotyped sixteenth-century figurations,
3) figuration deriving from rhythmic subtleties,
4) harmonically inspired figurations,
5) figuration depending upon abstract rhythmic motives, and
6) figuration depending upon features uniquely related to the keyboard.

---

[50] For another classification upon which this depends to a large degree see van den Borren, *op. cit.,* chapter iv.

[51] J. A. Fuller-Maitland, and W. Barclay Squire (editors), *The Fitzwilliam Virginal Book,* reprint, New York: Dover Publications, 1963, I, 1.

Even though the virginalists frequently departed from the contrapuntal ideal of Renaissance music, they did not leave it altogether. They maintained a distinctly disciplined control over polyphonic resources as one element of their writings. Often in a set of variations the more polyphonic sections will directly follow the announcement of the theme, probably in order to set a stamp of seriousness on the composition as a whole. Similarly such variations at times will conclude a set. Most often the counterpoint is motivically structured:

Mus. ex. I-27.
Bull: Variations on *Walsingham,* var. 2, measures 1-3.

That the ornamentation common to Continental sixteenth-century music would have been used by the virginalists was, of course, natural. In one variation Bull fashions his figurative lines in accordance with Venetian practice. The use of the turn and the descending run are two of the most common patterns of the older keyboard elaboration. The variation is distinctly conservative in tone:

Mus. ex. I-28.
Walsingham, var. 6, measures 1-2.

The most frequent types of rhythmic subtleties are:

1) the juxtaposition in different voices of different levels of rhythmic motion. Each voice is given its own stratified rhythmic independence.

Mus. ex. I-29.
Walsingham, var. 15, measure 1.

2) the consistent use of syncopation.

Mus. ex. I-30.
Walsingham, var. 4, measures 1-3.

3) the use of polyrhythmic patterns. This may be a conservative feature carried over into virginal style from English music at the conclusion of the fifteenth and beginning of the sixteenth century.

Mus. ex. I-31.
Walsingham, var. 20, measures 1-2.

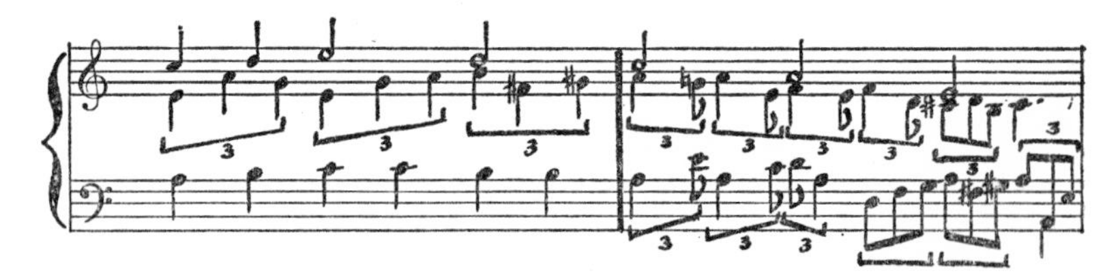

4) the use of triplet and sextolet figurations. Occasionally these may occur at two levels simultaneously.

Mus. ex. I-32.
Walsingham, var. 22, measures 1-2.

It should be observed that the figurative patterns themselves often condition the rhythmic organization of the music. In Continental keyboard music of the period rhythm is conditioned in much the same way it is in vocal music, by the exigencies of the melodic line. Any type of mechanical rhythmic pattern is generally avoided, for such patterns are antithetical to the freedom of one polyphonic line in its interplay with others. Mechanically-oriented rhythmic organization, which appears here in virginal music and in Italian concerted music after 1600, becomes an important element in seventeenth-century style.

Figuration originating in harmonic structure is perhaps the most important and revolutionary of all of these types. Here the stress laid on the vertical element effects a change in musical structure unlike anything else in previous keyboard music. Almost without exception, the music we have studied has depended upon a solid foundation of counterpoint. Here, however, the old foundation is replaced by harmonic considerations, considerations which become the building stones of the new seventeenth-century musical edifice. The most important types of harmonically-conceived virginal figurations are:

1) arpeggiated chords

Mus. ex. I-33.
Walsingham, var. 12, measure 1.

2) broken chord patterns

Mus. ex. I-34.
Walsingham, var. 21, measure 1.

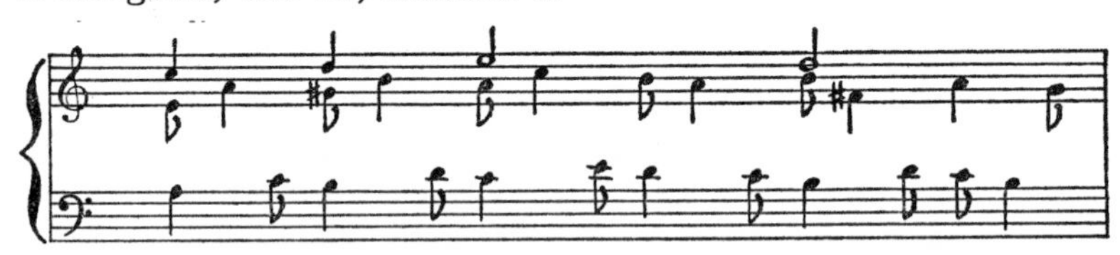

3) figuration in broken thirds and sixths

Mus. ex. I-35.
Walsingham, var. 18, measure 3.

Of almost equal importance is figuration which originates in rhythmic ideas of motivic and abstract character. The mechanical rhythms of seventeenth-century music are based on a limited number of motives used repeatedly in one composition after another. In the set of variations we are discussing the following common motives are presented:

var. 10

var. 21 (and)

var. 14

var. 26

var. 19

var. 28

One can find these same motives in literally thousands of Baroque compositions — they become some of the more frequently used elements of the new musical vocabulary.

The final category of figuration is that associated with certain features which are unique to instrumental playing in general and keyboard playing in particular. Important in this category would be:

1) the use of rapidly repeated notes

Mus. ex. I-36.
Walsingham, var. 28. measure 4.

2) the exploitation of wide leaps

Mus. ex. I-37.
Walsingham, var. 17, measure 4.

3) the use of sequentially repeated scale passages

Mus. ex. I-38.
Walsingham, var. 24, measure 1.

It should be pointed out that a single figuration could fall into several categories. For instance, one which exploits wide leaps is probably also conditioned by harmonic progression. It is the virginal composers who finally provide us with a modern keyboard vocabulary. Unlike their Continental contemporaries, whose music to some degree always depends upon its vocal origins, the English struck out in a new direction. Their approach was simply to create a style of music native to their instrument, a style which depended very little on vocal traditions but very much upon the imagination and dexterity of the player. This English tradition was rapidly absorbed into Continental music largely through the works of Sweelinck, whose compositions already appear in the virginal repertory, and his many German pupils.

The sixteenth-century heritage which the early seventeenth-century composers built upon consisted, then, of the following elements:

1) a thorough foundation in contrapuntal practice applied to keyboard writing.
2) the formal patterns of the *canzone*, the *ricercar*, the toccata, the *cantus firmus* setting, and the variation.
3) a tradition of keyboard ornamentation.
4) a concept of motivic writing, and
5) an extensive vocabulary of keyboard figuration, which was the heritage from the English.

Upon these elements the seventeenth-century keyboard tradition was built. The breakdown of the polyphonic choral tradition in the last decade of the sixteenth century betokened greater and greater concern for instruments in all aspects of music. The importance of the Italians, particularly the Florentines and Venetians, in establishing the new traditions is too well documented to comment upon. As in other musical fields, the most radical departures from the old styles of keyboard music were first effected in Italy. Our next task will be to turn to Italian organ music of the first half of the seventeenth century and to the works of Frescobaldi.

CHAPTER II.

ITALY

THE SOUTHERN ITALIAN KEYBOARDISTS BEFORE FRESCOBALDI

At perhaps no other time in history, unless it might be in the early years of our century, did music change as rapidly and completely as it changed in the years from 1590 to 1610. We have already discussed the common musical language which existed in the sixteenth century, a language with various dialects, but yet a language spoken in large degree by all composers of the period. During the last decade of that century and first decade of the next, that common language largely disintegrated into a myriad of new tongues. Elements of the old language remained, particularly its firm dependence on contrapuntal syntax. No longer, however, did composers feel compelled to write in similar fashion, and even single composers changed their stylistic grounds radically from one moment to another. The Renaissance goals of clarity, balance, and restraint of expression were replaced by an art which seemed often to stress the bizarre, the non-symmetrical, and the whim of the moment. Serenity was replaced by turbulence and stability by constant flux. The seventeenth-century composer appears to have taken his own individuality far more seriously than did his predecessor, and he allowed his imagination a far freer reign in the development of unique musical ideas. No doubt the chaotic scene which the early part of this century manifests would have produced utter musical confusion had there not at that time been an unusual number of musical minds of first rank. Monteverdi, Schütz, Sweelinck, Schein, Carissimi, Frescobaldi, and many others provided a wealth of sheer genius which prevented music from sinking in a morass of unbridled individuality.

While many important technical elements of the new language of the seventeenth-century keyboard music have their roots in the northern alliance between the English virginalists and Sweelinck and his many pupils, the most important emotional roots of this new art lie in the works of the Southern Italian keyboardists active from about 1585 until about 1640. It is well known that in most other genres of music, the early Baroque had its beginnings in northern Italy particularly in the cities of Florence and Venice. The development of opera, the rise of concerted music, the modification of the madrigal into the chamber cantata, and the development of the opulent polychoral style are all northern developments. We have already examined the organ music of the Venetian school of the late sixteenth century. Instead of revealing a radically new style, this music manifested typical features of Renaissance music. The stability of a toccata of Merulo, with its long held chords and statically conceived runs, or the vocally-oriented style of one of Andrea Gabrieli's *ricercari* hardly seem typical of the flux and rapid change characteristic of early Baroque music. The Venetian composers were as conservative in their keyboard works as they were radical in other areas of composition. Apel has convincingly demonstrated[1] that the roots of Italian Baroque keyboard music lie in a little known school of composers who worked in Naples and Rome. There they developed a keyboard art in which one can see the emergence of just those elements which are so singularly obvious in the style of Frescobaldi. The major composers of this school whose works antedate those of Frescobaldi are: Ercole Pasquini (c. 1560 to c. 1620), Frescobaldi's predecessor at Saint Peter's; the Belgian composer Giovanni de Macque, whose works we have already mentioned; Asconio Mayone (d. 1627); and Giovanni Trabaci (c. 1575-1647). A limited amount of the music of these composers is available to students. Pasquini's works are available in *CEKM*.[2] The second of two large keyboard collections which Mayone published has appeared in a modern performance edition.[3] His first collection, however, is unfortunately not yet available. Trabaci likewise published two anthologies of keyboard works. A large portion of the first collection (1603) is now available in the initial two volumes of an intended complete edition

[1] See: Willi Apel, "Neopolitan Links between Cabezon and Frescobaldi," *MQ* XXIV (1938), 419 and "Die süditalienische Clavierschule des 17 Jahrhunderts," *Acta Musicologica* XXXIV (1948), 128.

[2] Ercole Pasquini, *Collected Keyboard Works,* ed. W. R. Shindle, *CEKM* XII, 1966.

[3] Ascanio Mayone, *Secondo libro di diversi capricci,* ed. Kastner, *Orgue et Liturgie,* 63 and 65, Paris: Editions musicales de la Schola Cantorum, 1965.

of his works.[4] The *ricercari* which open the second publication (1615) are also available in performing edition.[5] Organists should be forewarned that the favorite instrument of these southern Italians was the harpsichord. Trabaci indicates that it is the king of instruments. Many compositions are conceived with the harpsichord idiom clearly in mind. In most general keyboard collections the composers designate the harpsichord before the organ in the title, a practice which is in sharp contrast to such collections published elsewhere in the seventeenth century. Although most compositions can be played with success on the organ, we must recognize that the situation is similar to that of English virginal music in which a body of music designed for stringed keyboard instruments influenced the subsequent history of organ music. With these facts in mind, the author has somewhat arbitrarily elected to discuss the toccata, the *ricercar,* and the *canzone* as genres native to the organ. The many variation sets and other works of a decidedly secular origin have been omitted in the following discussions. The reader should be aware of the difficulties this selection may produce.

The Toccata

The toccatas of Pasquini and Mayone are radically different from the type of toccata written by the Venetians. This new toccata depends upon: 1) a more firmly conceived harmonic basis, 2) a much wider variety of figurative patterns, 3) the use of unusual harmonic progressions for their own unique effect, and 4) a continual restlessness resulting from the rapid shift from one figurative or harmonic idea to another. These compositions have an improvisatory quality about them which suggests that the genre may have had its roots in *ex tempore* playing at the harpsichord. Due largely to the greater emphasis on harmonic progression, these compositions have a modernity that those of Merulo and his school distinctly lacked. A remarkably functional approach to harmonic thinking underlies many figurative passages. No longer do chords stand as

[4] G. M. Trabaci, *Compozioni per organo e cembalo, Monumenti de musica Italiana.* Series I, Vol. III (1964) 12 Ricercate dal Libro I, 1603 and Series I, Vol. IV (1969) Canzoni, Capricci, Canti Fermi dal Libro I 1603, ed. Mischiati, Brescia: Paideia.

[5] G. M. Trabaci, *Ricercate (Il secondo libro de ricercate),* ed. Bonfils, *l'Organiste Liturgique,* 54 and 57, Paris: Schola Cantorum.

static pillars above which endless scale passages move; the figuration is now shaped and directed by the harmonies. In the following example from Pasquini the figuration is as clearly directed by the harmony as such a passage would be in late Baroque music. Particularly interesting, however, is the clear distinction the composer evidences for melodic versus harmonic motion in his simultaneous use of C-natural and C-sharp:

Mus. ex. II-1.
Pasquini: *Toccata* V, measures 9-14.[6]

Unusual harmonic and melodic situations are frequent throughout Pasquini's toccatas. In the following passage the sixteenth-note figuration in the first measure shows intentional juxtaposition of dissonant notes in contrary motion without consideration for the traditional rules of consonance. The harmonic effect in the third measure where the composer concludes his ascending scale on an E-flat against the bass D is a striking moment. Although we should guard against the temptation of using modern harmonic analysis in situations in which it may not be applicable, the composer has nonetheless outlined the dominant ninth chord in the accented notes of the scale.

---

[6] Pasquini, *op. cit.,* 10.

Mus. ex. II-2.
E. Pasquini: *Toccata IV,* conclusion.[7]

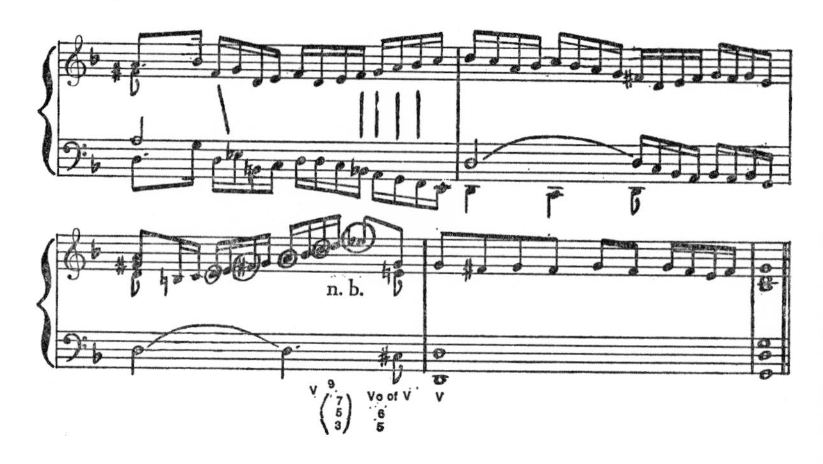

Pasquini's toccatas are all short compositions with a continuous spirit of excitement and restlessness. There seems to be little doubt that Frescobaldi knew these compositions of his predecessor at Saint Peter's. Although the quality and inventiveness hardly rival the toccatas of Frescobaldi, Pasquini's compositions no doubt served as models for the younger and more gifted composer.

The toccatas of Mayone are conceived on a larger scale than those of Pasquini. Frequently they are made up of alternation of sections in figurative style with sections in either chordal or imitative style. In this they share a superficial resemblance to the Venetion toccata. The spirit of these pieces, however, could hardly be more different from the staid, rather unimaginative Northern toccata. Extensive scale passages are rather rare in Mayone's works, and when they do occur they are buttressed by clear harmonic progressions. Moyane's chromatic toccatas, numbers four and five of his publication of 1609, are particularly interesting pieces. Both alternate sections in *durezza* style with passages in figuration. In the second of these toccatas the composer shows considerable proficiency in using such innovative harmonic features as the dominant seventh chord on the extreme sharp side of the key circle:

---

[7] *Ibid.,* 9.

Mus. ex. II-3.
Mayone: *Toccata quinta per il cimbalo cromatico,* measures 9-16.[8]

The figurative sections of this toccata are all built on *formulae* derived from the written out trill. Such undulating figuration is very typical of numerous other Mayone works as well as works of other Southern Italian composers:

Mus. ex. II-4.
Mayone: *Toccata quinta,* measures 1-3.[9]

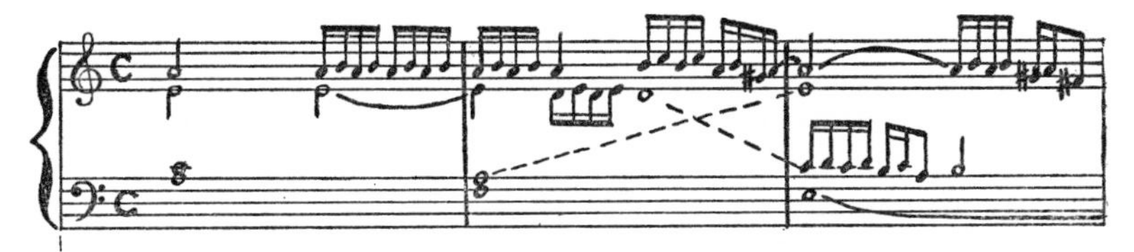

The Ricercar

The *ricercar* is very important in the productions of these Southern Italian composers. Both Mayone and Trabaci open each book of their keyboard works with a set of such compositions, and it is obvious that each composer lavished great care on these pieces. As one would expect, these composers show in the *ricercar* their most conservative side. Three of Mayone's *ricercari* are based on *canti firmi* set out in long note values and handled in the most reserved manner. As a whole the *ricercari* of these composers show

[8] Mayone, *op. cit.,* vol. 65, 53.
[9] *Ibid.,* 52.

none of the imaginative harmonic thinking or cleverness of idomatic keyboard writing so characteristic of their other writing. It is to the solution of formal problems that they seemed to have given their greatest attention.

Trabaci established a type of *ricercar* which remains common throughout Italy in the century. In this type the composer reduces his thematic material to from one to four thematic bits. To a large extent the contrapuntal texture of the entire composition is based on these bits of melodic material. The composer normally indicates in his titles the number of themes upon which his composition is based (*con una fugha, con due fughe, con tre fughe, con quattro fughe*); and also indicates in the title certain alterations, such as inversion, if such are to be used in the course of the piece. The *ricercar,* then, becomes a thematically bound composition. The multi-thematic approach of earlier Renaissance examples is replaced by an approach that strictly limits the thematic material throughout the composition. In a Trabaci *ricercar* the subjects are visible in almost every measure and frequently are used simultaneously.

In Trabaci's *ricercari,* the subjects lack the contrasting quality we might expect. Indeed, these subjects lack any particular individuality, and it is sometimes difficult to differentiate one from another in the musical texture. The composer, however, is relying less on the processes of modern thematic development, than on the integrity of a contrapuntal texture based consistently upon a few constantly recurring melodic ideas. In the process of developing this thematically derived texture such traditional devices as *stretto,* inversion, and simultaneous use of themes very frequently occur. In one instance Trabaci manages to present his initial theme simultaneously with his theme and its inversion:

Mus. ex. II-5.
Trabaci: *Ricercar del quarto tona* (*Secondo libro*), measures 39-41.[10]

[10] Trabaci, ed. Bonfils, Vol. 54, 20.

For the most part Trabaci retains the vocally-oriented texture characteristic of the sixteenth-century *ricercar*. In view of the revolutionary sound of the toccatas and *canzoni* of this school, the remarkable thing about Trabaci's *ricercari* is their thoroughly conservative sound. The *ricercar* seems to have stood for these composers as a genre in which they could prove their contrapuntal proficiency. Unusual individuality would have been inappropriate, and it rarely occurs. To the modern ear these compositions suffer particularly from a conservative modal harmonic structure, again uncharacteristic of other works of Trabaci and Mayone. What is significant is that the problem of the multi-thematic *ricercar* has been solved. Frescobaldi frequently borrows the Trabaci solution but adds to it his greater levels of harmonic and figurative imagination.

The Canzone

If the conservative format of the *ricercar* restricted the fiery imagination of the Southern Italians, the *canzone* provided them a medium in which their innate freedom could find expression. Both Mayone and Trabaci treat the *canzone* as a wide open form made up of small, concise sections of an indefinite number. Each section succinctly develops its own musical idea, which may or may not be related to ideas used in other sections. Diversity and a certain keyboard flamboyance are the chief characteristics of these pieces. No two compositions follow the same pattern, and while several pieces may have common characteristics, no single feature seems common to all *canzoni*.

Most compositions show some evidence of variation technique in the derivation of thematic material from one section to the next. The simplest pieces, such as the first *canzone* in Mayone's second book[11] make consistent use of the variation principle. Most other compositions, however, do not show this consistency. Sometimes, as in the second *canzone* from the same set, a theme for a subsequent section will be formed as a variation of material which appeared initially as the counterpoint to the principal theme.

---

[11] Mayone, *op. cit.*, Vol. 63, 17.

Mus. ex. II-6.
Mayone: *Canzone francese seconda,* themes.[12]

Mayone introduces into some of his *canzoni* a combination of the texture of the toccata with the principle of the *cantus firmus.* Both features seem essentially foreign to the lighthearted quality of the *canzone.* In such sections the principal theme of the composition appears in a chordal harmonization in one hand, while the other hand performs figuration made up of stereotyped ornamental patterns and scales. No doubt the feature of this technique which Mayone sought to exploit was keyboard virtuosity, a feature which the *canzone* otherwise rarely exhibited.

Mayone often derives from his theme motivic bits which he is capable of exploiting in a most modern way. The concluding section of the fourth *canzone* from this set is made up completely of motivic development of htis type, and it bears study as an indication that the older polyphonically derived texture of keyboard music will soon largely be replaced by a texture developed from motive. Some measures from this section are given below:

Mus. ex. II-7.
Mayone: *Canzona francese quarta* (Secondo libro), measures 65-68.[13]

[12] *Ibid.,* 20, 21.
[13] *Ibid.,* 29.

The seven *canzoni* from Trabaci's *Libro primo* (1603)[14] are even more diverse in structure than those of Mayone. Some, as for example the first in the set, are highly organized around a single theme presented in rhythmic variations in the various sections. In such examples the traditional contrapuntal approach associated with the *canzone* is used. In other examples the composer gives up this approach in favor of one in which the texture becomes more vertically conceived, homophonically conditioned, and motivically oriented. The use of concise sections strung together, which we observed in Mayone's works, is also characteristic of these compositions. Some such sections may have no more than a dozen measures, and there may be as many as eight sections within a single composition. The following measures are the opening of a section from the fourth *canzone,* a section which manifests the motivic and harmonic orientation we have just described:

Mus. ex. II-8.
Trabaci: *Canzona franzese quarta* (Libro primo), measures 32-37.[15]

The second and fourth *canzoni* of this set open with chordally structured preludes. The prelude to the latter piece[16] has an emotional quality as striking as anything in keyboard music of the period. It seems to herald the impact of some opening sections in the mature North-German style. The opening of the second *canzone* provides the simple rhythmic motive from which the entire composition is generated. Trabaci uses this motive at several levels of diminution in duple time and also presents a modification of it in triple time. The flamboyant codas which the composer uses to conclude many sections of these compositions bear mention. The following, from the same *canzone,* is typical of numerous others.

14 Trabaci, Mischiati, *op. cit.,* IV.
15 *Ibid.,* 11.
16 *Ibid.,* 10, also printed in *Apel K.,* 441.

Mus. ex. II-9.
Trabaci: *Canzona franzesa seconda* (Libro primo), measures 42-44.[17]

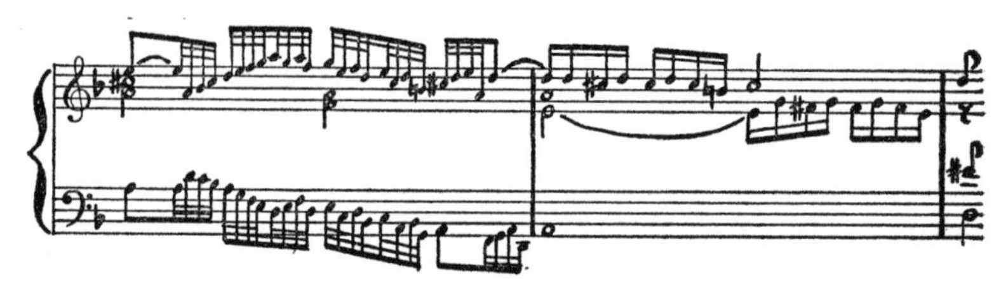

The seventh *canzone* from this set is one based on a theme which ascends chromatically through the interval of a fourth. Such chromatic themes either ascending from the dominant to the tonic or descending from tonic to dominant will become very frequent as the century progresses. Trabaci senses immediately the harmonic aspects in the theme's suggestion of consecutive secondary dominants. Such innovative harmonic considerations are characteristic of other passages in Trabaci's *canzoni*.

Mus. ex. II-10.
Trabaci: *Canzona franzesa settima cromatica* (Libro primo), measures 18-20.[18]

These *canzoni* of Trabaci deserve not only the most serious study on the part of the student of seventeenth-century keyboard music but also introduction into the performance literature. These compositions are unusual for their very careful and thoughtful construction, their highly innovative content, and an emotional quality of unique individuality often lacking in much early keyboard music. They cannot be too highly recommended to the serious student and performer.

[17] Trabaci, *op. cit.,* 6.
[18] *Ibid.,* 18.

THE WORKS OF FRESCOBALDI

In the following discussion of the works of Frescobaldi (1583-1643) the easily available edition of Pidoux[19] will serve as our source. While the compositions recently published from manuscript sources provide excellent new material, they do not significantly alter the nature of the composer's music as it is revealed in the Pidoux edition. The student is, however, warned of a difficulty inherent in the use of in this edition. The editor in a number of cases chose to base his edition on other than the earliest editions of the material involved. Hence dates which appear prominently on the covers of several volumes are misleading. The situation may be clarified by the following:

Pidoux, volume ii: *Das erste Buch der Capricci, Ricercari und Canzoni 1626.* The *ricercari* and *canzoni* first appeared in 1615 and the *capricci* followed in 1624. All works appeared in the 1626 edition used by Pidoux.

Pidoux, volume iii: *Das erste Buch der Toccaten, Partiten usw. 1637.* The toccatas originally appeared in 1615. The other contents appeared with them in the edition used by Pidoux.

Pidoux, volume iv: *Das zweite Buch der Toccaten, Canzonen usw. 1637.* All this material appeared originally in 1627.

The Ricercari and Similar Works

Ricercari or works in *ricercar* style occur in the body of Frescobaldi's works in three places: 1) the fantasias of 1608, 2) the *ricercari* of 1615 and 3) the various *ricercari* scattered throughout the *Fiori Musicali* (1635). Three distinct types of *ricercari* exist in Frescobaldi's works. The first is the Neopolitan type similar to examples by Trabaci and also to others by later Italian composers. In this type multiple themes are initially presented and generally developed simultaneously. The second type is that developed by Andrea Gabrieli in which a theme is initially presented in a fugal exposition and then appears as a *cantus firmus* in long-note values against which the other voices move. The *cantus firmus* generally

---

[19] Girolamo Frescobaldi, *Orgel und Klavier Werke,* 5 vols., ed. Pierre Pidoux, Kassel: Bärenreiter, 1963-1970.

appears in ever larger augmentations. The third type of *ricercar* is that which we might term experimental. Each composition in this classification explores the possibilities inherent in a particular problem set up by the composer, such as compositions in which one voice must be sung by the performer, compositions which avoid all stepwise motion, or compositions exploiting some other unusual contrapuntal procedure.

The Fantasias of 1608

Frescobaldi began his career as a keyboard composer by the publication in 1608 of a set of twelve compositions to which he affixed the inexplicable title "fantasia". These compositions are by no means free or fantasy-like in nature: They are precisely opposite, seriously conceived, contrapuntally complex *ricercari* of the Neopolitan type. The young composer seems to have taken as his first task the thorough mastery of the most difficult and restrictive of forms before he allowed himself the luxury of the freer genres of toccata, *canzona, capriccio,* and variation. With these fantasias Frescobaldi must have been attempting to fix his status as a contrapuntalist, a status which would have been mandatory for a budding Italian composer of the early seventeenth century. This set of fantasias has a clear overall structure. The initial three compositions are on a single subject, the next three are on two subjects, the next three on three, and the last three on four subjects.

The multi-sectional format of these compositions is atypical of earlier *ricercari* and also atypical of later *ricercari* of Frescobaldi himself. The themes are initially presented and developed in a section in duple time with a texture and metric organization typical of most *ricercari.* Rhythmically contrasting sections follow, either in faster motion, triple time, or a combination of both. Frequently the composer will conclude his composition by a return to the meter and mood of the initial section. Perhaps it was freedom and variety of rhythmic structure which led Frescobaldi to the title of fantasia.

No doubt the greatest interest in these pieces lies in the subtle thematic transformations the composer is able to effect. This level of subtlety is certainly more than the ear alone can comprehend. Frescobaldi often retains merely the overall melodic outline of this subject, and exposes it to rhythmic variations, at times completely obscuring the relationship of the variant to the original model. In the eighth of these fantasias the variations of the second subject alone produce the following material:

Mus. ex. II-11.

When one multiplies this level of complexity applied to a single subject by the number of subjects with which the composer began, in this case three, the difficulty in perceiving the composition becomes apparent. These compositions represent the most complex contrapuntal texture Frescobaldi ever attempted.

Some of the most interesting passages in these pieces lie in sections in faster note values. Here Frescobaldi frequently employs a texture built on lively rhythmic motives derived from his subjects. The result is a texture which contrasts strikingly with the more vocally-oriented texture which opens the compositions. The following passage is typical.

Mus. ex. II-12.
Frescobaldi: *Fantasia settima,* measures 73-76 (Pidoux I, 27).

The success of these early compositions of Frescobaldi can certainly be questioned. Apel suggests that to a large degree their failure lay in the composer's attempt to derive the entire texture of the pieces from the thematic material itself.[20] The balance between thematic material and free counterpoint, which normally acts as its foil, is thereby distorted. As a result the listener becomes confused by a constant stream of material all largely of equal importance. Another explanation for this confusion lies in a texture which is constantly too thick and opaque for ideas easily to shine through. Too much occurs simultaneously, and the ear demands a release from a too-complex structure, a release Frescobaldi too rarely provides. One certainly marvels at the difficulty of the task the young composer set for himself. That he may not fully have succeeded is understandable.

The Ricercari of 1615

The ten *ricercari* of the publication of 1615 show nothing of the overenthusiasm or youthful insecurity of the fantasias we have just studied. There is no attempt in these later compositions to overexpand the implicit limits of the *ricercar,* an attempt evident in the 1608 edition. Instead Frescobaldi remains within the formal and textural limits of the form as it stood in the early seventeenth century. Although each composition is unique in some way, the composer seems more willing to let tradition guide him. Borrowings from both the Neopolitan and Venetian traditions are blended with ideas which are distinctly the result of Frescobaldi's own genius. *Ricercari* numbers one and nine are of the conventional multi-thematic type typical of Trabaci and the Neopolitan school. Number five, likewise, is a multi-thematic example. It has, however, a unique form. Its three themes are introduced in the seventeen measure duo which opens the composition. Each theme then becomes the subject for one of the next three expositions. A final exposition uses the themes in combination. The resulting form may be diagrammed:

ABC – A – B – C – ABC.

Another variation of the Neopolitan type is found in number two. Here the composition is made up of three independent and lengthy expositions. Each exposition has its own two themes, and there is no attempt to reintroduce thematic material used in earlier expositions. In any one exposition each theme is presented in inversion

---

[20] *Apel K.,* 453.

as well as in its original state. The resulting form may be diagrammed:

AB with inversions — CD with inversions — EF with inversions.

Ricercari numbers four, six and seven show the influence of the Venetian or Andrea Gabrieli type. Number four, on the solmisation syllables Mi-Re-Fa-Mi, uses its theme in progressively larger augmentations in exactly the manner of examples by Gabrieli himself. In the sixth *ricercar*, on Fa-Fa-Sol-La-Fa, the theme appears consistently in the alto voice where it is subjected not only to the expected augmentations but also to an odd diminution and an appearance in syncopation. Although the unusual rhythms of the subject do not appear, the seventh *ricercar* follows essentially the same plan. Here we have a tenor *cantus firmus* juxtaposed against a *ricercar con due soggetti* which is developed in the other three voices: Frescobaldi has effected a blending of the Neopolitan and Venetian types of *ricercari*.

Numbers eight and ten show evidence of distinctly experimental undertakings. The first of these carries the title "One must not move by step." The composer carries out here an absolutely unique self-imposed task in writing a successful composition in which not a single example of step-wise motion exists. The last *ricercar*, on La-Fa-Sol-La-Re, again juxtaposes the notes of a *cantus firmus* against a three-voice tri-thematic *ricercar*. Here the *cantus* is given to the soprano. What is unique about this composition, when compared to others using the *cantus firmus* procedure, is that the interjections of the subject made throughout the composition by the soprano voice are in all manner of unusual rhythmic variations. The result is a kind of free *ostinato* imposed atop the other three voices engaged in a very conventional *ricercar*.

The variety of the formal patterns shown in these ten *ricercari* is ample evidence that Frescobaldi treated the form in exactly the manner of the late sixteenth century, *i.e.* as essentially a genre in which particular compositional problems could be worked out. The procedure used in these pieces retains the serious quality of contrapuntal craftsmanship which had been characteristic of the form since its inception. What is particularly unusual about these compositions is the variety of problems which the composer deals with so effectively. Italian composers after Frescobaldi tended to regard the *ricercar* much more conservatively. It became more and more merely a parody of the type perfected by Trabaci.

The Ricercari from the Fiori Musicali

In each of the three masses which make up the *Fiori Musicali, ricercari* are provided for use directly after the *credo*. Another very unusual *ricercar* follows the toccata for the elevation in the second mass. Two of these *ricercari* have short toccatas before them, an early example of the combination of a free with a fugal form, *i.e.* a prelude and fugue. For the most part the *ricercari* from the *Fiori* are more modest in scope than those in the edition of 1615. There is little evidence of attempts to pose and solve difficult compositional problems. No doubt this is due in large part to the liturgical function the music was destined to serve, a function in which a too-intellectual approach would have been out of place. Two of the most appealing examples are on chromatic subjects with a strong tonal impact.[21] As a result of the exploitation of the harmonic implications of these subjects, particularly the use of secondary dominants suggested by the second of them, the music of these pieces has a modern flavor lacking in many more modally-directed *ricercari*. In both chromatic *ricercari* the theme is subjected to simple, and only to simple, augmentation. It is evident that the composer's use of this device is more restrained here than it would have been in other situations.

Two specialized compositions should be mentioned. Both employ unusual *ostinato* techniques. The first of these, the *ricercar* after the elevation of the second mass,[22] indicates in a rubric that the bass is to be a special voice. This bass is structured on a theme in even whole notes which appears fourteen times in an order of key relationships moving around the key circle from C Major to E Major on the sharp side, and then from C Major to E-flat Major on the flat side. The complete order of presentations of the theme, which appears only in major tonalities, is:

C – G – D – A (A) – E – D – G – C – F – B-flat –
E-flat – F – C.

This exploitation of further reaches of the key circle coupled with the modulations which were necessary is ample evidence of the development in the early seventeenth century of a wider tonal pallet. The limitations of modal harmony must have been very real, and

21 Pidoux, V, 34 and 54.
22 *Ibid.*, 44.

the more inventive composers sought new ways in such technical devices as chromatic writing and modulation to broaden their tonal language on the one hand and to direct it, on the other, by the implications of harmonic movement.

The second experimental *ricercar* employing an *ostinato* idea[23] requires that the *ostinato* voice be added in the tenor register as a fifth voice to be sung by the performer. A similar technique is used by Frescobaldi in one of the *capricci* from the edition of 1626. In the composition from the *Fiori* the student is warned that the Pidoux edition is misleading. Frescobaldi's clear ternary notation, which Pidoux provides before the composition, indicates that the *ostinato* is to be sung in a cross meter with the portion of the piece which is to be played. This explicit demand that one sing a voice which the composer desired to stress is an interesting one. Does it possibly suggest that in other situations, where a similar need ot bring out a particular voice in a complicated texture exists, that a similar procedure might be in order?

The Canzone

Canzoni occur in the works of Frescobaldi in four publications:

Recercari et canzoni francese 1615—five *canzoni* (Pidoux II)
Il secondo libro di toccate, canzone 1627—six *canzoni* (Pidoux IV)
Fiori Musicali 1635—five *canzoni* in the context of the organ masses (Pidoux V)
Canzoni alla francese 1645 (posthumous)—eleven *canzoni* (Pidoux I)

There is little doubt that it is within the *canzone* that Frescobaldi produced his most natural and appealing works. The rigidities and scholarly implications of the *ricercar* hardly suited the boundless energies characteristic of early Baroque music, and although Frescobaldi produced some exceptional examples in this form, it must have imposed limitations which were not native to him. In the lighthearted, sectional *canzone* the situation was different. Ideas could be set out and developed concisely, new ideas introduced and contrasted with the old, mood could change rapidly and easily, and the concern was no longer with serious restrained contrapuntal invention.

---

[23] *Ibid.*, 57.

Of all the forms of seventeenth-century keyboard music, it was probably the *canzone* which was most clearly representative of the mentality of the century. Having divested itself of any direct relationship to the vocal *chanson,* the form had now become a medium for the development of concise keyboard ideas. The sectional nature of the form, originally derived from the sectional nature of the *chanson* model, had now been expanded to include more or less regular alternations between sections in duple and sections in triple time. As we have seen in the examples of Trabaci and Mayone there was often no thematic connection between one section and another. In this type of *canzone,* the so-called contrast *canzone,* the composer attempted to juxtapose different thematic developments and various textures and meters. Unless the composer exercised the soundest of judgment in the selection of his material, there was a threat that his composition would break down into endless short fragments, each independent and stable within itself, but taken together, disunited and poorly related.[24]

The most common means of providing unity to as diversified a structure as the *canzone,* one we have already several times observed, lay in binding the various sections together by use of modifications of a single theme. Thereby the best of both possible worlds was obtained. The ever-changing unbound quality of the multi-sectional format was preserved on the one hand, but unity of these sections was provided, on the other hand, by the process of thematic variation. The composer was free to maintain the level he sought of relation of one section to the next. He had merely to regulate the level of variation to which he subjected the theme. If he desired to make two sections similar in tone he had merely to present his theme in unaltered or slightly altered versions. If he wished to contrast one section with that which immediately preceded, he had merely to devise a more opaque variation in which the relation of the new to the old was less apparent. The requirements of both unity and variety were adequately met by this exceedingly simple device. The sectional variety of the form could be retained without the attendant confusion of endless thematic variety.

---

24 Another name often applied to the contrast *canzone* is quilt *canzone.* In a quilt no scrap of material necessarily relates to any other, but yet the result of piecing together unrelated scraps should be to produce an integrated whole.

In the course of his lifetime Frescobaldi gradually simplified his procedures in the writing of *canzoni.* The five-section format, duple — triple — duple — triple — duple, favored in his early *canzoni* was abandoned in favor of a three-section format, duple — triple — duple. The variation procedure we have just described was used more consistently in later than in earlier works. The contrapuntal texture, which is relatively complicated in his *canzoni* of 1615, became much less complex and more transparent in later examples. The ornate codas in toccata style, which the composer introduced in his 1627 *canzoni,* are more disciplined when they occasionally occur in the *canzoni* in the *Fiori* and the 1645 edition.

As we have just suggested, the earliest examples are the most complex. All but the last of the 1615 *canzoni* are in five sections. Actually Frescobaldi often divides the opening section, and sometimes others, into two or more clear-cut expositions each using the thematic material in slightly different ways. The result is even greater fractionization than the meter signatures themselves suggest. Thematic variation is not consistently applied, and even when it is, it is not always used in relation to the initial theme. The composer is almost as likely to apply this technique to subsidiary themes as he is to apply it to principal ones. Frescobaldi appears to have given great consideration to formal relationships between sections in these *canzoni.* There is a seriousness about the structural process which is similar to that which we have already encountered in his fantasias published in the same year. The following analysis of the fourth *canzone* from this set demonstrates the care with which the composer approached formal problems in these pieces:

Section I Based on theme A, itself divisible into two sections:

Two expositions: one based on the entire theme, the second on the theme minus its opening two notes. A homophonic bridge leads to the next section.

Section II Based on theme B:

Section III Based on a variation of B:

Section IV Based on a new variant of B and a derivative motive:

Section V Based on a return to the A theme with contrapuntal elaboration provided by use of a motive related to this initial theme:

The resulting overall form, then, becomes: A B B′ B″ A′.

The *canzoni* from the 1627 collection are unique in several respects. In many of these pieces Frescobaldi seems to obscure the line which traditionally separated the *canzone* from the toccata. Not only does he introduce very lengthy toccata-style codas into most of these compositions, he also allows the contrapuntal texture frequently to break down in favor of a more homophonic and motivically derived one. This latter procedure we have already observed in some *canzoni* of Trabaci. In the fourth *canzone,*[25] for instance, there is only one clear-cut imitative exposition and that opens the composition. Subsequently the structure is based on short sections based largely on motivic writing. The ascending notes of the fourth, which the composer draws from his opening theme, are used in ever-varying ways as a unifying device. On the whole the style of this composition is as much like a Frescobaldi toccata as it is like a traditional *canzone.*

There is about the thematic variations used in these *canzoni* a subtlety which requires study to extricate.[26] Some variations are apparent to the ear; others are not. The last section of the first *canzone* uses the following quarter-note pattern a number of times:

---

25 Pidoux, IV, 62.

26 See Apel K., 472, on this point.

Its origin is unclear until one realizes that it is merely an inversion and simplification of the secondary theme in the opening section of the *canzona*:

At one point in the second *canzone* the composer fashions a variation of his theme which produces *stretto* at the narrowest of intervals:

The last two *canzoni* from this set are peculiar in that they lack any duple sections. All sections are in simple triple meter or some type of compound meter. They depend on the most subtle type of thematic variation, and they lack any toccata-like writing. No similar examples appear to exist elsewhere in the repertory.

The *canzoni* from the *Fiori Musicali* and from the posthumous print show a greater simplification and clarity of structure than those of earlier publications. The three-section format becomes standard although there is an example of a two-section *canzone* (duple-triple) in the *Fiori* and two examples without meter change in the 1645 collection. One of these last two compositions is merely a very simple *ricercar* on two subjects. The other is a variation *canzone* without meter changes. Other evidence of the desire for clarity and simplicity lies in the lack of toccata-like codas in many of these pieces. Where such codas do exist they are shorter and less complicated than those of 1627. Frescobaldi also gives up his effort to merge the styles of toccata and *canzone*. The prevailing texture in all these *canzoni* is that of imitative counterpoint.

The process of thematic variation has by now become a standard one with Frescobaldi, and it will continue to be so in *canzoni* of his successors. The subtle and largely inaudible variations we encountered in earlier *canzoni* no longer occur. In his desire for clarity the composer devises variations which are almost always easily perceptible, and the evolution of the themes can be detected without deep study. Often a characteristic progression of intervals will relate subject to variation:

Mus. ex. II-13.
Subjects: *Canzon decima*, 1645.[27]

Frescobaldi's *canzoni* are important in the development of the fugue. Thematic material is now distinctly instrumental in nature. The tonal nature of the themes, which often depend upon the notes of the tonic chord or progressions from I to V or V to I, is similar to many later fugal themes.

Mus. ex. II-14.
Themes from the 1645 Canzoni, numbers one and five.

The concise manner in which Frescobaldi is able to contrive a fugal exposition as well as his ability to exploit the motivic implications of his subjects are further forward-looking qualities. The three-sectional *canzone* format based on thematic variations will still be commonly used by North-German composers of Buxtehude's generation. Beyond these features of historical significance, the *canzoni* of Frescobaldi are as appealing to modern performers and listeners as the whole of any early seventeenth-century composer. The lighthearted, easily perceivable style the composer developed in the *canzone* is much more easily grasped than the more personal and learned styles of the toccatas and the *ricercari*.

[27] Pidoux, I, 74.

The Toccatas

Frescobaldi published two complete books of toccatas (1615[28] and 1627[29]) as well as the shorter examples which appear at various points in the *Fiori Musicali.* In no other genre of music does he express himself so uniquely and personally as he does in the toccata. These compositions are infused with the restless and energetic qualities of early Baroque music. In an even more thorough way than did his Southern-Italian predecessors, Frescobaldi destroyed the stable and static Venetian toccata. With Frescobaldi the form becomes a fabric of constantly changing, ever-fluctuating musical textures. Despite the evidence in his *canzoni* and *ricercari* of his ability to create strict formal constructions, Frescobaldi shows in his toccatas compositions which seem to defy formal analysis. One idea follows another, each is transient, and none is likely to reappear in the course of a composition. The rhapsodic nature of the music is apparent throughout, and elements which would dispute this rhapsody are strictly avoided. Any single musical moment is important not so much as it relates to the whole, but in and of itself. One moment may lead to the next, but there is no necessity that one moment grow thematically or structurally into the next.

There is a certain timeless quality about a Frescobaldi toccata. As one plays or listens to one of these pieces, there is little sense of the direction or the limits of the composition as a whole. One can often predict the order and structure of a *ricercar* or *canzone.* It is not so with the toccata. Time seems to be suspended. The composer himself revealed that he cared little that an entire composition be completed. In his famous preface to the reprint of the first book of toccatas,[30] a preface which is a veritable treasure of clues to performance practices of the period, Frescobaldi indicated that the compositions are so constructed that a player may conclude at any of the many convenient cadences; and in so doing he may tailor the piece to the time he has available. We have already suggested that the origin of the Southern-Italian toccata lies in improvisation. The vocabulary of keyboard figurations which we will next discuss no doubt made up an improvisational vocabulary. What we may have

[28] Pidoux, III.
[29] Pidoux, IV.
[30] Published in the prefaces to both the volumes cited above.

in the toccatas of Frescobaldi are written-out improvisations. The style certainly suggests an *ex tempore* origin.

The toccatas in the three publications are so similar that they may be easily studied together. A toccata is made up of a series of short, rather clearly defined sections, each ending with a more or less obvious cadence. These sections may be as little as two measures in length or may run up to perhaps a dozen measures. Each such section consists of a development of one or more distinct figural motives. The motives change constantly from section to section, and none dominates the structure for an extended period or takes precedence throughout a piece. Frescobaldi reveals his imagination largely through his creation of varied, flexible, and ever-changing keyboard figuration. The fascination lies in the constant flux of this figuration, in the consistent development of new and varied ideas.

The motivic figurations Frescobaldi employs are not unique. Many motives are similar to those we have already analyzed in our study of virginal figurations. Others are similar to motives used by other Southern-Italian composers. Figurations used in these toccatas can be classified into four groups: 1) figurations developed from the common upbeat rhythmic motives and , 2) figurations based on dotted rhythms, 3) figurations based on trill-type ornamentations, and 4) motives derived from syncopated and so-called Lombard rhythms.

We have already observed that the motive is a generic unit which underlies much Baroque music, and it is also the most common of the motives used by Frescobaldi. Extensive passages of sixteenth-note motion are frequently developed by extension and repetition of this motive. The most typical patterns derivative from this motive are the following:

Mus. ex. II-15.

Frescobaldi is particularly fond of beginning this motive by the more hesitant method of the tied note as in the last two of the patterns above.

While the pattern (𝄾)♫ ♩ is by no means as omnipresent as that we have just discussed, it is still very frequent. Its combination with the syncopated rhythm of the Lombard snap becomes almost a mannerism of the composer:

Mus. ex. II-16.
Toccata IV, Book I, measure 2.[31]

We have already encountered figurations which have their origin in the expansion of the written-out trill. These are as common in Frescobaldi as they were in Mayone. Patterns which appear with frequency are:

Mus. ex. II-17.

Passages in dotted rhythms occur in almost all toccatas. Possibly many other passages which appear in the score in even note values were dotted in performance in a manner similar to the French *notes inégale*. Sometimes Frescobaldi seems to suggest this by indicating a dotted rhythm in the inception of a passage and then continuing the notation in equal notes:

31 Pidoux, III, 14.

Mus. ex. II-18.
Toccata V, Book I, measures 20-21.[32]

Certainly the most characteristically Italian rhythm is the so-called Lombard one in which the short note precedes the long. Frescobaldi uses this rhythm not only in situations in which the inherent syncopation gives accentuation to a masculine line, but also in situations in which he seeks a most intimate and feminine quality. The Lombard rhythm is particularly common in the most serious toccatas of Frescobaldi, those he specifies for use during the Elevation in the Mass. The most common patterns in which the Lombard rhythm occurs are:

Mus. ex. II-19.

The myriad shifts of figuration typical of these toccatas would be largely meaningless were it not for one element of Frescobaldi's style, his remarkable grasp of harmonic progression. No other element in these pieces is more strikingly modern than is their harmony. The figurations move in an environment of very calculated chordal progressions whose function it is to provide direction to the figural structures. Despite the fact that the figurations are so much more varied than those used by Merulo and other composers of the late Renaissance toccata, it is really the modern harmonic background of Frescobaldi's examples which places them in an entirely new musical world. Harmony in the Renaissance toccata acted as stable pillars for the largely static figurations. It changed relatively infrequently, and when it did so the progression was governed less by any harmonic logic than it was by the requirements

---

[32] Pidoux, III, 18.

of consonance and dissonance. The harmonic rhythm of Frescobaldi is much quicker. Changes occur generally at the rate of the half note although faster progression is not uncommon. More important than the mere rate of change is the obvious election of progressions in terms of harmonic potential. Any one section of a toccata, then, is largely directed by the harmonies which underlie it.

The harmonic vocabulary of the late sixteenth century had been expanded by Frescobaldi's time to include the dominant seventh chord, used by Frescobaldi in all positions; the free use of secondary dominants; and the ii_7 and $ii^6{}_5$ combinations. Each of these newly added harmonic entities gave directional force to the harmonic language. The sudden appearance of a dynamic harmony in the early years of the seventeenth century is closely connected to the simultaneous expression of dynamic emotion. Nowhere is this new harmonic order easier to observe than in the two *durezza*-style toccatas (Book I, Number 12; Book II, Number 8). The following passage is illustrative of the complexity of the harmony. It includes examples of secondary dominants, the use of the dominant seventh in root position and inversion, as well as a well developed modulation to the dominant.

Mus. ex. II-20.
Toccata XII, Book I, measures 16-21.[33]

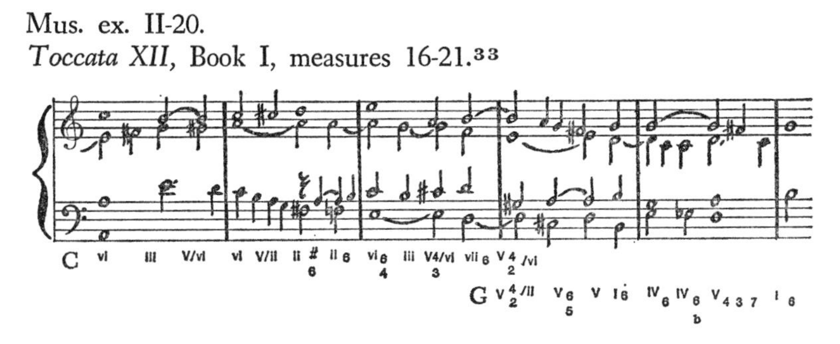

The toccatas in the second book are similar to those in the first. Frescobaldi does introduce into some of them passages in contrasting meter, a procedure he avoids in the earlier volume. One gets the impression that the toccatas of the second book are a bit more disciplined, that the figuration is pruned of excesses, and that the harmonic order is even more carefully calculated. The two toccatas on pedal points, numbers five and six, constitute a particular

33 Pidoux, III, 43.

genre which will be imitated by Southern- and Middle-German composers throughout the century. The *Toccata cromatica* from the *Fiori Musicali*[34] is another particular case. It is essentially a chromatic *ricercar* on two themes which opens with a short, six-measure introduction in *durezza* style.

The Capricci of 1626

The term *capriccio* in Italian music of the seventeenth century designates a composition which does not fall under the more conventional forms of *ricercar, canzone,* variation, or *cantus firmus* setting, but yet one which may partake of elements of any of them. A composition so named may vary from a piece which is largely studious and academic in tone to one in which the music is all lightness and gaiety. The term relates more to the freedom the composer himself felt in leaving the more stereotyped genres than to any unusual liberties he hay have taken in the music itself.

There is an unusual variety in the twelve compositions which make up the Frescobaldi *capricci.* The nature of these pieces ranges from the serious tones of the fantasias on the hexachord to sets of secular variations. A number of these pieces, such as the *Capriccio sopro il Cucho* and the sets of variations, are without doubt intended for the harpsichord. Others, such as the fantasias on solmization themes, the two pieces in *durezza* style, and the composition which specifies an added voice to be sung, were more likely designed for organ performance.

The two opening compositions, the *capricci* on *ut, re, mi, fa, sol, la* and on *la, sol, fa, mi, re, ut,* are obviously companion pieces. They are in reality on the same theme since in each the composer uses his theme in retrograde. Frescobaldi also introduces chromatic inflexions in both the ascending and descending hexachords. These pieces as well as the other *capriccio* on a solmization theme (*la, sol, fa, re, mi*) are made up of numerous sections in which the theme serves as the basis for varied and elaborate figuration and contrapuntal elaboration. These three *capricci* contain passages in which the writing is as flamboyant as any of Frescobaldi. The following passage is characteristic:

[34] Pidoux, V, 18.

Mus. ex. II-21.
Capriccio sopra la, sol, fa, mi, re, ut, measures 131-139.[35]

The *Capriccio di durezza* is similar to the chromatic toccata from the *Fiori Musicali* in that it is essentially a *ricercar* employing the texture of the *durezza* toccata. This composition, with its carefully constructed theme in which the downward leap of a minor sixth is characteristic, is one of Frescobaldi's most beautiful. The *Capriccio cromatico con ligature al contrario* is another of the composer's experimental compositions. In it he avoids the normal suspension and leads all tied notes upwards instead of downwards. The procedure leads to an unusual texture in which consonance is almost universal. The other experimental piece bears the title *Capriccio di obligo di cantare la quinta parte.* In this piece, which is similar to an example in the *Fiori Musicali* which we have already discussed, Frescobaldi provides for a sung *cantus firmus* to be interpolated wherever the performer finds it will fit. He does not provide the clues. The Pidoux edition[36] indicates only some of the possible entrances.[37]

The Liturgical Music

Music based on *cantus firmus* occurs only two places in Frescobaldi's keyboard works: the four hymn settings and three *Mag-*

---

[35] Pidoux, II, 14.

[36] Pidoux, II, 42.

[37] On this point see note, *Apel K,* 466. Using Burns' suggestion of transposing the theme, I would like to suggest two more possible entrances of the subject. Pidoux 44, brace 2, measure 2 and Pidoux 47, brace 2, measure 3. By use of all suggested entrances the sung part is maintained almost constantly throughout the piece.

nificat settings affixed to the first publication of the second book of toccatas and the settings of the *Kyrie* in the three organ masses that make up the *Fiori Musicali.* We would naturally expect this body of music to be conservative in tone, but what is so surprising is to find how very conservative it is. In the settings of liturgical *cantus firmus* the radical Frescobaldi becomes not only conservative but in reality reactionary. Hardly a trace of any of the new techniques of keyboard style or harmonic language is revealed in any of these settings. With few exceptions these compositions could be the work of Cavazzoni or Cabezon. The techniques employed by Frescobaldi are just those used by Renaissance composers of similar pieces. Most versets are either a short point of imitation with a theme derived from the appropriate chant or a setting of the chant in long-note *cantus firmus* style. Frescobaldi adheres to a contrapuntal style that is essentially sixteenth-century, and one finds little evidence of the new contrapuntal style based on the development of motivic figuration. Similarly the harmonic language is conservative, and even the appearance of a tiny bit of chromaticism is unusual.

One type of verset which seems to be unique with Frescobaldi sustains a pedal point throughout. The material in the other voices is derived from chant. As an example the conclusion of the last *Kyrie* from the first mass is given below. The circled notes are related to the chant melody.

Mus. ex. II-22.
Kyrie, *Fiori Musicali,* Mass I, conclusion.[38]

Very rarely Frescobaldi manages to make his versets sound more modern. In one such place, the third verse of the *Magnificat primi toni,* he elaborates the tenor *cantus firmus* with other voices based on a clearly perceived motive. This, coupled with the modern

[38] Pidoux, V, 13.

harmonic environment, makes this verse suggestive of verses in later chorale variations.

Mus. ex. II-23.
Magnificat primi toni, verse iii, measures 1-3.[39]

It should be pointed out that the masses which make up the *Fiori* are not complete. The composer provides no music for the ordinary outside that for the *Kyries.* When one compares the examples from this collection which are based on *cantus firmus* with the imaginative *ricercari, canzoni,* and toccatas it also contains, one concludes that the composer was far more interested in forms unbound by liturgical tradition. Perhaps he felt some obligation to restrain the tone of music designed to alternate with chant. He may have thought the newer musical language incongruous with the conservative tone of the chant. Thus to the composer the writing of such pieces may have been less challenging than the newer forms and styles. In all respects the liturgical organ music of Frescobaldi is less revolutionary and perhaps less interesting than the remaining body of his work.

ITALIAN ORGAN MUSIC AFTER FRESCOBALDI

After Frescobaldi the history of Italian keyboard music became even more closely related to the harpsichord than it had been in the earlier part of the century. Individual dance movements, dance suites, and variations on secular melodies became much more common in the literature. Some composers had already limited their output to such idiomatic harpsichord literature and have left nothing which seems suited to the organ — for instance the keyboard compositions of Martino Pesenti (c. 1600 to c. 1650) consist only of dance-oriented compositions. In the second half of the century the important publication of Bernardo Storace (1664) is made up

---

[39] Pidoux, IV, 76.

almost entirely of similar pieces. Bernardo Pasquini, the most prolific keyboard composer of the period, likewise produced far more works which were obviously intended for harpsichord performance than works which seem idiomatically suited to the organ.

The preeminence of the harpsichord is evidenced not only in the forms of music the composers favored, but also by the very texture of the majority of keyboard compositions of the period. A light, transparent, effervescent style depending upon those figurations which by their nature sound more convincing on the harpsichord replaced the essentially contrapuntal style of the earlier part of the century. While we must be careful not to attribute to the composers of the seventeenth century a feeling of differentiation of idioms which they may not have had, it does appear that their favorite instrument became more and more the harpsichord, an instrument which better suited the lighter quality of Italian music of the period. We will note a similar trend in France in the last half of the century.

Even in those works which seem by their nature most suited to the organ there is a feeling of a lack of vitality in the music itself. It seems as if the organ idiom was outdated, decidedly old-fashioned, and dependent more upon tradition than upon lively creative imagination. This lack of vitality is partly attributable to the harmonic idiom of Italian music of the period, an harmonic idiom which had become pristinely tonal. To a large degree the vitality of the music of Frescobaldi and his precursors is explained in the fortuitous combinations of the forms of late Renaissance keyboard music and the novelties of early Baroque harmonic structure. The constantly fluctuating harmonies; the harmonic experimentation; and the presence of the unexpected, even of the bizarre — all combined to enliven the basic structures already set out in the late sixteenth century. The complete ascendency of tonally directed harmony in the middle of the seventeenth century was, in comparison to the earlier idiom, much more conservative and less imaginative. The old forms of *canzone*, *ricercar*, and toccata continue; but they are now bereft of the major element of harmonic interest which had been so characteristic in Mayone, Trabaci, and Frescobaldi.

Nowhere is this tension between the older harmonic instability and the newer harmonic overstability more obvious than in a set of toccatas published initially around 1640 by the violinist Michelangelo

Rossi.[40] The influence of the toccatas of Frescobaldi is unmistakable. There is the same impetuous quality, the constant flux, the ever-changing mood characteristic of the older master's style. But what is different in Rossi's toccatas is the juxtaposition of sections in blandest tonal harmony with passages in which the older harmonic freedom and surprise suddenly reappear. In the following illustrative example the music has been moving in two-voice passage work largely built on scales in the key of B-flat major. Suddenly Rossi breaks to an E-major triad in the function of the dominant of the dominant of the original key of the piece, D-minor.

Mus. ex. II-24.
Rossi: *Toccata settima,* measures 14-16.[41]

The same short sections which characterize Frescobaldi's toccatas also make up those of Rossi. Rossi, however, has quite an imagination when it comes to key progressions. He is prone to cadence each short section in a related key. For instance, major cadences in the fifth toccata lie on:

> Tonic Key: C major — G major (measure 20) — A major (measure 27) — D major (measure 32) — B-flat major (measure 41) — F major (measure 50) — C major (measure 54) — G major (measure 57) — B-flat major (measure 67) — and through F major to the conclusion in the tonic key.

Rossi also has a broad vocabulary of figurative patterns which he exploits with considerable skill within the framework of a single short section. The texture varies considerably from serious four-voice *durezza* style to facile two-voice writing based on motivic interplay, a texture of which Rossi seems particularly fond. While Rossi's toccatas have life and verve they lack the emotional fervor of

---

[40] Michelangelo Rossi, *Works for Keyboard,* ed. John White, *CEKM* XV, 1966.

[41] *Ibid.,* 17.

Frescobaldi. While one must certainly attribute this partially to the obvious difference in genius, to some degree it is also explicable in a change in the nature of music from compositions of high emotional impact, characteristic of the early Baroque, toward more facilely contrived compositions of limited emotional content typical of much middle-Baroque music.

The publication of Giovanni Salvatore (1641)[42] is devoted entirely to compositions in the organ idiom. This work contains eight *ricercari,* two toccatas, four *canzoni,* and three complete organ masses. The *ricercari,* which are well-crafted compositions, are in the genre introduced by Trabaci. All are on multiple themes used in the conventional procedures which by now seem standard for this form in Italy. The last of these *ricercari* is based on a Gregorian hymn, *Iste Confessor,* and uses a long-note *cantus firmus* which presents the entire melody in one voice after another in the course of the piece. Salvatore is borrowing a procedure from an earlier Southern-Italian, in this case Mayone.

Salvatore's *canzoni* are very appealing and sometimes inventive music. The first three employ the traditional three-section format: duple—triple—duple, with thematic variation being used, although not consistently throughout any composition. The composer's selection of thematic material is highly idiomatic, generally sprightly and full of life. Salvatore breaks down the larger duple sections into sub-sections, some based on the principal theme of the composition and some based on newly introduced themes. Frequently he punctuates the juncture between such sections with short chordal insertions, frequently of unique harmony. The following example shows the use of augmented sixth chords in such a situation:

Mus. ex. II-25.
Salvatore: *Canzona francese terza,* measures 30-32.[43]

[42] Giovanni Salvatore, *Collected Keyboard Works,* ed. Hudson, *CEKM* III.
[43] *Ibid.,* 46.

The fourth of these *canzoni* is in reality a set of freely conceived variations on a popular tune of the day. The two toccatas in the collection are no more than very excellent imitations of those of Frescobaldi.

If Salvatore merely copied the style of Frescobaldi in his toccatas, he was more independent in the versets which make up the three organ masses. He appears to have had a unique talent for composition in this small format, and he shows none of the conservatism which Frescobaldi displayed in this idiom. For the majority of the verses Salvatore composed a short fugal setting. The variety, however, is amazing. The composer's ability to derive fresh subjects from the same material is obvious in the *Kyrie* settings of these masses. Here each new subject is derived from the same chant presented in the initial verset in long-note *cantus firmus* style. Some subjects seem to have been conditioned by the text which the verset is designed to replace. The masculine subject based on the notes of the tonic triad is obviously suggested by the text *Domine Deus Rex Coelesti* which the music replaces:

Mus. ex. II-26.
Salvatore: *Domine Deus,* Mass I, beginning.[44]

Another publication containing works suitable for the organ is that of Gregorio Strozzi (c. 1615 – c. 1690), the *Capricci da sonare cembali et organi* (1687).[45] Although published late in the composer's life, the *Capricci . . .* seems to contain much earlier work, as it is made up of compositions more typical of the middle than the latter part of the century. The conservative tone of the work is obvious from its opening composition, a lengthy (449 measures) *capriccio* on the notes of the hexachord. It is certainly doubtful that any composer would have written such a piece in the last years of the century. This *capriccio* is divided into nine distinct sections, each treating the notes of the hexachord in its own particular

[44] *Ibid.,* 54.

[45] Gregorio Strozzi, *Capricci da sonare cembali et organi,* ed. Hudson, *CEKM* XI.

fashion. In some sections the contrapuntal style is so scholarly and unimaginative that one suspects the composition may have been intended for pedagogical use. The same pedantic approach is obvious in the three *ricercari* in the collection. As with those of Storace, these *ricercari* are of the multi-thematic type. The counterpoint, however, has such a rigid quality to it that the compositions can hardly be called successful.

The four toccatas from this collection superficially show the imprint of Frescobaldi and other Southern-Italians. Again the emotional core of the earlier pieces is lacking in Strozzi's imitations, which tend to roam pointlessly from passage to passage and from figuration to figuration. The first toccata imitates the pedal point toccata introduced by Frescobaldi.

The most interesting of Strozzi's compositions are those in the style of the *canzone,* two *capricci* and three sonatas. In the later part of the century the term *capriccio* often refers to a composition in the style of the *canzone* but with a sectional order less defined than that of the traditional *canzone.* Strozzi's compositions of this type are in three sections and consistently use thematic variation. The sections, however, are in the order duple - duple - triple. The sonatas, on the other hand, are essentially *canzoni* using the normal duple - triple - duple format. The middle sections of these pieces, however, are of a larger scale than normal, and the compositions thus take on the structure of three distinct movements. At the conclusion of the triple movement the composer interpolates a free section as a bridge to the final duple one. Strozzi's other published compositions are distinctly for the harpsichord.

The most prolific Italian composer of keyboard music in the latter half of the century was Bernardo Pasquini (1637-1710).[46] As we have said, the majority of his works are certainly for harpsichord. Less than a dozen contrapuntal compositions would seem appropriate for the organ, and the toccatas, some thirty-seven in number, seem appropriate for either instrument. The most interesting of the contrapuntal compositions are the two *capricci* and the second of the two *ricercari.* The *capricci* are multisectional compositions, the first in seven sections and the second in five, in which the initial theme is subjected to the technique of variation. Pasquini has the

[46] Bernardo Pasquini, *Collected Works for Keyboard,* ed. M. B. Hayes, *CEKM* V, 7 vols.

ability to formulate easily perceptible themes and equally perceptible variations. The subtle complexity of Frescobaldi's variation technique is not to be found here.

Although the first of the two *ricercari* is nothing more than a mediocre example of the bi-thematic type, the second example, with the title *con fuga in piu modi,* is unique. Its form is similar to that of the two *capricci,* an extended multi-sectional development of a single theme. In this case the composition runs to 345 measures, and the sections vary from the stern texture of the chromatic *ricercar* to sections in lively figurative style and finally to a gigue. The theme with some of its more interesting permutations is given below:

Mus. ex. II-27.

In the numerous toccatas, or *tastati* as Pasquini sometimes calls them, one again has the impression that the composer is following the outward form of Frescobaldi without the inner content. The imaginative elements so characteristic of Frescobaldi are absent, and even the unusual harmonic moments characteristic of Rossi do not occur. What remains is largely figuration made up of the most common patterns and directed by the most predictable harmonies. Sequential progressions are used to excess. Particularly common are those employing progression of harmonies based on descending fifths:

Mus. ex. II-28.
Pasquini: *Toccata* (*CEKM V*, 5, number 85, p. 69), conclusion.

Even in the sonata, (in reality a toccata) designed for the elevation, Pasquini seems unable to muster any greater emotional depth. It is inconceivable that one could find as banal a passage in any early seventeenth-century example as the following excerpt typical of the texture of Pasquini's example:

Mus. ex. II-29.
Pasquini: *Sonata for the Elevation* (*CEKM V*, 6, number 105, p. 69), measures 21-23.

One cannot repress the feeling that after Frescobaldi Italian music for the organ suffered from adherence to formal procedures which no longer had viable content. Particularly is this true of the use of thematic variation as a cure-all to structural problems. In music for other instruments the older forms were transformed into the sonata and the concerto. In organ literature they tended to remain more or less static. The newer instrumental idioms had little in common with the essentially contrapuntal medium of the organ. Only conservative, pedantic composers continued to concern themselves with *canzoni* and *ricercari.* The harpsichord, by nature better adapted to the newer textures of the late seventeenth century, became more and more the only keyboard instrument acceptable for Italian musical style. The organ was left to its own conservative, liturgical tasks.

CHAPTER III.

FRANCE

A complete, historical study of the organ music of France during the seventeenth century is an impossibility and will probably remain impossible. A step by step process similar to that which we can observe in Italy and Germany is not revealed by French material available to us today. The gap of nearly a century which separates the publications of Attaignant (1530) and those of Titelouze (1623 and 1626) and the gap between his publications and the *Premier Livre d'Orgue* of Nivers (1665) are filled by only minor examples of organ music, examples which rarely reveal or suggest any continuity of developing organ style. The mysteries are many and intriguing. Titelouze's works show a fully developed, stylistically mature, and monumental musical language, a language we should have expected to see preceded by a host of composers contributing to its evolution. Yet it stands almost in a total vacuum. We would certainly expect to see a school of composers develop around so esteemed a teacher, but if Titelouze had a circle of composition students, as his contemporary Sweelinck did, that circle has vanished completely. From the publications of Nivers onward, the Classical style of French organ music is fully developed. It constitutes a cohesive, regimented style; its various forms are regimented; and there are only limited stylistic deviations from one composer to another. Yet prior to Nivers there is little in the existing literature to suggest how this cohesive style came into being. We are left chiefly to speculation.

One of the real enigmas in the pre-Classical history of French organ music lies in the fact that we have ample documentation of a sophisticated development in French organ building in the century from 1550 to 1650.[1] As early as 1580 an organ at Gisors[2] shows

[1] See: Fenner Douglass, *The Language of the Classical French Organ*, New Haven: Yale University Press, 1969.

[2] *Ibid.*, 59.

with astonishing consistency the characteristic features of the mature Classical instrument. That an equally sophisticated tradition of organ registration existed is proven by Mersenne's very complete instructions on the subject (1636).[3] The thoroughness with which he describes compound registrations of great complexity suggests that the organists of the period had a developed sense of organ sonority and color. Even more baffling is the fact that the type of registration suggestions Mersenne gives suggest the existence of an organ style which would have had little in common with Titelouze's severe contrapuntal one. Mersenne describes one solo register after another, registrations which suggest the dominance of a single voice in a musical texture and not an equality of multiple voices.

How can we reconcile the existence of a fully developed instrument with its associated registrational tradition on the one hand with a largely absent repertory on the other? The answer would seem to lie in the nature of the use to which the organ in France was put. No other country developed the practice of alternation as did France. The French placed the organ squarely in the midst of their liturgical practices. As we will see, the organ was required as an alternation medium for all important services in Parisian churches. Alternation, although common elsewhere, was mandatory in Paris. The short versets required by alternation coupled with its chant associations had always suggested improvisation in lieu of composition. Without doubt the French cultivated an extensive improvisatory tradition. Only in the last third of the century when it became fashionable to impose Parisian tastes on the provinces was it found necessary to commit this tradition to paper. Titelouze alone, whose musical style of conservative polyphony must have been completely atypical of music around him, felt earlier any similar compulsion to publish.

As the general musical style in France changed from a basic contrapuntal Renaissance orientation to the dance- and opera-oriented tradition of the mid-seventeenth century, organists must have rapidly followed suit. The newer styles demanded sharply differentiated voices to set out lively and expressive melodies. These are the voices which Mersenne so clearly describes. The short dance movement, typical in France from the 1630's onward was an appropriate medium in which to set a short organ verset. The conservative, poly-

---

[3] *Ibid.*, 63.

phonic tradition which underlay German and Italian organ music largely ceased to exist in France after Titelouze. Even in the organ mass, where one might have expected the chant to have maintained a conservative hold, the effects of dance and opera *récit* were rapidly felt. Movements based on *plein-chant* became fewer and fewer until in many masses they ceased to exist at all. By the time of the publications of Nivers, this newer tradition is fully developed. His works reveal no hesitant approach or insecure stylistic base. In this chapter we will first try to reconstruct as accurately as possible the history of the French organ tradition prior to Nivers. Then we will turn our attention briefly to the French Classical organ and then explore the Classical style itself.

FROM ATTAIGNANT TO TITELOUZE

There is not a single significant example of music intended especially for organ during the period from the publications of Attaignant (1536) to that of Titelouze (1621). An insignificant fantasy by Guillaume Costeley (c. 1531-1606) designated either for organ or spinette reveals a keyboard style no more advanced than that of Attaignant.[4] Its light three-voiced texture is built upon stereotyped keyboard motives similar to those in much Renaissance literature. A posthumous publication of the works of Claude le Jeune (1530-1600), the *Second Livre des Meslanges* (1612), contains three fantasias;[5] but these are almost certainly designed for ensemble instrumental performance. One passage in the first of these fantasias reveals the French composers were not unaware of experimentations in harmonic practice:

Mus. ex. III-1.
Le Jeune: *Première Fantasie,* measures 126-130.

[4] See: *Apel K* 207.

[5] Claude Le Jeune, *Trois Fantaisies Instrumentales,* ed. Bonfils, *Orgue et Liturgie,* 39, Paris: Schola Cantorum, 1956.

A publication of forty-two fantasias of Eustache du Caurroy (1549-1609)[6] likewise is certainly ensemble music. These compositions, as were those of Le Jeune, are typical of the ensemble *ricercar*. There is nothing in the works of either composer which could be regarded as essentially French, and they contribute nothing to defining a native instrumental style.

A manuscript in Munich (Bavarian State Library, Ms. 2987) contains *chanson* transcriptions which Bonfils asserts are of French origin.[7] The manuscript, however, is written in German keyboard tablature, a notation decidedly not French. These pieces are in no way different from hundreds of other *chanson* transcriptions. They do, however, suggest an interesting problem. Why did the French not leave a keyboard repertory based on their native *chanson*, a medium which we have seen from our study of Italy to be ready-made for instrumental music? We can only guess that such pieces were typically improvised in France. They would have represented a style so indigenous that formal composition would have been unnecessary. It would have been only the Italians, who were imitating an idiom not natively theirs, who felt compelled to commit to paper music based on the *chanson*.

An anonymous manuscript of obvious French origin now in the British Museum (Add. 29486) provides an excellent glimpse of the types of liturgical organ music in use directly before the time of Titelouze. This manuscript, dated 1618, contains several sets of preludes and intonations, three complete organ masses, a setting of the *Te Deum*, ten settings of the *Magnificat*, two fantasias, and a number of short fugal movements. Other than Sweelinck, the composer of one of the fantasias, and Giovanni Gabrieli, the composer of one set of intonations, no other composers are mentioned. The remainder of the pieces, however, shows such a strong stylistic similarity that they must all be the work of a single composer.

The organ masses and *Magnificat* settings are the most interesting works in the collection. These alternation settings are firmly based on chant and show the same restrained features we have observed in similar works by Cabezon and Frescobaldi. The music has a conservative, modal complexion having more in com-

[6] Eustache du Caurroy, *Fantasies à 3, 4, 5, et 6 Parties*, ed. Bonfils, *Les Grandes de l'Orgue*, Paris: Schola Cantorum, n.d.

[7] Jean Bonfils (ed.), *Chanson françaises pour Orgue, Le Pupitre*, Paris: Heugal, 1968.

mon with the sixteenth than the early seventeenth century. Harmonic surprises, idiomatic keyboard writing, and other evidences of early Baroque style hardly appear at all. All these *alternatim* movements are short and only a few exceed fifty or so measures.

From the point of view of the subsequent history of French organ style, the most interesting pieces are several compositions which conclude some of the *Magnificat* settings. These pieces have titles which indicate that a solo melody is to be played on either *les registres couppez* (divided registers) or on the cornet. What we have here, then, are the earliest known examples of the type which in French classical organ style became the *récit en dessus*. Following is an excerpt from the concluding movement of the *Magnificat Quinti Toni* from this collection:

Mus. ex. III-2.

THE WORKS OF TITELOUZE

It can be argued that French organ music never came under the influence of the Baroque. The classical style is dominated by a spirit having nothing in sympathy with either the experimentalism and emotional fervor of the Italians or the large compositional constructions of the Dutch and Germans. Only rarely does the style transcend the light elegance of the age and approach the seriousness of other seventeenth-century organ traditions. We might expect to find some elements of Baroque grandeur in the works of the one composer in the early half of the century who has left us any significant body of music. We are to be disappointed, however, if we hope to find the spirit of the Baroque in the works of Titelouze. Only in their monumental conception do these works have anything in common with the Baroque. Titelouze reveals himself to be a composer of ultra-conservative nature, a composer who evidences no sympathy for the new compositional techniques of the early seventeenth century. His works represent the last flowering of the organ style of the late Renaissance. As a spiritual descendant of Cavazzoni and Cabezon he writes as if the early-Baroque had made no dent in the polyphonic edifice of the sixteenth century.

His two publications reveal the conservative nature of their author. Both the *Hymnes de l'église* (1623) and *Le Magnificat* (1626)[8] are based consistently on chant. We find in these works no longing on the part of the composer either to free himself from the limitations of a *cantus firmus* or to create new formal procedures suggested by it. As we have seen, Frescobaldi frequently employed a *cantus firmus* in his organ writing, but one has the feeling he bent his material for his own fantastic ends. Titelouze lacked such brazen individuality. Those procedures developed by the Italians and the Spaniards in the last half of the preceding century consistently underlie Titelouze's compositions. It is interesting to note that the composer was born and raised in the Spanish Netherlands. The spirit of the Spanish Renaissance, and not that of the Italian Baroque, breathes throughout his works.

The general characteristics of the style of Titelouze are:

1) conservative, polyphonic texture generally of four distinct voices, occasionally of only three.
2) thorough domination of the contrapuntal structure by Gregorian melodies.
3) melodic lines conditioned by vocal considerations and rarely by idiomatic keyboard figuration.
4) avoidance of clearcut cadence structures with melodic overlapping of all internal cadential points.
5) use of the most conservative formal structures such as the long-note *cantus firmus* technique or motet-like constructions based on consecutive points of imitation.
6) A tonal idiom modally conditioned without evidence of modern functional harmony.

---

[8] Jean Titelouze, *Oeuvres completes d'Orgue,* ed. Guilmant, *Archives de Maitres de l'Orgue,* Mainz: Schott, 1967.

7) Avoidance of all "modern" harmonic elements such as dissonant chordal combinations and chromatically conditioned harmony.
8) Similar avoidance of unusual rhythmic or melodic surprises.
9) A resulting structure conservative in sound, consistent in texture, essentially in the spirit of the sixteenth century, and most serious in tone.

A rigid format shapes a hymn setting of Titelouze. The majority of these settings contain three verses, although a few contain four. The opening verse is always built over a long-note *cantus firmus* generally in the bass voice. The material in the accompanying voices is generally derived from the Gregorian melody. The second verse is normally in motet style and is built on consecutive points of imitation. The themes are chant derived. If there are four verses in the setting, the third is likely to be made up of two canonic upper voices over the hymn in long notes in the pedal. Such verses are the only concession Titelouze makes from his normal four-voice texture. The final movement is again based on the long-note *cantus firmus,* but here it often moves from voice to voice in the course of the movement. This migrating *cantus* is a technique we have already observed in the works of Andrea Gabrieli.

The hymn settings reveal only one type of movement in which the composer is willing to free himself from the restraints of vocally-oriented melodic line. Several hymn settings conclude with movements based on extended pedal points either in the bass or soprano voices. The free voices in these movements are built on small bits of motivic material. The resulting structure is much more modern in sound than is typical for Titelouze. These movements generate their excitement and interest not from the severe interweaving of contrapuntal lines, but through an idiomatic use of organ sonority. The following example is typical of the texture of such movements:

Mus. ex. III-3.
Titelouze: *Annue Christe, Amen,* measures 35-38.[9]

[9] *Ibid.,* 75.

The second volume of Titelouze's works reveals that the composer relaxed somewhat his severe musical style. He remarks in his preface to the settings of the *Magnificat* that many who had studied his hymns had found them technically too difficult. These new pieces, he says, should satisfy this criticism. The musical style here is, all in all, less complex and more direct; and in many small points these pieces show the composer's awareness of more modern styles of keyboard writing.[10] The most obvious stylistic difference between the two publications lies in the fewer long-note *cantus firmus* pieces in the *Magnificat* collection and a greater number of fugal movements there. Those pieces also show a greater comprehension of the nature of harmonically-conceived writing:

Mus. ex. III-4.
Titelouze: *Magnificat Septimi Toni, Deposuit potentes,* measures 15-20.[11]

Unlike the hymns, which avoid all chromatic writing, the *Magnificats* contain some of it, though it is exceedingly restrained.

Mus. ex. III-5.
Titelouze: *Magnificat Primi Toni, Deposuit potentes,* Alter ver, beginning.[12]

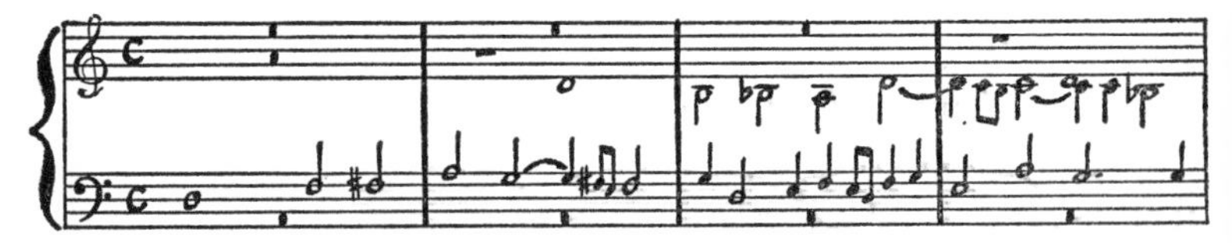

10 We know that the Magnificats were written after 1623. It is possible that the hymns were composed much earlier, and would, then, have represented an earlier style.

11 Titelouze, *op. cit.,* 153.

12 *Ibid.,* 107.

There are also passages in which the composer completely gives up his vocally-oriented style and writes motivically conditioned passages in a very bold manner.[13] Some of the fugal subjects he constructs are as instrumental as any in Frescobaldi:

Mus. ex. III-6.
Titelouze: *Magnificat Quarti Toni, Gloria Patri,* beginning.[14]

We must not, however, view the citations above as typical of the *Magnificats* as a whole. These passages are extraordinary intrusions into a structure that remains essentially conservative in nature. As we might expect Titelouze's works had but limited effect upon the subsequent course of French organ music in the century. Only in the *plein jeu* of the late seventeenth-century organ masses can one sense that his serious style had continued at all. Titelouze did, however, stand as the spiritual father of the most serious of the French Classical composers, De Grigny. It was certainly no accident that De Grigny chose the hymn as the basis for some of his most moving works.

FROM TITELOUZE TO NIVERS

As we have already remarked, there is no evidence that Titelouze had around him a school of pupils or that his works inspired similar works from other composers. In the period from the *Magnificat* settings (1626) to the first publication of Nivers (1665) there exists but a single work of similar seriousness. However, this example, a fantasia by Charles Racquet (active in Paris c. 1618 to 1643), is not liturgical music, bears no relationship to the subsequent development of French style, and shows a closer relationship to Sweelinck than to Titelouze. A handsome and extended composition, it treats the same theme contrapuntally in four contrasting sections:

[13] See the conclusion of *Suscepit Israel, Magnificat Quinti Toni, ibid.,* 141.
[14] *Ibid.,* 133.

Section 1: Fugal exposition in *ricercar* style
Section 2: Exposition of an elaboration of the theme moving in eighth-note motion
Section 3: The original theme used as a long-note *cantus firmus* with new contrapuntal material
Section 4: Theme presented against elaborate sixteenth-note passage work.

The concluding dominant and tonic pedal points are particularly exciting and modern sounding writing.

Another fantasia by Etienne Richard (d. 1669)[15] is on a far smaller scale. While it demonstrates a secure sense of harmonic direction, it suffers by being broken into too many small sections. The sections in ternary meter show clearly the influence of dance rhythms. Whether these two fantasias are all that remains of a distinguished line of such compositions we cannot know. In any event their consistent contrapuntal approach has nothing in common with the French Classical style.

What little evidence we do have concerning the development of this style must come from the scanty works of two composers, Henri DuMont (1610-1684) and Louis Couperin (1626-1661). The limited number of keyboard works of DuMont[16] indicate specifically the instrument or instruments for which each composition was intended. Some are for organ, some for organ and *clavecin,* and some for *clavecin* or a trio of stringed instruments. It is interesting that the composer indicates that dance movements are as appropriate to the organ as to the *clavecin.* The serious, chordal texture of the first *allemande grave* is identical to that of the Classical *plein jeu.* It can be distinguished from the latter genre only by being cast in binary dance form.

---

15 André Pirro, *L'Art des Organistes, Encyclopédie de la Musique* VII, 1272.

16 Henri Dumont, *L'Oeuvre pour Clavier,* ed. Bonfils, *L'Organiste Liturgique,* XIII Paris: Schola Cantorum, 1956.

Mus. ex. III-7.
DuMont: *Allemanda Gravis,* beginning.[17]

Another Classical texture is anticipated by DuMont in four preludes *en duo.* Duo compositions with very lucid, dance-oriented counterpoint are an important genre of the Classical style. DuMont provides each of these pieces with an alternate third voice, and, in so doing, he anticipates the equally important trio. The Bonfils edition is woefully misleading, however: The two upper voices were intended to be taken by the right hand and the bass voice with the left. The use of pedal in trios was reserved only for the slower moving pieces, and it certainly would not have been used in allegro movements similar to these. The opening of one of these preludes is given below:

Mus. ex. III-8.
DuMont: Prelude Number 7, beginning.[18]

No doubt the history of organ music in France at mid-century could be greatly clarified if the contents of a manuscript containing some seventy works of Louis Couperin were made readily available. Unfortunately we have only a description of the manuscript and a

[17] *Ibid.,* 4.
[18] *Ibid.,* 10.

detailed list of its contents.[19] This volume is definitely the work of the composer himself, and he carefully dated from 1650 to 1658 each of its many items. From Oldham's description we learn that two pieces are preludes (*pleins jeux* ?), six are *basses de trompette,* two are duos, thirty-three are fugal movements often termed fantasias, and twenty-seven are plain-song settings. A few of the titles, such as that of number 29 "*Fugue qu'il fault jouer d'un mouvement fort lent sur la tierce du Grand Clavier avec le tremblant lent,*" provide evidence of specific registrational requirements. The designations of numbers 5 and 6 indicate the practice of thumbing from one manual to another to sustain a *cantus firmus* while playing a moving voice simultaneously with the right hand. Save for such tantalizing bits of information, we can gain no access to a manuscript of great historical and musical value.

Three organ pieces of Couperin, a fantasia, a duo, and a carillon have fortunately come down to us from another source.[20] The fantasia is the earliest available example of the *basse de trompette.* Couperin handles this genre with mature skill. His theme has the heroic quality associated with this type of piece. The solo line has the characteristic wide leaps found in nearly all later examples:

Mus. ex. III-9.
Louis Couperin: *Fantasia,* measures 23-29, bass.[21]

The *gigue* rhythm so often found in later duos is found in the Couperin example. This composition, however, concludes with a

[19] Guy Oldham, "L. Couperin: A New Source of French Keyboard Music of the Mid-seventeenth Century," *Recherches sur la Musique française* I (1960), 51.

[20] Louis Couperin, *L'Oeuvre d'Orgue, Orgue et Liturgie* VI, ed. Dufourcq, Paris: Schola Cantorum, 1954, 24, 27, and 30. The other works in this collection are not necessarily for the organ.

[21] *Ibid.,* 25.

somewhat unusual coda in binary rhythm and shows an unusually firm grasp of harmonic direction in a two-voice instrumental idiom.

The *carillon* is without doubt designed to be played on the brilliant registers of the *grand jeu*. The exploitation of echo, so often associated with this registration, is important in the piece. Couperin shows in these three pieces a mature concept of the new Classical style. We must await, however, the appearance in print of the Oldham manuscript, which will, no doubt, confirm Couperin as the father of the new style.

An attempt was made by François Roberday (1624-1680) to introduce the Italian style of organ music into France. His publication, *Fugues et Caprices* (1660),[22] contains a series of *ricercar* movements. Most of these movements are followed by a three-sectional variation *canzone* entitled "caprice." Roberday admits in his preface that some of these pieces belong to Frescobaldi and some to Froberger and that the themes of other compositions had been provided him by other composers. The work was published in the Italian manner of open score, a procedure rare in France. Since we have extensive biographical information about Roberday[23] which makes almost no mention of his musical activities, the *Fugues et Caprices* are most likely not works of Roberday himself, but merely an anthology of Italian compositions he had grown to admire and collected for publication under his own name. In any event, the publication seems to have had little influence in the subsequent history of French organ style. Of the Classical composers, only Gigault made any attempt, and that very brief, to write in the Italian manner.[24]

THE FRENCH CLASSICAL STYLE: SOME GENERAL CHARACTERISTICS

A decidedly Germanic outlook (resulting from the importance of Bach) in the study of seventeenth-century organ literature tends to put French music in a poor light. The Classical French style of organ writing depends upon a completely un-Germanic set of criteria, criteria which stress qualities largely outside the style of seventeenth-century German music for the instrument. For instance,

22 François Roberday, *Fugues et Caprices*, ed. Jean Ferrard, Paris: Heugel, 1972.

23 P. Hardouin, "François Roberday," *Revue de musicologie*, July 1960, 44.

24 This composer left some fugues in the Italian manner.

to expect to see in François Couperin the same qualities one finds in Buxtehude is to misunderstand the place of both composers. The first step in understanding the French Classical style is to understand what qualities it stressed and what qualities it largely ignored. The following are general characteristics of this style:

1) The French Classical style stresses grace, sensitivity, melodic nuance, and small scale. These qualities are best developed in compositional formats of limited extent. Large formal orders with complex thematic transformations, intricate contrapuntal workings, and the like are not only inappropriate: Had they been employed, they would have destroyed the style itself. This is an art which could exist only in the miniature.
2) French Classical organ music is designed only for liturgical use within the practice of alternation. Autonomous compositions standing outside this tradition do not exist. This fact to a large degree determines the limited size of the typical French composition. Only in the offertory did the French organist have any opportunity for use of extensive compositions.
3) French Classical organ music is intimately tied to a conception of an instrument. The instrument and the style are two sides of the same coin. The French composer expected a precise registration for each genre of composition in the tradition. His works, then, depend upon a highly regimented conception of registration, unknown in other countries.
4) French Classical organ style is not tightly tied to the traditions of older contrapuntal styles as are the German and Italian. Instead the musical style of the French was derived largely from the current styles in opera, dance, and *clavecin* music.
5) The French Classical style is so defined that highly individual writing is unknown and does not appear to have been sought. French composers worked within the bounds of clearly understood types of compositions, bounds which they rarely violated. The regimentation of organ composition is certainly as complete as that effected by Lully in opera. Apel suggests, probably correctly, that some external influence, possibly the Jesuits, was responsible for the organization of the style within such narrow limits.[25]

[25] *Apel K.*, 723.

THE FRENCH CLASSICAL ORGAN

Although this book has studiously avoided discussion of seventeenth-century organ design, an attempt to discuss the French tradition without a brief introduction to the instrument is an impossibility. The type of instrument which the French composer required was as explicitly delineated as were the musical genres in which he wrote. The many registrational directions provided by French composers[26] amply attest to the unique relationship between instrument and musical style. These directions have a uniformity about them which indicates once again a thoroughly organized tradition which placed little premium on individual tastes. A study of the requirements in the sources on registration reveals that the composers expected an organ similar to the following hypothetical disposition:

Grand Orgue	*Positif*	*Récit*
Montre 16′	Montre 8′	Cornet V (treble)
Bourdon 16′	Bourdon 8′	Trompette 8′
Montre 8′	Prestant 4′	
Bourdon 8′	Flûte 4′	
Prestant 4′	Nasard 2⅔′	*Écho*
Flûte 4′	Doublette 2′	Cornet V
Grosse Tierce 3⅕′	Tierce 1⅗′	
Nasard 2⅔′	Larigot 1⅓′	*Pédale*
Doublette 2′	Fourniture	Flûte 8′
Quarte de Nasard 2′	Cymbale	Flûte 4′
Tierce 1⅗′	Cromorne	Trompette 8′
Sifflet 1′		Clairon 4′
Cornet V (treble)		
Fourniture		
Cymbale		
Trompette 8′		
Clairon 4′		Tremblant fort
Voix humaine 8′		Tremblant doux

The instrument was structured around the *Grand orgue* and its diminutive, the *Positif*. Smaller instruments had only these two manuals and in some cases they were less complete than the list above. Auxiliary manuals were used for solo and echo purposes.

[26] These are all translated in Douglass, *op. cit.*, 178 following.

CARL A. RUDISILL LIBRARY
LENOIR-RHYNE UNIVERSITY

The *Pédale* functioned either to provide the bass for simple trio playing or to provide the assertive *Trompette* 8′ to carry the *cantus firmus* in the bass and tenor voices.

Two distinct ensemble registrations were employed. The sounds of one were never confused with the other:

1) The *Plein jeu: Montre* 16′, *Bourdon* 16′, *Montre* 8′, *Bourdon* 8′, *Prestant, Doublette, Fourniture,* and *Cymbale.* This was normally coupled to the *Petit plein jeu (Positif): Bourdon* 8′, *Montre* 8′, *Prestant, Doublette, Fourniture,* and *Cymbale.* This registration was reserved for the more serious, sedate pieces in the literature, pieces in which a contrapuntal four-voice texture was sustained, possibly over a pedal *cantus firmus.*
2) The *Grand jeu: Bourdon* 8′, *Prestant, Nasard, Quarte de Nasard, Tierce, Trompette, Clairon, Cornet* V and often the *tremblant fort.* The *Petit Grand jeu* was normally coupled to the above: *Prestant, Bourdon* 8′, *Nasard, Tierce, Cromorne.* The *cornets* and reeds of the *Écho* and *Récit* were also incorporated, if possible. The registration emphasized the brilliance of *cornet* and reed registrations taken together. The most brilliant pieces in the literature were invariably assigned to this ensemble registration.

Duos were played on registrations which juxtaposed reed and *tierce* colors. Typical registrations were:

1) Treble: *Petite tierce (Bourdon, Prestant, Nasard, Tierce)* on the *Positif.*
   Bass: *Grand jeu de tierce (Bourdon* 16′, *Bourdon* 8′, *Flûte* 4′, *Grosse tierce, Nasard, Quarte de nasard, Tierce)* on the *Grand orgue.*

   or

2) Treble: *Cornet (Récit)*
   Bass: *Trompette* with its foundations (*Bourdon* 8′, *Prestant*).

Trios were played on similar registrations, the right hand taking two voices. Slower trios employed the *Flûtes de Pédale* with each of the hands on a separate manual with stops similar to the above.

CARL A. RUDISILL LIBRARY
LENOIR-RHYNE UNIVERSITY

Fugues were generally played on reed stops with their foundations (*Bourdon, Prestant, Trompette* or *Bourdon, Prestant, Cromorne*) or, if the fugue were particularly brilliant, on the *grand jeu*. The *plein jeu* was not used for fugal movements.

The largest number of compositions in the repertory are associated with solo registrations characterized either by reed or *tierce* colors. The accompanying voices were played on the *jeux doux* made up either of two eight foot stops (*Montre* and *Bourdon*) or an eight foot with a four foot (*Bourdon* and *Prestant*, or *Bourdon* and *Flûte* 4′). The solo voices used were:

1) *Trompette* with foundations (*Bourdon* and *Prestant*)
2) *Cromorne* with foundations (*Bourdon* and *Prestant*)
3) *Voix humaine* with *Bourdon, Flûte* 4′, and *tremblant*
4) *Cornet* V (either on the *Grand orgue* or *Écho*)
5) *Jeu de tierce* (*Bourdon, Flûte* 4′, *Nasard, Doublette, Tierce, Larigot*)
6) *Grand jeu de tierce* (similar stops on the *Grand Orgue* based on the *Bourdon* 16′).

The unique relationship between registration and musical styles is evident in that each of the standard sonorities had connected with it an appropriate musical genre. For instance terms such as *Plein jeu, Grand jeu, Jeu de tierce,* and so forth are at the same time designations of specific registrations as well as the genres appropriate to each registration. The intimate relationship between registration and musical style demands in performance of this music sounds similar to that for which it was conceived. Otherwise the music becomes meaningless. The other traditions of seventeenth-century organ music are relatively translatable to organs unlike that for which they were originally created. The French Classical style, attached as it was to so definite a concept of an instrument, resists such translation.

TYPES OF COMPOSITION

The Plein Jeu.

The most conservative style in the French repertory was reserved for the *plein jeu*. The musical texture associated with the *plein jeu* is closely related to the Italian *toccata con ligature et durezza.* Unlike most other types in the French repertory, the integrity of four, occasionally five, contrapuntal voices is preserved in the *plein jeu*. These voices, however, move within a clear harmonic framework. Whatever contrapuntal integrity any one voice may have is carefully conditioned by the prevailing chordal organization. The result is a severe texture relying for its interest on a strong sense of harmony, the limited use of melodic figuration, and control of non-chord tones, particularly the suspension dissonance. The majority of these compositions are in duple meter, with half-note harmonic rhythm maintained throughout. Melodic motion in values smaller than the eighth-note is practically non-existent, and even eighth-note motion is limited and reserved. The intent is to produce a composition of dignity, restraint, conservative sound, and solemnity, a style which contrasts strikingly with the dance- and opera-oriented origins of the remainder of the repertory.

The *plein jeu* was reserved for opening movements of the major sections of the Mass and the opening movement of *suites*. Less frequently it is also used as a concluding movement of such a set of pieces. Composers apparently found it appropriate and perhaps respectful to begin with the most restrained and conservative idiom before breaking into more modern sounding styles. One has the feeling that composers paid homage to the severity of Titelouze's strict style, but once having paid their obeisance rapidly turned their pens elsewhere.

Compositions organized entirely upon harmonic movement must of necessity be short. The liturgical context already demanded this, and few *pleins jeux* exceed fifty measures in length. Unlike its Italian equivalent, the *plein jeu* contains no harmonic experimentation or excessive use of chromaticism. Elements of surprise would have been foreign to a style so carefully regimented, and without exception they do not occur. The harmonic language of the *plein jeu* is that of typical middle-Baroque writing. The newly-found device of the secondary dominant is the only important intrusion into the consistently diatonic harmonic framework. Internal cadences are carefully placed to provide points of reference in the musical structure. These are always closely related to the tonic key. The following example from Boyvin is typical of the texture and harmonic language of the *plein jeu*:

Mus. ex. III-10.
Boyvin: *Grand plein jeu, Premier ton,* measures 1-7.[27]

Compositions for the *petit plein jeu au positif* occur frequently, generally as brief concluding movements of suites or sections of the Mass. The texture of these pieces is lighter and thinner than the *plein jeu* itself. Scale passages in sixteenth-note motion as well as motivic writing are typical. The consistent four or five voice texture of the *plein jeu* is avoided. The following example is characteristic:

Mus. ex. III-11.
Guilain: *Suite de quatrième ton, Petit plein jeu,* measures 1-4.[28]

Sections for the *petit plein jeu* were often interpolated into the *plein jeu* itself. In so doing the composers relieved the serious texture of the genre on the one hand and expanded its length on the other.

The *plein jeu* was always the medium against which the long-note *cantus firmus* in the pedal was set. This tradition, which finds its origin in Titelouze, was never violated. The chant melody could

---

[27] Jacques Boyvin, *Premier Livre d'Orgue,* ed. Bonfils, Paris: Les Editions Ouvrières, 1969, 15.
[28] Jean Adam Guilain, *Pièces d'Orgue,* ed. Guilmant, *Archives des Maitres de l'Orgue,* Mainz: Schott, 1969, 46.

appear in either the tenor or bass voices, but always it was assigned to the assertive Trompette 8′ of the pedal and disposed in consistent whole- or half-note values. In many cases there is no musical connection between the manual voices and the chant melody. In many situations the manuals are provided with a texture which would be entirely satisfactory with complete omission of the pedal:

Mus. ex. III-12.
De Grigny: *Premier Kyrie,* measures 1-5,[29] (pedal *cantus firmus* omitted).

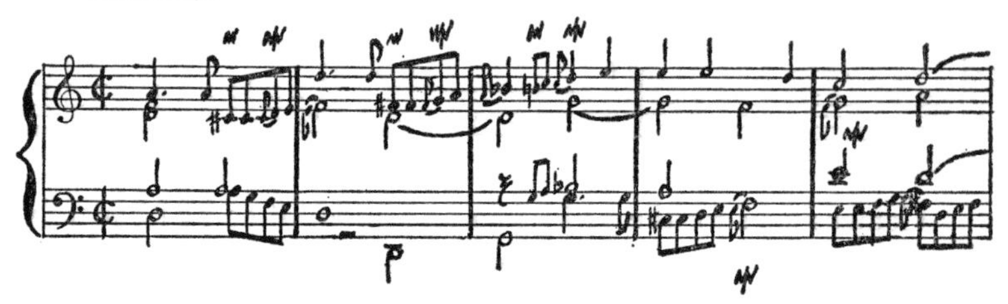

At other times there are simple efforts to relate the manual voices to the pedal melody.[30] These relationships always represent obvious thematic derivation. One never finds hidden, esoteric constructions in French music of the period. These would have been regarded as tiresome intrusions into a style which depended so much on clarity and directness of musical statement.

Finally we should mention two examples of the *plein jeu* in which the pedal is employed not for the function of bearing the *cantus firmus,* but for virtuoso effects. The *plein jeu* which opens the suite of Marchand[31] employs a double pedal. The right foot bears a second tenor voice and the left foot plays a parody of the bass voice otherwise carried in the left hand. The piece has a certain awkward quality about it which suggests this Germanic procedure was hardly acceptable in the French idiom. The other composition, the prelude to the suite on the third tone of Jullien[32] is much more

[29] Nicolas De Grigny, *Livre d'Orgue,* ed. Guilmant, *Archives des Maitres de l'Orgue,* Mainz: Schott, n.d., 1.

[30] See the *Gloria* from the Couperin *Messe pour les paroisses.*

[31] Louis Marchand, *Pièces d'Orgue,* ed. Guilmant, *Archives des Maitres de l'Orgue,* Mainz: Schott, 1967, 15.

[32] Gilles Jullien, *Premier Livre d'Orgue,* ed. Dufourcq, Paris: Heugel, 1952, 35.

successful. Here the *Pédale* is assigned a moving tenor voice of considerable interest.

The Fugue

Considering the importance of fugal forms in other seventeenth-century traditions, the French organ fugue is insignificant. We have already observed that serious contrapuntal writing was alien to the French style, and although such writing was not avoided entirely, it played a much smaller part in this tradition than it played in either the Italian or German. The French fugues were typically even shorter than the *pleins jeux* and most were no longer than fughettas. A typical plan was to have two expositions, the first complete with the theme in all voices, the second incomplete. The first exposition generally cadenced on either the dominant or relative key. A short bridge section might connect the expositions. Entire compositions might consist of no more than twenty-five measures.

The thematic material was fittingly simple. Subjects were short and generally contained some characteristic rhythmic motive or intervallic progression which gave the theme its integrity. The French differentiated two types of fugues, the *fugue grave* and the *fugue de movement.* These roughly correspond in type to the Italian styles of *ricercar* and *canzone.* Chaumont's *Suite du deuxième ton* contains examples of both types of fugue. The beginning of each is given below:

Mus. ex. III-13.
Chaumont: *Suite du deuxième ton.* [33]

33 Lambert Chaumont, *Pièces d'Orgue sur les huit Tons*, ed. Farrard, Paris: Heugel, 1970, 21 and 24.

The use of fugal devices is rare. Thematic inversion occurs occasionally, but *stretto,* augmentation, and diminution are almost unknown. Dance rhythms, particularly the *bourée* and *gigue,* dominate the *fugue de movement.*

Only De Grigny elevated the fugue of the French style to a higher level. His preference for five-voice texture in which the pedal receives an *obbligato* voice and the voices carried by each hand are played on independent registers is indicative of his more serious attitude toward the fugue. His fugue subjects are often derived from parody of the appropriate chant melody. The fugue in the *Kyrie* of the Mass consists of an archaic series of expositions each based on a subject derived from successive lines of the chant.[34]

De Grigny retains organization of the fugue into clear-cut expositions, although he often expands the format to three instead of two. In the fugue from *Veni creator* the middle exposition is based upon the most natural and unaffected inversion of the subject.[35] When such rarely-used devices appear in French music they are so unobtrusive that they may be entirely missed in the natural levity of the style.

The fugue from the hymn setting *Pange lingua* is unusual for the technical complexity of the pedal voice. De Grigny expects from the pedal, which was not normally used in French fugues in any case, a fluency unknown outside of Germany.

Mus. ex. III-14.
De Grigny: *Pange lingua,* fugue, measures 20-24.[36]

[34] De Grigny, *op. cit.,* 2.
[35] *Ibid.,* 55.
[36] *Ibid.,* 69.

De Grigny's contribution to the development of the fugue lies less in radical changes in its format than it lies in the expansion of it, in a more serious attitude toward contrapuntal writing, and greater care in voicing and registration.

Duos and Trios

The duos and trios are the first compositions we have encountered which fall completely under the influence of the dance. Every major category of music of the *grand siècle* showed the influence of the rhythms, mood, and elegance of the French dances; organ music was no exception. Raison's famous quotation makes clear how important understanding of the dance was to the organ performer:

> You ought to observe the direction of the piece you are playing and consider if it has relation to a sarabande, gigue, gavotte, bourée, canaris, passacaglia and chaconne . . . and give it the same atmosphere you would give it on the clavecin, except that the movement should be a little slower because of the sanctity of the place.[37]

One wonders if the last suggestion was ever taken seriously, for the dances in the organ music seem not the least more serious or churchly than those in secular music. All duos and trios in the repertory show the influence of the dance, an influence which defines the tempo and mood of a composition in question.

The French duo has no real parallels in the organ music of other traditions, the German *bicinium* notwithstanding. The duo is derived from a transfer to the organ idiom of one of the most common Baroque textures, soprano voice over basso continuo. The French composers showed a positive genius in being able, within the two-voice idiom, to outline very clearly the harmonic progressions in the music. Although the bass line participates in imitative and motivic writing, its basic function remains that of a continuo line. If their origins were unknown, passages from these organ duos would be indistinguishable from the continuo polyphony of Baroque solo sonatas. The following passage is characteristic of the nature of the writing:

[37] Translated: Almonte Howell, *The French Organ Mass*, Dissertation: Chapel Hill, The University of North Carolina, 1953, 27.

Mus. ex. III-15.
Boyvin: *Suite du premier ton,* Duo, measures 1-15.[38]

Similarly the organ trio is no more than an adaptation of the texture of the trio sonata. In a trio the bass is freer of responsibility in imitative and motivic passages and hence functions even more as a continuo line. Particularly in those trios in which the pedal assumes the bass voice, there is a large degree of differentiation between the melodically constructed upper voices and the harmonically conceived lower one.

The dances favored for the duos were invariably the more lively ones: the *gigue,* the *bourée,* and the *gavotte.*

Gigue: Couperin, Duo from *Messe pour les paroisses.*

[38] Boyvin, *op. cit.,* 20.

Bourée: Clérambault. Duo from *Suite du deuxième ton.*

Gavotte: De Grigny, Duo from the Gloria, *Livre d'Orgue.*

Although it is difficult to arrive at generalizations, the more moderate ternary dances seem favored for the trios. Although it is rare that the ground bass type of chaconne or passacaglia appears in organ literature, it is these dances and the minuet which are typically used in the trio. We might observe, however, that there was a wide latitude in the tempo of various examples of the minuet. Composers often were forced to specify the mood and tempo of ternary dances in order to avoid confusion in performance. The following example is obviously influenced by the moderate minuet:

Mus. ex. III-16.
Jullien: *Trio pour une élévation,* measures 48-53.[39]

A rhythmic mannerism characteristic of such ternary dances is the use of hemiola at cadence points:

Mus. ex. III-17.
Guilain: *Suite du premier ton,* Trio, measures 17-23.[40]

---

39 Jullien, *op. cit.,* 55.
40 Guilain, *op. cit.,* 6.

The qualities of grace, charm, gaiety, and directness which apply to the entire French Classical style are nowhere more evident than in the duos and trios. These unpretentious pieces in which dance-oriented rhythms combine with continuo polyphony are always kept within the bounds of *bon goût.* No contrapuntal surprises, no complex thematic developments are to be found here, only cheerful and appealingly direct music.

Compositions for Solo Registers

The largest number of compositions in the French literature are pieces for selected solo registers (*Cornet, Jeu de Tierce, Cromorne, Trompette, Voix humaine,* and occasionally *jeu de Nasard*) either alone or in dialogue with one another. In all cases the musical texture is the same. One hand plays a homophonic accompaniment on the *jeu doux* while the other hand performs the melody. The pedal, particularly in compositions *en taille,* may be involved in this accompaniment. The melody may skip phrase by phrase from one hand to another (*dialogue de dessus et bassus*) or it may remain in one register.

The French composers had very clear concepts of the type of composition appropriate to each solo register. Hence there are subtle differences between two genres as closely related as the *tierce en taille* and the *cromorne en taille.* More striking differences would be evident between *récits* for dissimiliar stops. A *récit en dessus de tierce* is a very different type of piece from a *récit en dessus de trompette.* An understanding of these important differences is a prerequisite to the understanding of the style itself. The French organists would no more have treated the *voix humaine* as a *cromorne* than the contemporary chamber composer would have treated a recorder as an oboe. Each type of solo composition, then, requires our special consideration.

Récits for the jeu de tierce and the cromorne en taille

Récits for the tierce in either the soprano or tenor and *récits* for the cromorne in the tenor were invariably serious in tone, meditative in character, and lacking in the lighthearted gaity of the dance evident in most other *récits.* The grandest of these pieces, both in elegance and scope, was the *tierce en taille,* a genre upon which the composers lavished particular care. In these meditative *récits,* one finds highly ornate melodies of asymmetrical phrase lengths assigned to the solo voice. This melody exists against a background of slow harmonic rhythm and carefully calculated chordal progressions. The unique quality of these pieces comes from a blending of the greatest of melodic nuance operating in a well-constructed harmonic environment. The following example shows the care with which the two elements are put together:

Mus. ex. III-18.
Couperin: *Messe pour les paroisses, Tierce en taille,* measures 14-21.[41]

The origins of the meditative organ *récit* lie in the vocal *récit* of the Lully opera. The overriding consideration of the seventeenth-century opera composer was the expression of text. Music functioned as a means to enhance the inflexion of the French language in such a way that its every nuance would find a musical parallel. As a result of this principle, the musical texture in page after page of Lully's

[41] François Couperin, *Pieces d'Orgue,* ed. Brunold, Monaco: Editions de l'Oiseau-Lyre, 1952, 30.

writing is a curious style halfway between recitative and aria. It has too great a structure to relate solely to the first, too little structure to relate solely to the latter. Foreigners complained that they never knew when a recitative ended and an air began. The free melodic style of the *récit* was enhanced by the tradition of ornamentation added by the performer. Below we have the beginning of Lully's *Récit de la beauté* from *Le Mariage Forcé* (1664) in both its original version and an ornamented one by Michel Lambert, Lully's father-in-law and a composer himself:[42]

Mus. ex. III-19.

If the ornamented version of this piece is played on a registration of a *récit de tierce* the result is identical in sound with a similar *récit* composed originally for organ. The organ genre is but an adaptation of its opera equivalent.

It has been suggested that in some cases the relationship of text and music did not escape the consideration of the organ composer. The relationship may go deeper than general mood. The ease with which the text of the *Benedictus* may be fitted to the

42 Jean Baptiste Lully, *Oeuvres Completes* I: Les Comédies-Ballets, 13.

melodic line of the *cromorne en taille* from Couperin's *Messe pour les paroisses* is hardly accidental:

Mus. ex. III-20.

Subtle differences in style exist among the *récits* for *tierce en dessus, tierce en taille,* and *cromorne en taille.* When the *tierce* was used in the soprano the movement tended to be of smaller scale and far less weighty than either of the tenor types. The *Tierce en taille* was the most serious composition in the repertory, generally more lengthy than other *récits,* and provided with accompanying voices played on the *fond d'orgue* (16, 8 and 4) (and not on the *jeux doux*) with the bass being always assigned to the *Pédale.* The accompaniment was often motivically related to the solo voice and generally more sophisticated in structure than that of other *récits.* Perhaps the most characteristic feature of the melodic line itself was the flamboyant running passages which left the tenor register and moved in soaring fashion into the soprano.

The *cromorne en taille* differed from the *tierce en taille* in being a more restrained composition, generally smaller in scope, and more vertically conceived. The running passages previously mentioned are normally absent. The range of the melody rarely exceeds the tenor register. Both types share the same general musical qualities of seriousness, severity, and dignity. As rococco taste made itself felt in the later years of the century, the *en taille récits* became less favored. They are, for instance, notably absent in the *suites* of Clérambault.

Récits for trompette and the basse de cromorne

The *récits* for trompette (basse et dessus) and the *basse de cromorne* were based on sharp, clear-cut, clearly recognizable subjects in the rhythm of the *bourée* and less frequently of the *gigue.* These compositions normally open with a short fugal exposition on the accompanying manual. The solo voice enters as one voice of that exposition. The relationship between these genres and the fugue is very close. Indeed composers often labeled these pieces fugues for the trompette or cromorne. Other fugal characteristics are the monothematic character of these *récits* and subsequent brief expositions which occasionally occur.

The extension of the solo phrase is accomplished by figurative patterns of a mechanical nature. Particularly characteristic of such patterns are disjunct figures with abnormally large leaps which give to the *basse de trompette ou cromorne* its particular sound.

Mus. ex. III-21.
De Grigny: *Basse de Trompette ou Cromorne* for the Mass, measures 60-63.[43]

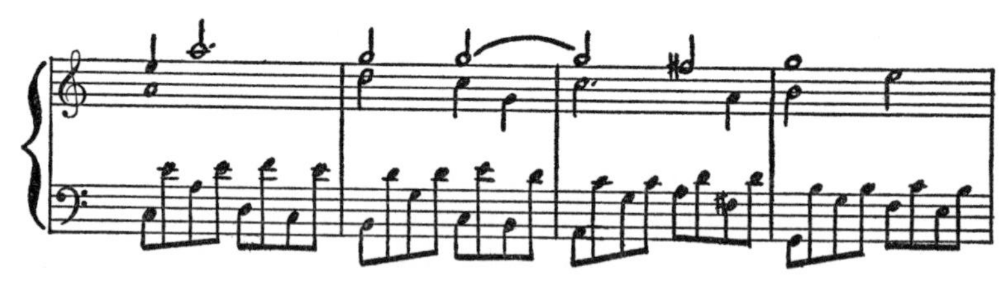

The origin of this unique type of writing lies in the relationship of the attack characteristic of these reed stops and the attack characteristics in viol playing. The figurations of many passages in solo viol writing are very similar to those used for the trompette and cromorne and this suggests that the composers for organ were imitating a chamber sonority.

Mus. ex. III-22.
Marin Marais: *Boutade, Pièces à Une et à Deux Violes,* 1686, measures 9-15.[44]

[43] De Grigny, *op. cit.,* 22.
[44] Clyde Thompson, *Marin Marais,* 1656-1728, Dissertation: University of Michigan, Ann Arbor, 1956, Appendix, 10.

There were Spanish antecedents for the *basse de trompette* which also appear to have influenced the French form. The predilection of the Spaniards for reed sounds is, of course, well known. Two compositions by Sebastian Aguilera de Heredia (c. 1565- ?) have textures remarkably similar to the *basse de Trompette* and often employ dance-like rhythms:

Mus. ex. III-23.
Aguilera: *Vajo de 1° tono,* measures 51-54.[45]

Composers were fond of contrasting the bass of the *trompette* with its treble. In such dialogues alternate phrases of the solo melody were taken on the bass and treble registers. The *cromorne,* whose treble lacked the appropriate bite, was not used in this fashion. As an alternate to the treble *trompette,* one of the *cornets* was often suggested. The French drew a clear distinction between the assertive *cornet,* which they tended to treat with the reed voices, and the more tender and meditative *jeu de tierce.*

Dialogues for voix humaine

The French composers used the plaintive sound of the *voix humaine* in pieces of considerable restraint and intimacy. The places in which such pieces are used in the Mass (for example as the *Benedictus* in one Mass of Raison and as the *Elévation* in another) confirm that none of the assertive qualities of the other reeds stops was attached to *voix humaine.* That the music which fitted this stop should be played slowly and with dignity is suggested by Raison's marking of *lentement* for the *Benedictus.*

Most compositions for the *voix humaine* are dialogues between its soprano and bass registers. Frequently such compositions conclude with sections in which all voices are to be played on the

[45] Willi Apel (ed.), *Spanish Organ Masters after Antonio de Cabezon. CEKM* XIV, 105.

solo register. It is obvious that the French were fond of the pungent sound of ensemble playing on this stop, a pungency which was accentuated by the frequent direction that the *voix humaine* was to be played with the *tremblant doux.*

The musical style of the *dialogue sur le voix humaine* was even more homophonic than other *récits.* Simple, rather square-cut melodies generally with note-against-note harmony are characteristic. Compositions are found in both duple and triple meter. The slow forms of the minuet and the gavotte are the prevailing rhythms. The following passage is typical of the style:

Mus. ex. III-24.
Guilain: *Suite du Second Ton, Dialogue de voix humaine,* measures 9-17.[46]

Dialogues for solo registers

We have already mentioned dialogue between the bass and soprano registers of the same solo stop. Dialogues also exist contrasting the bass register of one stop with the soprano register of another (*i.e. basse de cromorne avec le dessus sur le cornet*) as well as dialogues which contrast the soprano registers of two or more stops. The format of such compositions does not differ radically from the simple *récit* except that the melodic lines are generally cut into somewhat smaller phrases to allow frequent alternation of registers. Contrasts were normally made between registers of similar dynamic and emotional quality. Hence dialogues between the trompette and cornet are com-

[46] Guilain, *op. cit.,* 27.

mon while dialogues between the trompette and *voix humaine* are unknown.

A careful study of the juxtaposition of registers reveals the sensitivity the French felt for what was appropriate to each. Raison writes a dialogue made up entirely of brief echo passages followed by a cadential formula. The echo passages, which are marked *guayment,* have a direct and assertive quality; the cadential formula, which is always more restrained and melodic, is assigned to the cromorne to be played *lentement*:

Mus. ex. III-25.
Raison: *Messe du premier ton, Qui tollis,* measures 5-7.[47]

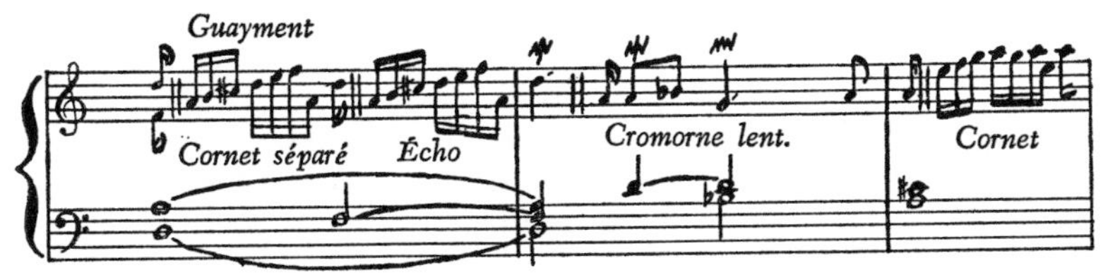

In a dialogue between *Cornet* and *Tierce,* Couperin reshapes the *Tierce* melody into a more direct one when it is echoed on the *Cornet*:

Mus. ex. III-26.
Couperin: *Messe pour les paroisses, Tu solus altissimus,* beginning.[48]

Certain articulation peculiarities inherent in the playing of each solo register further delineated their respective qualities. In many dialogues there is a concluding section in which the two solo registers are played in trio over a pedal bass.

[47] Raison, André, *Premier Livre d'Orgue, Orgue et Liturgie* 55, ed. Dufourcq. Paris: Schola Cantorum, n.d., 14.

[48] François Couperin, *op. cit.,* 35.

Compositions for flûtes alone

Concerts or trios for *flûtes* alone occur occasionally in the repertory. These pieces are always in the meter of a moderate ternary dance (minuet or sarabande). The musical structure is unabashedly homophonic. The three or four voices which make up the musical texture tend to move simultaneously, and the resulting structure is more chordally conceived than that of any other genre. Beyond this, the periodic structure of the dance is often strictly maintained, and these compositions tend to be based on even phrase lengths of two and four measures. The following is typical:

Mus. ex. III-27.
Guilain: *Suite du second ton, Trio de flûtes,* measures 1-8.[49]

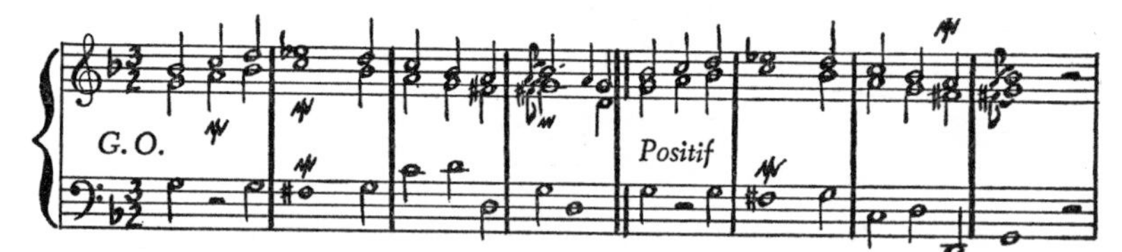

A consistent feature of these pieces is the dialogue between the *flûtes* of the *Positif* and the *flûtes* of the *Grand orgue* and *Positif* coupled. One phrase is taken on the lighter registration, the next on the heavier. The mood of the *concert pour les flûtes* was always one of simple grace and charm. This mood coupled with the prevailing periodic structure made such pieces favorites with the composers of *noëls.*

Compositions for le grand jeu

The most flamboyant and extensive pieces in the repertory were reserved for the registers of the *grand jeu.* The striking sonorities of a large ensemble dominated by reeds and cornets gave rise to equally striking compositions which, more than any other pieces in the repertory, epitomize the optimistic dance spirit of the age. The composers gave to the *grand jeu* the most conspicuous places in their *suites* and masses. Hence this type of composition was normally used as the conclusion of a *suite,* the conclusion of the *Gloria in excelsis,* for the

[49] Guilain, *op. cit.,* 18.

large offertories, and frequently as conclusion to the *Kyrie* and *Sanctus*.

The *grand jeu* depended upon the following stylistic features, although no one composition is likely to reflect them all:

1) The French overture: Many *grands jeux* are patently organ adaptations of the French overture. The opening solemn section with its characteristic dotted-note figures and *tirades* as well as its ebullient fugue are transferred from the orchestral to the organ idiom.
2) The rhythms of the faster, more exciting dances: the bourée, gavotte, and gigue.
3) Fugal writing: The fugues in the *grand jeu* are often more extensive than those which stand separately.
4) The texture of the *basse et dessus de trompette.* Extensive passages indistinguishable from this genre are common in the *grand jeu.*
5) Echo writing: Elaborate echo writing frequently concludes the *grand jeu.* It is rare that such a composition exists without some evidence of echo technique.
6) Florid technical display: The *grands jeux* are the only compositions in the repertory which employ technical virtuosity for its own sake.

The simplest type of music allotted to the *grand jeu* is represented by the concluding movements of the *Kyries* and *glorias* of the Raison Masses. These movements are no more than homophonically conceived bourées, gavottes, canaris, and gigues with completely symmetrical phrase structure. One phrase is given to the *petit jeu* and the next to the *grand jeu.* These movements may conclude with a more embellished coda. The following style is characteristic:

Mus. ex. III-28.
Raison: *Messe du premier ton, Amen* from the *Gloria,* measures 1-4.[50]

None of this type of *grand jeu* exceeds the limits of a routine liturgical composition. Similar in scope are brief fugues on dance-oriented subjects. Such pieces often begin and end on the *Grand orgue* with an extensive episode in the middle to be played *en duo* on the *Positif* and the *Récit.* An example of this type of composition is the *Amen* of the *Gloria* from the Couperin *Messe pour les paroisses*

Either the homophonic type or the fugal type is often introduced by a slow, dignified section certainly derived from the French overture. These sections may be chordal with limited adornment, a style not unlike that for the *plein jeu,* or they may reflect the traditional dotted notes of the opening section of the overture sometimes with the characteristic fast scale passages (*tirades*):

Mus. ex. III-29.
Marchand: *Premier livre, Dialogue,* measures 1-7.[51]

The slow introduction from one of De Grigny's hymn settings, that on *Ave Maris Stella,* is unique. This introduction is based on elaborate scale passages not unlike those more typical of the *tierce en*

---

[50] Raison, *op. cit.,* 18.
[51] Marchand, *op. cit.,* 38.

taille. The cursive and recitative-like writing is unusual for its emotional content.

Many *grands jeux,* whether they open with a slow introduction or not, conclude with a brief coda in dignified chordal style. It is again De Grigny who endows such codas with an harmonic language beyond the mere routine. The following example, in which the composer writes over a descending chromatic bass, is a case in point:

Mus. ex. III-30.
De Grigny: *Dialogue* from the *Agnus* of the *Mass,* conclusion.[52]

If the fast sections of the *grand jeu* are to be expanded beyond the limits we have already described, it is usually accomplished by having sections in the style of the *basse de trompette* introduced into the fugal writing, or by the addition of echo sections, or possibly by the addition of both. Some dialogues are practically indistinguishable from large *récits* for *trompette.* The only difference might be in the scale of the composition and dexterity and elaborate quality of the solo line:

[52] De Grigny, *op. cit.,* 49.

Mus. ex. III-31.
De Grigny: *Dialogue, Amen* from the *Gloria* of the *Mass,* bass, measures 21-26.

Echo is such a consistent feature of the *grand jeu* that at times it runs the risk of becoming banal. Some dialogues may have fifty or more measures of consistent echo passages among the *Grand orgue, Positif,* and *Cornet d'Écho.* The vertically conceived motives of the dance were ready-made material for echo. De Grigny, who time and again rescued a style so close to becoming hackneyed, relieved the potential monotony of such passages by repetition of phrases in their parallel minor keys.[53]

Two offertories demand special consideration: that from the De Grigny Mass and that from the Couperin *Messe pour les paroisses.* These compositions transcend the normal limits of the French style, and by their size and grandeur become expressions of the Baroque in a repertory dominated by rococco tastes. Neither of these pieces has unusual technical features. What is unique is the manner in which the technical features we have already discussed are worked into compositions of such large dimensions.

The Couperin offertory is essentially a gigantic French overture with the insertion of a trio and slow fugue between its principal sections. The principal sections are in the major mode, the insertions in the parallel minor. There is a majesty in the first section rarely attained in the literature. To some degree this hinges on Couperin's sense of motivic writing and contrapuntal style. The harmonic borrowings from the minor mode which conclude this section are further evidence of a greater tonal perception than one usually finds with his contemporaries. The extensive fugal gigue which concludes the offertory shows this same consideration for motivic and contrapuntal writing. Couperin rarely allows accompanying voices to remain static, but gives these voices real participation in the

---

[53] *Ibid.,* 48.

motivic structure. The gigue is certainly one of the most interesting and effervescent in the entire French repertory.

The offertory of the De Grigny mass is a large bi-partite composition; the first section in duple time, (gavotte rhythm) and the second in 6/4 (gigue). The opening begins with a long and important section in *basse de trompette* style. Although the theme has its origins in gavotte rhythm, De Grigny gives it a more individual quality than many other such subjects possess:

Mus. ex. III-32.
De Grigny: *Offertory* from *Livre d'orgue,* bass, measures 10-14.[54]

The writing for the solo voice is some of the most elaborate one encounters in this idiom.

Mus. ex. III-33.
Bass, measures 44-47.

The opening concludes with a fughetta with echo passages built on the theme and related material. The gigue section begins and concludes with fugal writing. The center section is also developed with echo passages. In his writing De Grigny shows the same concern for motivic and contrapuntal writing shown by Couperin. This grand composition ends with an exciting pedal point reminiscent not only of Titelouze but also of De Grigny's own *Point d'orgue.*[55]

The Noël

In the last quarter of the century the introduction by Gigault and LeBegue of variations on *noëls* is clear indication that rococco

[54] *Ibid.,* 32.
[55] The concluding movement of the hymn *A Solis Ortus.*

taste was eroding the French Classical style. In the *noëls* the traits of simplicity, surface charm, naivete, and musical shallowness are substituted for the elegance, grace, polish, and grandeur characteristic of the literature as a whole. These variations inevitably became hardly more than formula composed music. Folk melodies imposed on the variation form the strict periodic structure which hampered musical imagination, forced the adaptation of simplistic textures, and largely destroyed the close connection between registration and musical style. In the *noël,* registrational subtlety was lost in a musical structure of too little import.

The formulas were simple. Page after page of duo writing exists in which the melody, only superficially ornamented, is accompanied by a mechanically conceived bass voice. Italian patterns, essentially alien to the French style, appear in abundance:

Mus. ex. III-34.
LeBegue: Excerpts from the bass, *Une Vierge Pucelle.*[56]

Any vestige of contrapuntal interest, any seriously conceived motivic writing, any rhythmic pliability is lost in endless superficiality and shallowness.

The French Classical style always lay dangerously close to the abyss of the superficial. But composers such as De Grigny, Couperin, Nivers, Clérambault, and du Mage refused to allow their works to fall from the tasteful to the shallow. In a sense the real value of the style lay just here. To derive a legitimate organ style from idioms of dance, chamber music, and opera was no easy effort. But as genius lies close to insanity, so magical success lies close to banality: this is proved by the eighteenth-century composers who attempted to follow in the seventeenth-century footsteps. The style was dead. The variations on the *noël* were partly to blame.

---

[56] Nicolas LeBegue, *Noëls variés, Orgue et Liturgie* 16, ed. Dufourcq, Paris: Schola Cantorum, 1952, 88 ff.

LITURGICAL PRACTICES AND ORGANIZATION OF PIECES INTO LARGER FORMS

We have pointed out several times that the entire seventeenth-century French repertory is liturgical music designed to be used in the elaborate *alternatim* practice which was common in Parisian churches of the period. Important information concerning this practice is available from directions contained in the *Caeremoniale Parisiense,* 1662, by Martin Sonnet.[57] This document indicates that the organ is required for Masses on Feasts of the first and second classes, but that it might also be used for all Sundays except those of penitential seasons. Moreover it specifies that the organ may be used not only at Mass, but also at Lauds, Matins, and Vespers. We also know that beyond its solo duties in alternation, the organ supported the singers and provided them intonations. A setting of the *Salve regina* written around 1710 by the minor composer Babou has included in it crude harmonic accompaniments for the portions of the chant which were to have been sung.[58] One hopes that the accompaniment practice of most churches would have been more sophisticated. In any event, this setting does provide evidence of organ accompaniment of the singers. The *Caeremoniale* also indicates that at certain portions of the Mass the organ is to maintain the chant and that it is not at those times to play free pieces. In those masses in the repertory which have *cantus firmus,* this procedure is followed very exactly.

The Mass

Organ music was invariably provided for the *Kyrie,* the *Gloria,* the *Sanctus* and the *Agnus Dei.* The larger, and by implication more festive, masses provided music for the Offertory, the Elevation, the *Benedictus,* and sometimes the *Deo Gratias.* There are rare examples of music for the Gradual and the Communion. Certain traditions dictated the nature of certain movements while other movements appear to have been open to the imagination, arbitrary though it seems to have been, of the composer. The following indicates the outlines of the practice:

---

[57] For this material I am indebted to Howell, *op. cit.,* 25 ff.

[58] Babou, *Treize Pièces,* ed. Froidebise, *Orgue et Liturgie* 43, Paris: Schola Cantorum, 1959, 27.

Kyrie I: Always for the *plein jeu* with *cantus firmus* if there was one.
Kyrie III: Generally a fugue on a subject derived from the *cantus firmus* if there was one.
Christe II: Freely elected movement.
Kyrie IV: Freely elected movement.
Kyrie VI: Either a *plein jeu* with *cantus firmus* if there was one or a dialogue for *grand jeu.*
Et in terra: Always for the *plein jeu* with *cantus firmus* if there was one.
Benedictus te: Generally a fugue on a subject derived from the *cantus firmus* if there was one.
Glorificamus te: Freely elected movement.
Domine Deus, Rex celestis: Freely elected movement.
Domine Deus, Agnus Dei: Freely elected movement.
Qui tollis peccata mundi, suscipe: Freely elected movement.
Quoniam tu solus: Freely elected movement.
Tu solus altissimus: Freely elected movement.
Cum sancto spiritu — Amen: Sometimes a *plein jeu,* with or without *cantus firmus.* More often a dialogue for the *grand jeu.*
Offertory: Always a dialogue for *grand jeu.* Often omitted.
Sanctus I: Always a *plein jeu* with *cantus firmus* if there was one.
Sanctus II: Freely elected movement.
Benedictus: Freely elected movement. Often omitted.
Elevation: Freely elected movement. Often omitted.
Agnus Dei I: Always a *plein jeu* with *cantus firmus* if there was one.
Agnus Dei III: Freely elected movement. Often a dialogue for the *grand jeu.*
Deo gratias: Often omitted. When present usually a *petit plein jeu.*

All *cantus firmus* masses in the repertory are based on one Gregorian mass, *Missa Kyrie Cunctipotens Genitor Deus* (*Liber Usualis,* 25). The consistency of this one *cantus firmus* is difficult to explain. Other organ masses, which apparently are free of *cantus firmus,* may yet have relationships to certain pseudo-Gregorian masses used at that time in Paris. For instance, there are a number of striking similarities between themes from the Couperin *Messe pour les couvents* and one of the masses in Gregorian style by Henri DuMont, composer of organ pieces already mentioned and composer to the Chapel of Louis XIV. Whether these relationships are accidental or intentional it is difficult to say. The following is one such example:

Mus. ex. III-35.
Benedictus te:

DuMont: *Missa 6ⁱ toni* (transposed to G) Couperin: *Convent Mass,* theme.

Masses which apparently have no *cantus firmus* still employ the tradition of *plein jeu* movements for those sections of the Mass which had formerly been based on the chant.

It should be pointed out that masses with which we are familiar generally come from published sources and are certainly not characteristic of the scope of the routine mass of the period. In most cases the music must have been improvised. One major factor in all French organ publications was the necessity of apprising provincial organists of Parisian tastes. Published works, then, would have reflected the type of music used only for the higher feasts of the church year. For an idea of the type of music used for more ordinary occasions the reader is referred to a mass for a second class feast (unpublished in the seventeenth century).[59] The longest piece in this mass, the Offertory, is only forty-six measures in length. Several movements of the *Gloria* have only seven or eight measures.

The Suites

Many organ books: Nivers, *Premier Livre* (1665); LeBegue, *Premier Livre* (1676); Boyvin (1690); Jullien (1690); Chaumont (1695); Guilian (1706); DuMage (1708); and Clérambault (1710); consist of suites of compositions. The only consistent, unifying factor in a suite is its modality. There is no standard order or number of movements. Most suites begin with a *plein jeu* followed by a fugue and most conclude with a dialogue on the *grand jeu*. Beyond this no generalizations can be made.

There was never any intent that suites were to be performed straight through. They were no more than collections of pieces organized by mode from which the practicing organist could select for

[59] Published in: Almonte Howell, *Five French Baroque Organ Masses*, Lexington: University of Kentucky Press, 1961.

a particular liturgical need. The number and order of movements was, therefore, unimportant. Selected pieces from suites could be used at any time: Mass, Lauds, Matins, Vespers, or for any other service for which organ music was necessary. Some suites were designated for performances of the Magnificat. The *Second Livre d'Orgue* of LeBegue contains a series of such suites. Even here some latitude of selection was expected. These suites contain seven or eight movements. For an alternation of the Magnificat six organ versets are required. Obviously some freedom on the part of the organist was expected.

Gigault's *Livre de Musique pour l'Orgue* (1685) contains over one hundred pieces grouped first according to the church mode and then according to genre. For instance all the *pleins jeux* of one mode are grouped together followed by all the fugues in that mode. Here is a large anthology from which the player can select what he needs as he needs it. Except in the Mass and in hymn settings there was apparently no feeling that any one composition was meant to serve just one situation. In practice performers no doubt mixed, at will, compositions from varied sources, basing their selection solely on the tone of the chant and the appropriateness of a certain piece to the liturgical requirements.

Hymn Settings

It is interesting that only Nivers (*Deuxième Livre d'Orgue*), the first of the classical composers, and De Grigny, whose serious style stands out so strikingly against the Parisian, left settings of hymns. The performance of hymns in alternation must have been common practice, particularly in the monasteries. The presence of an unchanging *cantus firmus* no doubt made improvisation even more common here than elsewhere. The hymns of both Nivers and De Grigny generally contain but three or four verses. The initial verse is always a *plein jeu* with pedal *cantus firmus*; and the next verse, a fugue on a subject derived from the hymn. The third verse is often a *récit en dessus* with a melody again modeled on the opening phrase of the hymn. The following excerpts from Nivers' *Veni creator spiritus* indicate the techniques:

Mus. ex. III-36.[60]

De Grigny often expanded this format by the addition of movements which have nothing at all to do with the hymn melody. The *récits, duos,* and *grands jeux* he uses here are as free of the influence of *cantus firmus* as are similar movements elsewhere.

MAJOR PUBLICATIONS AND SOURCES OF THE FRENCH CLASSICAL STYLE

The following constitute the major publications and manuscript sources for music in the French Classical style. All appeared in the last third of the seventeenth century and the first decade of the eighteenth century. All of this material is available in modern performance editions and is indexed in the bibliography.

Boyvin, Jacques (1649-1706): *Premier Livre d'Orgue* (c. 1690) – Eight suites on the church tones.

Chaumont, Lambert (? -1712): *Pièces d'Argue sur les Huit Tons* (1695) – Eight suites.

Clérambault, Louis Nicolas (1676-1749): *Livre d'Orgue* (1710) – Two suites.

Couperin, François (1668-1733): *Pièces d'Orgue* (1690) – Two masses.

De Grigny, Nicolas (1671-1703): *Livre d'Orgue* (1699) – One mass and four hymn settings.

Du Mage, Pierre (1676?-1751): *Livre d'Orgue* (1708)–One suite.

---

[60] G. G. Nivers, *Deuxième Livre d'Orgue,* ed. Garros, Paris: Schola Cantorum, 1956.

Gigault, Nicolas (1625-1707): *Livre de Musique pour l'Orgue* – Two masses, numerous pieces in the church tones, and a Te Deum.

Guilain, Jean Adam (? - ?): *Pièces d'Orgue pour le Magnificat* (1706) – Four suites.

Jullien, Gilles (c. 1650-1703): *Premier Livre d'Orgue* (1690) – Eight suites in the church tones.

LeBegue, Nicolas (1631-1702): *Premier Livre d'Orgue* (1676) – Eight suites in the church tones; *Deuxième Livre* (1685) – A mass and nine suites for the magnificat; *Troisième Livre* (c. 1688) – Offertories, "Simphonies" (i.e. French overtures), *noëls* and elevations.

Marchand, Louis (1669-1732): A suite published posthumously probably dates from the seventeenth century. All other works show distinctly eighteenth-century traits. None of these was published.

Nivers, Guillaume Gabriel (1632-1714): *Premier Livre d'Orgue* (1665) – One hundred compositions in the church modes; *Deuxième Livre d'Orgue* (1667) – Contains one mass and numerous hymn settings; *Troisième Livre d'Orgue* (1675) – Compositions in the church tones.

Raison, André (c. 1645-1719): *Premier Livre d'Orgue* – Five masses; *Second Livre d'Orgue sur les Acclamations de la Paix tant désirées* (1714).

CHAPTER IV.

ENGLAND.

The history of English organ music in the seventeenth century shows little of the dynamic qualities we have seen on the Continent. In England this period represents an era of insecurity between the stable traditions of sixteenth-century liturgical organ writing and the mature voluntary for double organ of the eighteenth century. There is a demonstrable drop both in the quality and quantity of English organ music during this century, a drop which reflects an indecisive attitude toward the organ on the part of composers and the culture alike. This indecision had a religious basis. The English Reformation severed very completely the liturgical base upon which sixteenth-century practice had rested, yet it provided few incentives within its liturgical forms for new uses of organ music. If the reactions toward the organ on the part of the more radical elements in the Anglican reformation had been neutral, the results would have been disastrous enough. But these attitudes were hardly neutral and indeed often antagonistic. English organs had traditionally been situated on the elaborate rood screens which separated the choirs and the naves of English cathedrals. These screens became particularly hated symbols of Papal authority; and their destruction, one of the most common iconoclastic acts of the Puritan element of the Reformation. Unfortunately this element little discriminated between the screens themselves and the organs they supported. To the Puritan mind the organ was but another symbol of Rome to be destroyed along with altars, images, rood screens, and Masses. As early as 1563 a prohibition against the singing of polyphonic music and the playing of the organ narrowly missed passage in Parliament.[1] From the Act of Uniformity in 1559 which established the

[1] For a detailed account of the Puritan attitude toward the organ see: Percy Scholes, *The Puritans and Music* (London: Oxford University Press, 1934), Chapter XV, "The Organ in Church and Home in Puritan England."

norm of the *Book of Common Prayer* until the restoration of the monarchy in 1660 there is a century in which the official attitude toward ecclesiastical use of the organ was lukewarm at best. True there were periods in which the wholesale destruction of organs was temporarily replaced by a more moderate attitude which even saw some new organ construction during the century. As long, however, as the organ remained one of the symbols of the struggle between religious moderates and radicals, it could hardly thrive as a musical, much less a liturgical, medium. Certainly during the period of the Commonwealth, when Puritan ascendency reached its zenith, the history of the organ was at its lowest.

The strong liturgical base of sixteenth-century English organ music died slowly. Long after such music could have had any flourishing liturgical life, composers such as Tomkins were still writing *cantus firmus* settings essentially in the style of Blitheman and Tallis. However, this conservative polyphonic tradition found a more progressive outlet in the fantasia, which became the most important type of organ writing in the first third of the seventeenth century. Although Italian and Dutch influence is readily obvious in these fantasias, many of them still retain the complex contrapuntal orientation of sixteenth-century music. English organ music in the first third of the seventeenth century, then, is largely retrospective and conservative. Its most progressive feature lay in the adaptation into organ style of the techniques of the virginalists.

Almost no literature for the organ survives from the middle third of the century, and very probably little was actually written. We can only conclude that Puritan influence was successful in discouraging composition for the instrument. The last third of the century, from the Restoration onward, saw a gradual increase in serious concern for the instrument, a concern reflected in the works of Blow and Purcell. We must not, however, assume that the organ ever became a vital mode of musical expression in seventeenth century England. Purcell left only a handful of legitimate organ works and Blow left only thirty pieces, and many of them are insignificant. This latter third of the century was characterized by the importation of foreign influences, particularly those of Italy and France. The influence of the Italians was ultimately so strong that the eighteenth-century voluntary, which grew from the works of Blow and Purcell, was less natively English than an adaptation to English purposes of Italian style.

THE FIRST THIRD OF THE CENTURY

Ties to Virginal Music

The importance of the virginal to composers at the turn of the century could hardly have failed to influence writing for the organ. Composers for the virginal whose creative lives extended into the seventeenth century, Bull, Orlando Gibbons, and Tomkins, left us the most important compositions for the organ in the early years of the century. The organ tradition is inextricably bound to that of the virginal; so tightly bound is it that separating one from the other is often impossible. On the one hand the bond between the two instruments produced in organ style the progressive application of virginal figuration. On the other hand the essentially polyphonic basis of sixteenth-century oriented virginal style hampered the development of more modern formal procedures in music for the organ. Unlike Italy, wherein the sixteenth-century tradition was transformed by Frescobaldi and others into a radically different seventeenth-century style, England continued the conservative Renaissance style uninterrupted well into the next century. From Tallis to Tomkins there is a straight and direct stream; from Cavazzoni to Frescobaldi the original stream broke into numerous new rivulets.

It is most difficult to define the line of demarkation, if one existed at all, which lay between virginal and organ styles. The flamboyant, figurative style of the virginal transferred to the organ as easily as the stricter polyphonic style of *cantus firmus* composition transferred to the virginal. Any allocation of compositions to one instrument exclusive of the other is certainly partially arbitrary and open to conjecture. Some criteria, however, can be developed which will aid in the designation of pieces essentially designed for organ performance:

1) A composition for the organ, because of its liturgical purpose, would necessarily be of modest dimension. This precludes the extensive *cantus firmus* settings we find in the literature, particularly the majority of those on the famous *cantus In Nomine.* Such compositions normally subject the Gregorian melody to thorough working out by the mechanistic techniques of variation writing so favored by the virginalists. This suggests a second criterion:
2) The Puritan disposition would hardly have condoned the technical display so characteristic of the secular music of

the period. Pieces dependent upon such display would hardly have been found suitable for use in church. We can, then, expect to find compositions for the organ to be more serious in tone and contrapuntal in their texture.

3) In many cases the liturgical intent of compositions is revealed by the titles they bear. Hence we can assume that verses, voluntaries, and offertories were destined specifically for the organ. For the most part the validity of the criteria above are borne out by the nature of pieces bearing such titles.

There are certainly two objections which can be raised to the standards which have just been set. In the first place, they make the assumption that the only organs in England were in churches. Such was not the case, for small, chamber organs existed in domestic establishments, where they were used as alternates to the virginal. In the second place, there are a number of compositions of an extensive and very serious nature written by Tomkins near the end of his life. While it may be that he had no particular keyboard instrument in mind for their performance, their style suggests the organ and not the virginal.

The Fantasia (Fancy) and Related Forms of Voluntary, Verse, and Offertory

The English were never as explicit in the titles they chose for their organ works as were Continental composers. The designations fantasia (fancy), voluntary, and offertory indicate compositions usually free of *cantus firmus* and essentially in the same style. The term verse may indicate a free composition generally in fugal style, although examples based upon chant also exist. The terms fantasia and voluntary tell us something about the open-ended structure of English free composition. The term offertory refers, of course, to the one place in the liturgy in which the pre-Commonwealth Church allowed extensive organ performance.

It is impossible to define the meaning of fantasia in English practice of the period. One composition bearing this name may be stylistically worlds apart from the next. We can, however, point out three distinct types of fantasias, each dependent upon a nationalistic point of view:

1) The English type: This type is characterized by a very serious contrapuntal texture. It normally begins imitatively, although the initial theme is rarely developed throughout the composition. This type fantasia has much in common with the sixteenth-century motet, particularly in its dependence upon successive points of imitation each based on a new theme. In most pieces the texture becomes propressively more complex throughout as the composers tend to rely more and more on motivic development. The very opaque texture of this music rarely allows for the extensive dropping of voices. Also obvious cadential points are often avoided. The intent is to produce a consistently complex texture, a texture which reveals the probable origin of this type to be the ensemble fantasia for strings common in England during the period.
2) The Italian type: Here the obvious model is the Italian *canzone* modified to suit English tastes. The texture shows the same transparency typical of its model and none of the complexity of the English type fantasia. The reliance upon Italian models is revealed in the practice of borrowed thematic material, either from vocal works or other *canzoni* of the Italians. The practice of thematic variation, however, rarely interested the English. They tended to rely upon the technique of successive points of imitation and not upon attempts to develop mono-thematic structures.
3) The Dutch type: These fantasias, which exist only in the works of Bull, reflect his adoption of Continental musical style during the latter years of his life, years which he spent in Brussels and Antwerp (1613 until his death in 1628). These fantasias, one of which is based upon themes of Sweelinck, imitate the Dutch fantasia in which a single theme is initially treated in fugal style and then presented, often in augmentation, as the basis for elaborate keyboard embellishment based on the vocabulary of virginal figuration.

The Fantasias of Bull

The complete edition of the keyboard works of Bull[2] opens with nineteen compositions entitled "fantasia". Among these fantasias the composer demonstrates a wide latitude of styles, ranging from compositions made up of figurative patterns alone,[3] pieces which on the continent would have been termed prelude, to scholarly compositions of great length such as the first hexachord fantasia[4] in which the composer explores the limits of seventeenth-century harmonic relationships. Despite the rather simplistic statement which opens the introduction to the edition,[5] a number of these fantasias could hardly have been conceived with the organ in mind. Some of them, Numbers 5, 6, 10, 11, 14 and 18, are most certainly virginal compositions and can be omitted from our present discussion. Others seem to sound equally good on either instrument. Only Number 15, which in its simple and effective contrapuntal texture and small scope is certainly designed to serve as a verse, can be definitely assigned to the organ. Even the hexachord fantasia which we have just mentioned was not necessarily intended for the instrument. It probably was conceived by Bull as an abstract composition whose purpose it was to work out certain compositional problems. Although much has been made of this one piece, it is decidedly atypical of the English fantasia and has more in common with Italian harmonic experiments.

Dutch influence is very prominent in several of the compositions. The chromatic theme of Number 5 with its immediate double diminution and compound chromaticism is particularly Continental in spirit:

[2] John Bull, *Keyboard Music I, Musica Britannica,* XIV, ed., John Steele and Francis Cameron, London: Stainer and Bell, 1967. Volume II contains exclusively virginal works.

[3] *Ibid.,* Numbers 6 and 16.

[4] *Ibid.,* Number 17.

[5] *Ibid.,* xiii.

Mus. ex. IV-1.
Bull: *Fantasia* (Steele, Number 5),measures 1-10.[6]

The fantasia on a theme of Sweelinck[7] borrows more from the Dutchman than its initial material. The composition is unmistakably an effort to imitate the Sweelinck-type fantasia. Its theme appears initially in whole- and half-note motion in a serious, *ricercar*-style exposition. The theme then serves as the basis for a section of sixteenth-note running figurations and finally for a section based on sequential motivic patterns typical of Sweelinck's more contrapuntal writing.

The influence of the Italian *canzone* is evident in the third and seventh of Bull's fantasias. The first of these pieces[8] employs thematic variation typical of its models. This composition, which dates from the last years of Bull's life, reflects his relationship in Brussels with the Italian composer Guami. The seventh fantasia[9] is a far more original composition. This piece is composed of two expositions of entirely different material. Each exposition is repeated in an elaborate ornamented version resulting in a form A A′ B B′. While such written out elaborations occur in other Italian *canzoni,* this example is unusual for its figurative patterns, particularly that of repeated notes:

---

6 *Ibid.,* 15.
7 *Ibid.,* 12.
8 *Ibid.,* 10.
9 *Ibid.,* 20.

Mus. ex. IV-2.
Bull: *Fantasia* (Steele, Number 7), measures 88-90.

While Continental influence certainly dominates the fantasias of Bull, some natively English traits are also obvious. The English predilection for continuous, uninterrupted counterpoint, a feature which we will see is characteristic of Tomkins' writing, is most evident in the third of the hexachord fantasias.[10] Here the composer even avoids the clarifying technique of successive points of imitation, a technique Tomkins favored. Bull similarly avoids clear-cut cadences, and he even subtly disguises the hexachord progression in complex rhythmic variations. The resulting effect is a complex contrapuntal web of sound which contrasts strikingly with the lucid writing of the Italian and Dutch influenced compositions.

In the first fantasia Bull introduces another English type of writing, the composition for solo cornet. Such a texture seems to have been first developed by the English and then borrowed by the French in their more diminutive *récits*. The opening of Bull's fantasia is given below:

Mus. ex. IV-3.
Bull: *Fantasia* (Steele, Number 1), measures 1-12.

[10] *Ibid.*, 65.

The Fantasias, Voluntaries, Offertories, and Verses of Tomkins

The free compositions of Tomkins (1573-1656) show hardly a trace of the foreign influences which dominate Bull's work. Tomkins is unabashedly English in his outlook toward organ composition. His style is characterized by complex counterpoint relieved only by such devices as harmonic sequence and occasional keyboard figuration borrowed from virginal style. While Bull favors the clarity of counterpoint of the Italian *canzone* and the sparseness of texture of the Dutch fantasia, Tomkins favors the continuous polyphony of the English viol fantasia. He sustains four voices measure upon measure; he avoids clear-cut cadences; and thereby he produces a texture distinctly conservative in tone and English in flavor.

Several fantasias are monothematic (numbers 23, 30 and 31).[11] In these compositions the initial theme is developed in a *ricercar* texture that is almost entirely devoid of elements of keyboard figuration. This texture differs in one respect from the vocally-oriented texture of similar Italian compositions. English composers had a more pragmatic and instrumental attitude towards voice-leading. Their primary consideration often seems to have been that the various polyphonic parts divide comfortably between the two hands. Inner voices often contain erratic skips which conform more to this consideration than to normal concepts of melodic progression. Likewise English composers feel no qualms about adding extra notes to the texture when it serves to improve the sonority of a passage. The following passage is illustrative of Tomkins' use of these traits:

Mus. ex. IV-4.
Tomkins: *Fancy* (number 23), measures 45-47.[12]

The most progressive sound Tomkins achieved in his fantasias

[11] The numbers refer to: Thomas Tomkins, *Keyboard Music, Musica Britannica*, V, ed. Stephen Tuttle, London: Stainer and Bell, 1973. An offprint of nine organ pieces from this edition is also available from the same publisher (1955).

[12] Tomkins, *Keyboard Music*, 53.

invariably lies in those passages developing motivic ideas. The device of sequence, so successfully exploited in virginal writing, he fashioned to serve the needs of organ writing. The following passage is typical of the modern sound of such passages, passages which often contrast markedly with the prevailingly conservative texture of the surrounding material:

Mus. ex. IV-5.
Tomkins: *Fancy* (number 25), measures 27-31.[13]

In those fantasias which are not monothematic, Tomkins employs procedures further developed by both Orlando Gibbons and Thomas Lugge. Such compositions borrow the technique of successive points of imitation from the Renaissance motet. The themes which they employ, however, show little relationship to vocal style. Invariably they contain motivic germs upon which the development of the various points depends. There is rarely direct thematic relationship between one motive and another. What does occur, however, is a progressively more active texture, both rhythmically and motivically, from one section to the next. Each section is more lively than the one which precedes it; the final section, then, has the densest texture and most active motivic interplay. The complexity of these compositions is increased by Tomkins' reluctance to allow one section to cadence clearly before the next is introduced. He rather prefers the more conservative approach of dovetailing one point of imitation into that which came before. The result is an unrelieved contrapuntal sound saved from unintelligibility by the translucent motivic development derived from virginal style. As

[13] *Ibid.,* 57.

they stand, these fantasias of Tomkins have no parallel in complexity in Continental music of the period.

The Fantasias of Orlando Gibbons and John Lugge

Perhaps the most successful fantasias from the standpoint of modern performance are those of Orlando Gibbons (1583-1625). His ten examples vary from short compositions obviously designed to introduce an anthem[14] to fully worked out examples in the complex English style we have just discussed.[15] Two examples similar to Italian *canzoni* also exist.[16]

In the examples in English style the serious contrapuntal approach of Tomkins is evident. It is, however, considerably relieved by a strong and modern sense of harmonic direction, a sense which permeates Gibbons' style. The opening theme of the ninth fantasia,[17] which in many ways is the masterpiece of these compositions, employs the diminished fourth suggested by the b-flat to f-sharp relationship of g minor.

The harmonic outlines of the entire composition are strikingly modern. Gibbons makes no effort to conceal cadences in the manner of Bull and Tomkins. Instead he uses cadences in the manner of later Baroque composers, that is to define the tonal order of the developing composition. For instance the first half of this piece, down to measure 44, progresses through major cadences on the tonic (measure 19), the relative major (measure 36), the dominant (measure 41), and finally back to the tonic (measure 44). The passage leading up to the cadence on the relative major is amazing in its use of secondary dominant chords with irregular resolutions. This passage also contains an unusual augmented triad in first inversion. The d-sharp serves as a very pungent appoggiatura to the following e.

14 Orlando Gibbons, *Keyboard Music, Musica Britannica* XX, ed. Hendrie, London: Stainer and Bell, 1970, Numbers 5 and 6. An offprint from this edition containing nine organ pieces is also available from the same publisher.

15 Gibbons, *Keyboard Music,* numbers 9, 11, 12, and 14.

16 *Ibid.,* numbers 8 and 13.

17 *Ibid.,* 14.

Mus. ex. IV-6.
Gibbons: *Fantasia No. 9,* measures 26-35.

Gibbons follows the English procedure already discussed of progressively deriving motivic material from the developing texture. As with so many other English fantasias, the last section is the one in which the motivic writing is most complex. Here again Gibbons relies on his well-developed harmonic sense in organizing the musical material. The following passage is illustrative of the means by which the composer guides his figuration by carefully controlled harmony.

Mus. ex. IV-7.
Gibbons: *Fantasia 9,* measures 76-78.

One fantasia of Gibbons and three of John Lugge[18] introduce us into a type of native English composition we have not yet en-

[18] John Lugge, *Three Voluntaries for Double Organ,* ed. Susi Jeans and John Steele, London: Novello, 1956.

countered, the fantasia for double organ (*i.e.* organ with two manuals). Throughout the remainder of the century this type of composition is the most important English contribution to the literature for the instrument. From about 1600, English organs were characteristically built with two manuals, great and chair. The fantasia for double organ is an outgrowth of the implicit duality of this type of instrument. The double organ fantasias of Gibbons and Lugge have much in common with the English type fantasia we have already discussed. They share the serious contrapuntal approach as well as use of the technique of successive points of imitation. None of the four examples is monothematic. They all begin calmly in a vocally-oriented style and progressively move to more complex writing centered on motivic play. For the most part the four-voice texture of the conventional fantasia is here replaced by three voices, two to be assumed by the right hand and the solo bass line with the left. It is conventional to introduce each new thematic idea on the chair organ in all voices and reserve the entrance of the solo voice for several measures. There is no attempt to use the potential contrast between the soprano and bass of the solo register in the manner of the later French *récits*. It is typical, however, to move both hands to the solo manual for the lively codas which conclude these compositions. They characteristically end with elaborate writing which shows considerable flamboyance.

Mus. ex. IV-8.
Lugge: *Voluntary No. 1 for Double Organ,* conclusion.[19]

[19] *Ibid.,* 6.

Lugge maintains a sense of the dynamic in his fantasias by constantly increasing the rhythmic drive of each newly introduced motivic idea. The result is a movement from the beginning to the end of these pieces of increasing rhythmic activity. The following are the themes from his second fantasia:

Mus. ex. IV-9.

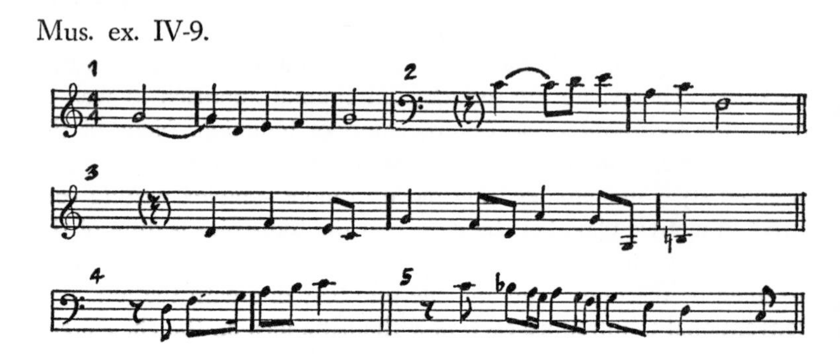

The English fantasia must be regarded as essentially a conservative type of seventeenth-century composition into which the more modern elements of keyboard figuration were introduced. The absence of concern with the processes of working through a single theme and the use of the Renaissance technique of successive points of imitation point up this conservatism. English composers were even more conservative in their treatment of *cantus firmus* pieces, to which we now turn.

Cantus Firmus Settings

In the treatment of the *cantus firmus* English seventeenth-century composers were much more rigid than their Continental peers. Not only did they set the same few Gregorian melodies time and again,[20] but they almost invariably presented these melodies in the long-note fashion of the otherwise outdated *cantus planus*. One would think that this conservative technique would be clear proof that these pieces were intended for the organ; this is not so. The large majority of these settings belong to the virginal repertory. The *cantus firmus* provided, as did the secular melody, merely a frame-

[20] The two most famous melodies were the antiphons *Gloria tibi trinitas,* known also as *In Nomine* (*Liber Usualis,* 914) and *Miserere mihi Domine* (*Liber Usualis,* 266).

work upon which the composers could construct keyboard elaborations. The compositional interest lay not in the melody itself, for it furnished little material for the construction of added voices. The Gregorian melody was the passive basis upon which the dynamic figurations were built. Hence there is as little reason to regard most *cantus firmus* compositions of the period as inherently organ music as to regard secular variations as such.

Based on the criteria of restrained technical display and a length reasonable for liturgical use, we can attribute to the organ only Tomkins' four short *Miserere* settings and one setting of *Clarifica me Pater.*[21] None of Bull's extensive compositions would qualify. Other seventeenth-century composers left none. Even in these small settings English composers resorted to few Continental devices in setting the *cantus firmus.* The derivation of added material from the existing melody is limited to opening imitations. Figuration is mechanistically added, and there is little attempt to retain any cohesiveness in the use of a single figuration throughout a setting. The English habit of moving from one idea to another with great freedom, a practice we have seen to be characteristic in the fantasia, is even more the practice here. The following measures excerpted from the *Clarifica me pater,* a composition only twenty measures in length, show how diverse figurative material can be in so short a composition:

Mus. ex. IV-10.

[21] Tomkins, *Keyboard Music,* numbers 14, 15, 19, 20, and 4.

One is led to believe that a medieval concept of *cantus firmus* writing in which the bare notes of the melody were used to support keyboard figuration continued uninterrupted in England well into the seventeenth century. Perhaps the use of the same few melodies over and over was dictated by a tradition which had become stereotyped. If the added voices were to be merely decorative, it was important that they be applied to melodies which were already well known: otherwise a composition would dissolve into chaos. In any respect this repertory has no subsequent effect on English or Continental organ music. The tradition did not survive the Commonwealth, and with a single exception no *cantus firmus* compositions exist in England after the turn of the century.

ENGLISH ORGAN MUSIC AT MID-CENTURY

As one might expect, little organ music from the middle of the century appears in English sources. The period of the Commonwealth marks the low point for the instrument, and this is certainly reflected in the limited repertory. The works of two composers, and neither of them of first rank, give us some glimpse of the state of affairs. Christopher Gibbons (1615-1676), the son of Orlando, left us five pieces now available in a modern edition,[22] and Matthew Locke (c. 1630-1677) left seven pieces originally published in his collection *Melothesia* (1673).[23].

The published works of C. Gibbons reveal a composer of limited technical skill and one completely undisciplined by concern for formal order. The openings of two of his compositions reveal in one case a blatant set of parallel fifths and, in another, an equally obvious example of an exposed fourth:

[22] Christopher Gibbons, *Keyboard Compositions*, ed. Clare Rayner, *CEKM* XVIII.

[23] Matthew Locke, *Organ Voluntaries*, trans. and ed. Thurston Dart, London: Stainer and Bell, 1968.

Mus. ex. IV-11.
C. Gibbons: *Voluntarie,* beginning.[24]

Mus. ex. IV-12.
C. Gibbons: *In A,* beginning.[25]

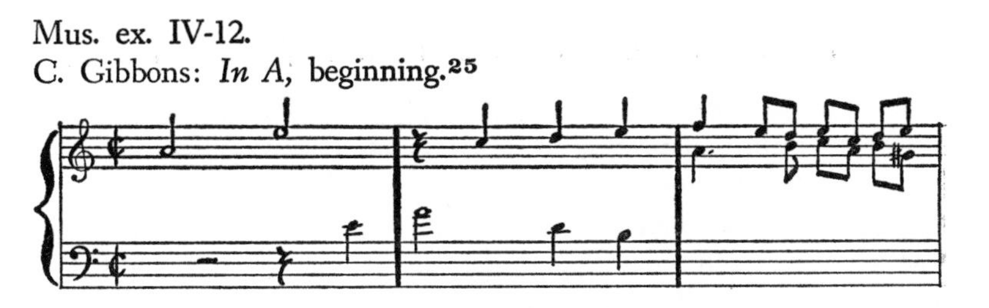

It is hardly likely that such crude openings suggest a more polished style in the remainder of these works. The first two pieces in the new edition are large voluntaries for double organ. Both compositions ramble from one idea to another without any cohesiveness or concern for relationship of one idea to the next. The most consistent stylistic feature is the promiscuous introduction of one figurative passage after another drawn directly from the vocabulary of the Italian concerto. None of these passages is in itself objectionable, but their lack of relationship to one another is. Both compositions exist in original versions which conclude at different points, an indication, no doubt, that the original copyists became somewhat tired of the rambling chaotic style of a composer unwilling to bend his material to any perceivable artistic end. When, in the second voluntary the composer lets the following passage intrude into this continuous froth, the result is almost laughable:

24 Gibbons, *op. cit.,* 29.
25 *Ibid.,* 32.

Mus. ex. IV-13.

C. Gibbons: *Voluntary for Double Organ Number* 2, measures 148-150.[26]

The fourth composition in the collection, a much shorter voluntary, has some rather interesting passages making use of echo. It too, however, degenerates into meaningless scale passages lacking any particular musical direction. One must conclude that the composer was a person of limited ability, one whose works would probably have been lost to us were it not for his illustrious father.

The more modest and restrained works of Locke are more interesting and musical. If Italian taste dominated the compositions of Gibbons, then French influence dominates the works of Locke. The most impressive of his organ compositions[27] is a work in the style of the French overture complete with an opening section in dotted rhythm and a bright fugal subject. Its brilliant coda, however, suggests that something of the virginal flair still remained in English keyboard playing.

[26] *Ibid.*, 22.

[27] Locke, *op. cit.*, 4.

Mus. ex. IV-14.
Locke: *Voluntary in A,* measures 34-37.

Most of Locke's compositions (numbers 1, 2, 3, 5 and 7) are short and competently written but hardly startling or highly original. They must have served as intonations for anthem performances, a liturgical practice which is documented in the Restoration Church. French influence is no less obvious in these small voluntaries. Number 2 is certainly in the style of the French *duo* and number 5 in the style of a *trio.* The influence of the solo *récit* is evident in the larger *Voluntary for Double Organ* (number 6), a composition which very successfully imitates the *récit pour le dessus et bassus.* Further evidence of Locke's French orientation exists in his adoption of the French signs of embellishment and the absence of the traditional English signs of / and //.

THE LAST THIRD OF THE CENTURY

During the last third of the seventeenth century only two English composers, Henry Purcell (1658-1695) and John Blow (1649-1708), left significant music for organ. Neither composer seems to have regarded the organ as central to his artistic output, and if we expect either of them to establish a native English organ style, we are to be disappointed. The works of both composers vacillate between compositions revealing French and those revealing Italian influence. Blow goes so far as literally to cite passages from the toccatas of Frescobaldi. It is obvious that both composers felt no strong national ties to the older English keyboard tradition and that each was willing to borrow very freely from foreign traditions.

The revised edition of the organ works of Purcell[28] contains but six works. One of these, the *Voluntary on Psalm 100,* may be a work by Blow. Two of the remaining five compositions are identical in their opening twenty-five measures. The short *Verse in F* and *Voluntary in C* (numbers 1 and 2 on the new edition) are similar in scope and probable liturgical intent to the shorter works of Locke. These pieces reveal a two-sectional form favored by both Purcell and Blow. Different thematic ideas are developed in the two sections of such compositions. The material in the B section usually moves in faster note values that that in A. Both A and B may be fugal, although examples exist, such as this *Voluntary in C,* in which A is non-imitative.

The *Voluntary in G* represents Purcell's attempt to imitate the highly personal style of Frescobaldi's elevation toccatas. This piece has the recitative-like manner, the subtle harmonic surprises, and even the Lombard rhythms associated with the toccatas of the Italian composer. Purcell, however, uses this style as an introduction or prelude to a fugal movement in the style of an Italian *canzone.* The juxtaposition of two such dissimilar styles, a technique to which the Italians themselves never resorted, is an English habit.

The *Voluntary for Double Organ* is the most handsome of the Purcell organ compositions. In its alternation of the solo voice from bass to soprano, in the imitative introduction in which the theme is presented on the subsidiary manual, and in the practice of bringing the hands together on the principal manual for the conclusion of the piece, it contains outward similarities to the *récits* of the French. The figuration, however, is more influenced by Italian than French styles and has about it a flamboyance the French repertory distinctly lacked. The following excerpt from the soprano is illustrative:

---

[28] Henry Purcell, *The Organ Works*, ed. Hugh McLean, London: Novello, 1967.

Mus. ex. IV-15.
Purcell: *Voluntary for Double Organ,* soprano, measures 23-28.[29]

It is regrettable that Purcell did not turn more frequently to the organ. Again we are faced with the hesitancy of the English to regard the instrument as a valid and important musical medium. Fortunately, John Blow left some thirty compositions.[30] For the most part these pieces show little stamp of individuality. Most could have originated almost anywhere in seventeenth-century Europe. They are devoid of unusual features, rather bland in their fugal writing, and highly dependent upon Italian sources for the principal inspiration. Many of them use the two-sectional form described in the discussion of Purcell. Although normally there are no thematic relationships between A and B, in number 5 Blow uses an approximate inversion of the first theme as a subject in B. One of the most striking deficiencies of these pieces, also notable in other English music during this century, is the inability of the composer to devise an initial theme of adequate strength. Reliance is unfortunately placed on thematic ideas without any noticeable shape or striking characteristics. The following themes are typical:

Mus. ex. IV-16.

---

29 *Ibid.,* 8.

30 John Blow, *Thirty Voluntaries and Verses for the Organ,* ed. Watkins Shaw, London: Schott and Company, 1972.

Hardly one of these voluntaries does not end in a coda based on Italianate figuration. The codas often seem little more than icing on poorly baked cakes. We are left to conclude that these compositions must have served the liturgy in a most perfunctory way, and that the composer hardly lavished on them the care he spent on his other works.

We have already mentioned that in two places Blow quotes note for note from the works of Frescobaldi. One of these citations, the opening of number 2, leads into another English attempt to imitate the rhapsodic style of that Italian composer. The result, however, is hardly as successful as that in Purcell's attempt, partly because the composition degenerates into a development of the figure of the downward slide, a motive used so commonly by Blow and other English keyboard composers that its appearance produces the effect of cliché in a style demanding utmost seriousness:

Mus. ex. IV-17.
Blow: *Voluntary II,* measures 19-21.[31]

Blow's four voluntaries for double organ are by far his most serious and well conceived compositions for the instrument. Here again the undisguised influences of France and Italy appear. Number 28 is a very good adaptation of the *récit de cornet* to the English organ. The composer imitates the style so exactly that, were it not for the composition's unusual length, the piece could pass as French. The coloratura has a particularly authentic quality absent in other similar pieces in which Italian figuration has been allowed to intrude into an otherwise French line. The opening solo melody is given below:

[31] *Ibid.,* 3.

Mus. ex. IV-18.

The bolder solo lines of the other double voluntaries suggest the use of the trumpet as the solo voice. Here the same flamboyance is present which we mentioned in the Purcell example. Lines often conclude with flashy, thirty-second-note running passages. At one point Blow even allows the solo voice to move in consecutive thirds:

Mus. ex. IV-19.
Blow: *Voluntary XXVII,* measures 25-26.[32]

From the historical point of view, the last of these voluntaries is the most interesting; for it establishes the lines of the eighteenth-century English voluntary. The Italian origin of this composition is patently obvious. As if to underscore this origin, Blow quotes literally from Frescobaldi (measures 45-57). The two major themes are drawn directly from the idiom of the Italian *canzone* and even borrow the technique of Italian thematic variation:

Mus. ex. IV-20.

The figurative working-out of these ideas is based on the vocabulary of the Italian concerto. There is no longer evidence of the more

[32] *Ibid.,* 53.

sensitive French style. The tension we have noted throughout the last half of this centurry between French and Italian tastes has now been resolved completely in favor of the latter. The adoption of the Italian manner in the English keyboard music of the eighteenth century is but another manifestation of the complete musical victory achieved by the importation of Italian opera. There is hardly a trace of native English or French style in the eighteenth-century voluntary; the pendulum has swung completely towards Italy.

The last composition in the collected works of Blow, the *Voluntary on Psalm 100,* deserves brief mention. It is likely that the work is originally by Purcell, although the evidence is inconclusive. It stands as the only extant attempt to set psalm tunes in the manner of the Continental chorale prelude. It may represent a written-out example of an improvisational practice more common than we suspect. In any event, this composition is hardly of the quality we associate with either of these composers.

CHAPTER V.

SPAIN & PORTUGAL.

THE FIRST THIRD OF THE CENTURY

The conservative attitude in English organ music during the first third of the seventeenth century is closely paralleled in the music of Spain and Portugal.[1] As we have seen, this conservative attitude faded in England after the Restoration and was replaced by a new interest in the modern features of French and Italian styles. The situation in the Iberian peninsula, however, remained essentially retrospective throughout the century. There is from Cabezon to Cabanilles an unbroken stylistic line which largely ignores outside developments and remains remarkably stable and consistent. The seventeenth-century composers inherited from the Cabezon generation a tradition which blended pristine counterpoint and a well-developed system of keyboard elaboration, the practice of glossing. These two elements remained throughout the century as the pillars of the unique Spanish style of organ composition. Both elements, however, never lost their essentially sixteenth-century flavor. Linear, modal counterpoint is to be found frequently in works as late as Cabanilles. While the Spanish were not unaware of the newer harmonic principles of the Italian tradition, it is clear they resisted universal acceptance of them. Particularly they avoided the Italian practice of harmonic experimentation as an end in itself, and while restrained modern harmonic devices were used rather frequently, it is obvious these are additions to a basically reactionary concept of tonal order. We have already traced the sixteenth-century origins of the instrumental elaboration. The popularity in Spain of the vihuela and the harp, which as plucked instruments had to conceal beneath the addition of a wealth of figuration their inability to play true counterpoint, no doubt influenced the keyboard com-

[1] Portugal during the period under consideration was politically a part of Spain. The musical development of the two countries in the period is similar. In order to avoid confusion, and with due apologies to the Portugese, the term Spain will refer often in this chapter to the peninsula as a whole.

posers to move in a similar direction. Several early editions of Spanish keyboard music indicate that these instruments could be used as alternates to the organ and harpsichord. The tradition of decorative figuration, a tradition which in other countries was greatly modified by the exigencies of tonal harmony, remained essentially unchanged throughout the Spanish seventeenth century. The variation principle, then, is the essential element of this musical style.

Despite the central place which variation technique plays in this music, it is not the *diferencia* but the *tiento* upon which the composers lavished their attention. Liturgical music is relatively rare. Of the important composers of the period only Coehlo left any significant body of such works. The *tiento* is often defined as merely the Spanish equivalent of the *ricercar*. While this designation may be close to the truth for sixteenth-century examples, it is insufficient in the seventeenth century. Some modest *tientos* are indeed like the *ricercar*. The more extended examples, however, are closer in style to the northern fantasia. Such *tientos* are lengthy, sectional compositions most often held together rather loosely by the central theme. This theme is traditionally presented in a full contrapuntal treatment in the style of the *ricercar*. Thereafter it serves as the basis for variations of one type or another. The style is, then, open-ended. The sixteenth-century *tiento* had been a composition of modest dimensions; the fantasia-like seventeenth-century examples often reach three hundred measures in length. Overall length of a composition seems largely at the whim of the composer. He may stop after a single variation of his subject or he may write as many as a dozen such variations.

Within the style of the *tiento* are elements borrowed from the variation, the *ricercar*, the *canzone*, and the toccata. Such individual styles were not practiced in and of themselves by the Spaniards; instead, all was encompassed in the *tiento*, a single example of which can include variations from the most severe to the most flamboyant writing. The origin of the terms "*toccata*" and "*tiento*" are similar: *i.e.*, the respective Italian and Spanish verbs meaning to touch. "*Tentar,*" however, implies more than mere touching. Its meaning is more to probe and examine tactilely. The term *tiento,* then, implies a combination of the Italian *ricercar* (to research) and *toccata* (to touch). The word is an excellent description of the musical style itself. The principal characteristics of this new type of seventeenth-century *tiento* are as follows:

1) an opening exposition in conservative, *ricercar* style
2) a tendency toward overall monothematic structure
3) sectional treatment of the theme or themes. Each section develops a new and essentially different figurative idea
4) excessive length resulting from many such sections strung together
5) restrained attitude toward dissonance and harmonic complexity
6) consistent use of four-voice, contrapuntal texture.

We have been describing the *tiento* to be played on one manual, the so-called *tiento lleno* or *tiento pleno* (simple *tiento*). These are the most common. Also frequently written were *tientos* in which the musical line or lines played by one hand assume solo roles. Such compositions are called *medio registra* (*i.e.*, divided registers, from the necessity for different stops in such compositions). Examples exist for left- and right-hand solos of either one or two voices. Compositions similar to the French *basse et dessus* in which the solo moves from one register to the other do not exist, probably due to the limitations of Spanish organs.

Another sub-category of the *tiento* is the *tiento de falsas.* Apel equates this type with the Italian *durezza e ligature* prelude.[2] This is not entirely a satisfactory equation. In the first place, the Spanish form is contrapuntally, not harmonically, conceived as is the Italian. The *falsas* is almost always a clear development of a monothematic subject in *ricercar* style. The *durezza*-style prelude, on the other hand, rarely shows such development. While the *falsas* often contains passages in suspensions and occasionally somewhat more striking dissonances than other music by the same composers, the complexity of dissonance is low. Some compositions which bear the designation *falsas* are no more dissonant than vocal compositions of Victoria. In what ways such bland compositions appeared to their creators to be false is not clear. In any respect, the type rarely has the experimental qualities characteristic of its supposed Italian equivalent.

The works of three composers dominate Iberian keyboard music in the first part of the century: Sebastian Aguilera de Heredia (1585-1618), the Portuguese composer Manuel Rodriguez Coelho (c. 1555-c. 1635), and Francisco Correa de Arauxo (d. 1626). Often one is

[2] *Apel K.*, 514.

hampered in the study of Spanish music by the lack of published material. Fortunately the works of these three composers are available. Aguilera's works are published in two anthologies which are readily available and to be highly recommended.[3] The works of Coelho[4] and Correa[5] are available in complete editions, both unfortunately expensive and difficult to obtain. We turn first to the music of Aguilera.

Aguilera

The published works of Aguilera provide the easiest introduction into the Spanish style. These seventeen pieces form a cohesive body of material containing examples of the principal forms used by the other composers of the century. Augilera's music is also unburdened by compositions of excessive length, common in the works of Coelho and Correa. The *tiento lleno,* called by Augilera simply *tiento,* or at other times *obra,* is represented by five examples.[6] The clarity of structure of the *Obra de l° tono*[7] makes it a good example for study. The *ricercar*-style theme of this composition clearly defines the tonality of the piece. Augilera's principal themes often show in their tonality a distinctly modern flavor often out of keeping with the modal surroundings into which they are fitted.

Mus. ex. V-1.

This theme serves as the basis for the remainder of the composition. First it is subjected to two complete expositions in *ricercar* style.

---

3 Willi Apel, ed., *Spanish Organ Masters after Antonio de Cabezon, CEKM XIV,* and *Antologia de organistas españoles del siglo XVII,* 4 volumes, ed. Higinia Angles, Barcelona: Diputacion Provincial de Barcelona, 1968 (hereafter cited as *Angles A*).

4 Manuel Rodrigues Coelho, *Flores de Musica,* 2 volumes, ed. Santiago Kastner, *Portugaliae Musica,* Lisbon: Fundacao Calouste Gulbenkian, 1959.

5 Francisco Correa de Arauxo, *Libro de Tientos y Discursos de Musica,* 2 volumes, ed. Santiago Kastner, *Monumentos de la Musica Españolo,* Barcelona, 1948.

6 *CEKM XIV,* numbers 16, 17, 19, 20, and 21. Also in *Angles A.*

7 *Ibid.,* number 17.

Exposition B treats the theme in *stretto,* and a radical textural change occurs at the conclusion of it. Here the conservative style is given up in favor of one in which the theme, which remains in half-note motion, is the basis for extended sixteenth-note figuration. Such a radical change in texture is typical at this point in most extended *tientos.* In the texture of such figurative passages, the theme tends to retreat into the background and serves merely as the scaffolding upon which the figuration is constructed. The figurative ideas change rapidly from one to another. Aguilera employs the following ones in this *obra*:

Mus. ex. V-2.

A short coda, which again returns to the more severe style of the opening of the piece and which carefully conceals the theme in the alto voice, concludes the composition.

It is important to understand how differently Spanish composers of the century viewed the theme in composition. A major concern of the Italians was thematic development. The theme and what happens to it in the course of a piece are central to the musical style. Spanish composers, on the other hand, viewed the theme as hardly more than a point of departure. They were quite willing to relegate it to a subordinate position in the musical structure or to drop it altogether. The Spaniards were particularly uninterested in any elaborate, intellectual thematic development; it is foreign to their style. The Italian technique of thematic variation was, however, well known in Spain. Its use became commonplace as the century progressed. The presentation of the theme in a new rhythmic guise served more as a means to initiate a new variation than as a point of musical interest in its own right. Several of Aguilera's *tientos* have sections in triple time based on such variations. The theme and its variation from the *Tiento de 4° tono*[8] are as follows:

[8] *Ibid.,* number 18.

Mus. ex. V-3.

This *tiento* also introduces a rhythmic feature particularly favored by the Spaniards. One might view the rhythm $\frac{4}{4}$ ♩ ♪♩ ♪♩ as a simple syncopation within the middle of a measure. More careful analysis by Apel[9] reveals not a syncopation, as such, but a division of the measure into $3 + 3 + 2$. That this analysis is correct is revealed by passages in which the harmonies themselves move in this rhythm:

Mus. ex. V-4.
Aguilera: *Vajo, 1° tono,* measure 56.[10]

Aguilera provides three examples of the *tiento de falsas.* These bear out our assertion that this form is hardly like its Italian counterpart. Almost all the progressions in the *Falsas de 6° tono*[11] may be found in any composition by Vittoria. The opening is in the most controlled counterpoint; there exists not a single extraordinary harmonic progression in the entire piece; and the voice leading throughout is within the limits of sixteenth-century usage. What this piece does show is a sensitive feeling for harmonic order revealed in carefully controlled cadences, the occasional use of secondary dominants, and a restrained use of harmonic sequence. In terms of modern harmony, the use of the V^{6}_{5} of IV in the concluding measures of the piece offers its most striking moment:

---

9 Apel, "Drei plus Drei plus Zwei = Vier plus Vier," *AM*, XXXII, 1960, 29.
10 *CEKM XIV*, number 22.
11 *Ibid.*, number 15.

Mus. ex. V-5.
Aguilera: *Falsas de 6° tono,* measures 54-57.

One harmonic progression which occurs from time to time in these *falsas* is common in Spanish music throughout the century. The use of the augmented triad in first inversion is relatively inoffensive, even by sixteenth-century standards, since all voices are consonant with the bass and each is handled with melodic propriety:

Mus. ex. V-6.
Aguilera: *Tiento de 4° tono de falsas,* measures 69-70.[12]

One of Aguilera's compositions bears the title *ensalada* (hodgepodge). This type of composition is made up of short, contrasting sections hardly exceeding thirty measures in length, each thematically unrelated to the other. Here the composer seems to be imitating the Neopolitan quilt *canzone* in which as many as seven such sections were often so strung together. Stylistically this composition has much in common with the *canzone* style.

Aguilera is master of the *medio registro* with solo in the bass (*vajo* = *baixo* = bass). Four examples of his work in this form show a grasp of solo writing ahead of its time. We have already mentioned these compositions as possible models for the French *récit de basse.* What is amazing is how well they foreshadow the French form by nearly half a century. The *tiento lleno,* no matter how inventive its figurations, nonetheless was securely grounded in the equal-voice counterpoint of the past. The *vajo,* with its focus on the solo melody, was decidedly innovative and seventeenth-century in spirit.

[12] *Ibid.,* 58.

Each of the *vajos* opens with a set of imitative entries so fashioned that the bass solo enters last. At this point the connection to imitative writing ceases. The upper voices serve merely to provide the chordal background against which the solo moves. The interest lies in the direction taken by the bass and not in any interplay among the voices. Just as in vocal music the appearance of monody at the beginning of the century imposed a new conception of melodic construction, one finds Aguilera's melodies to be guided by new concepts of tonal harmony. The direction of the melody is no longer the result merely of the singable and graceful considerations of the sixteenth century. Its form is now suggested by basic harmonic goals. The rhythmic drive toward these goals is heightened by the surge of motivic writing and the use of melodic sequence. The opening of the solo in the *Registro baixo de 1° tono* is illustrative. The melody moves from its tonic beginning to the relative major, is extended to a full cadence on the relative, then returns to the tonic. The shape of the melody is thoroughly conditioned by harmonic considerations:

Mus. ex. V-7.
Aguilera: *Registra baixo de 1° tono,* bass, measures 11-23.[13]

Sequential melodic progressions, which play an important role in the extension of these melodies, are often guided by harmories descending through the circle of fifths:

[13] *Ibid.,* 110.

Mus. ex. V-8.
Registro baixo de 1° tono, measures 86-90.

Melodies are also often extended by repetition, generally of a two-measure phrase, at the dominant level.

Mus. ex. V-9.
Aguilera: *Vajo de 1° tono,* bass, measures 119-122.[14]

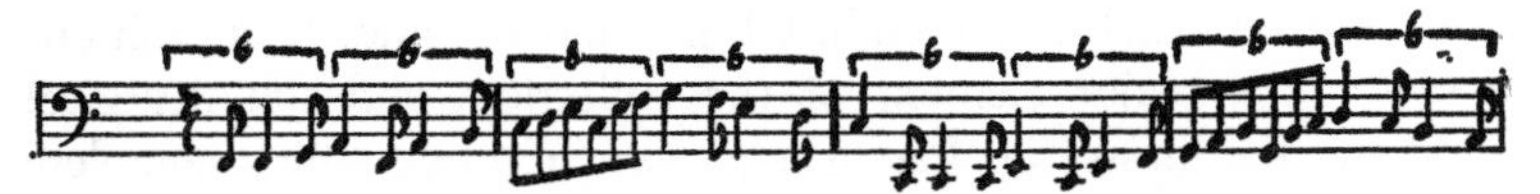

Such feeling for modern melodic writing shows that at least in this type of composition Aguilera is as progressive as his contemporaries in other parts of Europe. It is difficult to understand why such concepts did not more thoroughly permeate Spanish keyboard music of the period.

Aguilera left one example of composition for two bass solo lines (*dos vajos*). In it his writing is similar to certain viol *duos* in the French tradition, particularly in the interchange of a motive from one solo voice to another. The use of echo in this composition suggests again the many similarities between the Spanish *tiento* and the Dutch fantasia of Sweelinck. Throughout his *vajos* Aguilera uses figurations based on abstract patterns identical to those of Sweelinck. Such formulas as the following are typical:

Mus. ex. V-10.

The question of the origin of such patterns arises. Did the Dutch influence the Spanish or the Spanish influence the Dutch? The close

---

[14] *Ibid.,* 108.

political connection between Spain and the Netherlands no doubt explains the exchange of musical idioms. Their origin, however, remains in doubt.

Aguilera's music for use in the liturgy is minimal. The two compositions entitled *Salbe* (*Salve regina*) are no more than short *tientos* based on the opening notes of the chant. The trio setting of the *Pange lingua* places the melody in the soprano and forces a stylized rhythm upon it. The piece is similar to others in the English repertory.

Coelho

A major monument of Iberian keyboard music appeared in 1620, the *Flores de Musica* of the Portuguest composer Coelho. This well-organized anthology contains twenty-four *tientos* (Portuguese *tento*), three in each of the eight Church modes. These compositions constitute the major element of the collection, and the liturgical music and the glosses on Lassus' *chanson Susanna,* which complete the collection, are less important. It is the *tiento* upon which the composer lavishes his special care; these compositions assure him a place in the keyboard literature of the century. As in other collections of Iberian keyboard music, the organ is not designated as the medium of performance. The title page of the publication indicates the music is suitable for any keyboard instrument (the generic term *tecla* is used) or harp. Since a third of the collection is devoted to liturgical music and Coelho himself was an organist of no small reputation, we can conclude that the organ was the most likely instrument upon which this literature was originally performed. It is interesting, however, that this collection contains no *tientos de medio registro.* This is one of the few stylistic differences between the music of Coelho and the Spanish composers of the century. Perhaps the organs to which he had access had no divided stop capability.

Coelho's musical style is a curious mixture of the conservative and the progressive. On the one hand it is obvious he was well acquainted with English and particularly Dutch keyboard writing. The similarity of his musical syntax is again and again so strikingly similar to that of Sweelinck that, as Tusler observes,[15] it is difficult to tell which of the two composers wrote a given passage. Figurative ideas are conceived in Coelho's works in as abstract a manner as in

15 Robert L. Tusler, *The Organ Music of Jan Pieterszoon Sweelinck,* Bilthoven: A. B. Creyghton, 1958, 82.

Sweelinck's, and they are consistently developed by as modern a technique as Sweelinck employs. This progressive attitude toward figuration is, however, unmatched by modern concepts of formal order. The carefully worked out formal design of the Sweelinck fantasia, with its monothematic and sectional structure, finds no parallels in the meandering *tiento* of Coelho. The Portuguese composer seems curiously unconcerned with the overall design of a composition. He prefers a chain of loosely connected links, each interesting at the moment and dropped soon in favor of another.

This unconcern for tight formal order is particularly difficult to understand in view of the fact that Coelho's *tientos* are some of the longest pieces in the seventeenth-century keyboard repertory. Almost all exceed two hundred measures in length and some exceed three hundred. The explanation for such length, on the one hand, and non-existent formal order, on the other, is probably to be found in the intent with which these pieces were written. Kastner suggests[16] the *tientos* were written for the edification of the player himself, that they were introspective in nature, and, as such, hardly designed for public performance. The quasi-improvisational nature of these works is certainly in keeping with this function. Wandering from one interesting keyboard idea to another is the type of musical thinking underlying much improvisation. The novelty in the early seventeenth-century of this type of keyboard play is adequate explanation for the almost whimsical attitude toward more complex organization of musical material.

In their enthusiasm for Coelho's music, both Kastner and Tusler attribute to him the practice of developing a chain of figurative ideas from a single germ motive. One motivic idea gives rise to the next; and a composition consists, then, of ideas which have a common motivic origin. Were this consistently the case, the problem of formal cohesiveness would be largely solved. A careful examination of the *tientos* reveals, however, that only a few use this technique throughout and some others organize lengthy sections thus. Still others show no evidence at all of it. An example of a composition using this technique with some consistency is the *Segunda Tento do Segundo Tom.*[17] The initial repeated notes of the composition form the germ for a number of figurative ideas:

---

16 Coelho, *op. cit.*, xxvii.

17 *Ibid.*, I, 38.

Mus. ex. V-11.

Even in this carefully chosen example, there is a lengthy intrusion of an imitative section which has nothing at all to do with the leading motive (measures 130, following).

Similar in conception to the derivation from one germ of other figurative ideas is Coelho's practice of expanding a small melodic figure into an extensive section. Very often the initial presentation of such a figure may be so inconspicuous as to escape notice. These figures are invariably some of the most common decorative patterns of late sixteenth-century counterpoint and, as such, hardly draw attention to themselves. The listener or player may discover what seemed at first to be inconsequential to have become very important. The bracketed figure in the example below later is used in just this way.

Mus. ex. V-12.
Coelho: *Terceiro Tento do Segundo Tom,* measures 75-77.[18]

One must not think that Coelho's concern is for any high level of structural cohesiveness. Most *tientos* show no one theme central to the composition. Many are overtly polythematic, a feature which stresses the overall sixteenth-century flavor of this music. The effect of most compositions is that of a musical stream of consciousness in which one idea begets another in an imprecise, non-intellectual manner. One is almost unaware when one idea blends into another. The relationship of the new to the old is there, but it is nebulous.

[18] *Ibid.,* I, 50.

The sense of time in a *tiento* of Coelho is different from the sense of time in an Italian or northern composition. The compulsion to organize and structure the temporal relationships of musical events by means of intellectual devices, a compulsion to which Western music gives prime importance, is almost absent in Coelho's music. Were he an inept composer in other ways, one might attribute this unusual temporal sense to lack of ability; but he is everything but inept. His musical syntax has the perfection we expect from an Iberian composer oriented toward late sixteenth-century style. The lack of formal cohesiveness is an intentional part of his musical design and to fault the music for this is to miss the introspective nature of Coelho's art.

We have already mentioned the kinship between Iberian figurations and those of the Dutch and English. This kinship is particularly striking between Coelho and Sweelinck and Scheidt. Just as do these northerners, Coelho uses a relatively small number of keyboard motives. The most common are the following:

Mus. ex. V-13.

The closeness which exists between the styles of Coelho and Scheidt is further revealed by the triplet figurations used by both composers. There is hardly a *tiento* of Coelho which lacks such figuration.

One *tiento,* number 19 on the seventh tone,[19] is unique in that it has no keyboard figuration at all. This composition is Coelho's single *falsas.* Sections in *falsas* style occur in other *tientos* as a relief to figurative writing. In this *falsas* Coelho shows particularly good control of the dominant seventh chord in unprepared situations as well as of the ii^6_5.These limited modern harmonic devices are used frequently in the other *tientos;* but when they are, they stand out strikingly against the otherwise modal background of the harmony.

The *Flores de Musica* contains the most important and exten-

---

[19] *Ibid.,* I, 187.

sive body of seventeenth-century Iberian liturgical music. The publication contains four settings of the *Pange lingua,* four settings of the *Ave Maris Stella* and a set of five other verses on the same chant, twenty-three unusual verses for soprano voice and organ, thirty-four verses for the various tones of the Magnificat, and thirty-five settings of the Kyrie. It is interesting to compare Coelho's style in this body of music with the works of Titelouze published within the same decade. The rigidly complex contrapuntal style of the French composer is rarely to be found in Coelho's works. The same concern for keyboard elaboration and figuration underlies his liturgical music as underlies his *tientos.* It is difficult to imagine Titelouze resorting to a texture similar to that of the following passage. Such a texture, however, is common in Coelho's versets.

Mus. ex. V-14.
Coelho: *Pange lingua,* measures 120-123.[20]

Coelho's typical treatment of the chant melody is in long-note, *cantus planus* fashion. In the two settings of the *Pange lingua* the use of double-whole notes for the hymn produces over one hundred measures, a length incompatible with alternation use. No doubt these long settings were used, as were the *tientos,* for personal edification. The *cantus firmus* in these pieces moves so slowly that it, like so many themes in the *tientos,* retreats completely into the background. Our ears are drawn again solely to the figurative pattern. The first compositions on the *Ave maris,* although somewhat shorter, are similar in style.

The second set of versets on this chant deserves particular attention. Unlike the other liturgical compositions in the collection, the second set never includes the *cantus planus.* These versets are small *tientos* based on themes derived from the chant itself. The five movements are based on progressive phrases of the hymn tune in the following manner:

20 *Ibid.,* II, 8.

Verse I – First half of phrase one
Verse II – Second half of phrase two
Verse III – Phrase 2
Verse IV – Phrase 3
Verse V – Phrase 4

Progressive derivation of themes from subsequent lines of a hymn is unique in the liturgical works of the period. Since such a procedure hardly suggests alternation practice, is it possible that the five verses were designed to be played without interruption in the fashion of a lengthy, multi-sectional *tiento?*

The sung versets are also unusual. In these pieces the chant melody, the *Magnificat* in all cases save the last *Nunc dimittis,* is presented in unadorned fashion in the soprano register. The compositions are restrained in length and obviously designed for practical use. Suggestions are often made that the organ was routinely used in both Iberian and French practice to accompany sung chant. These pieces are undoubtedly examples of the manner in which this took place. The numerous settings of the *Magnificat* without voice, as well as the settings of the *Kyrie,* are also of practical length. They do not differ in technique from the larger chant settings we have just discussed.

Correa

An equally important collection of organ music appeared in the publication of Francisco Correa, the *Libro de tientos* (1626). It contains some sixty-three *tientos,* to the virtual exclusion of other types of music. The lengthy introduction to the publication is an unexplored treasure of information pertaining to contemporary performance practices, particularly ornamentation and possible rhythmic alterations of the score.

The *tientos* are grouped according to type and the composer has further pointed out the relative difficulty of his various compositions. The publication opens with a set of *tientos* in each of the Church modes; there follows a miscellaneous group of *tientos llenos.* The compositions for *medio registro* follow, grouped for single solo soprano, then single solo bass, then double solo soprano, and finally double solo bass. Correa uses the title *discurso* for some compositions. These pieces are *tientos* of more than normal difficulty.

Correa shows much more concern for tighter organization than does Coelho. A majority of his compositions are monothematic and none has the excessive length we associate with the Portuguese composer. This greater concern for thematic integrity is only one element which ties Correa even closer to Sweelinck than the other Iberians we have discussed. Correa in some cases uses the device of thematic diminution in the manner of Sweelinck. Further unmistakable evidence of the relationship between the two composers is to be found in Tiento XXIII, *Tiento tercero de sexto tono,* which is an unabashed imitation of the Sweelinck echo fantasia. The following passages could be the work of either composer.

Mus. ex. V-15.
Correa: *Tiento tercero de sexto tono,* measures 47-51.[21]

The chromaticism of Sweelinck is, as one might suspect, absent in Correa's works. Only one *tiento, Discurso de medio registro de dos baxones de segundo tone* is provided with a mildly chromatic theme. Correa, however, does have a curious habit of modifying a previously diatonic theme with chromatic inflexions. In the following example the theme, here in the alto, appeared in the opening exposition merely as C C C D B.

Mus. ex. V-16.
Correa: *Tiento V de quinto tono,* measures 42-45.[22]

[21] Correa, *op. cit.,* I, 130.
[22] *Ibid.,* I, 29.

Correa has a decided preference for the *tiento de medio registro* and nearly half of the examples are of this type. In these compositions he follows the lines already set by Aguilera. Correa, however, provides numerous examples in which the treble carries the solo and numerous examples in both bass and treble for two solo voices. The alternation of a figuration between the two solo voices over the held harmony of the accompaniment produces a texture not unlike that of the early trio sonata.

Mus. ex. V-17.
Correa: *Tiento LIV de medio registro de dos tiples de septimo tono,* measures 24-26.[23]

Toward the end of Correa's publication there are a number of *tientos* which are made up of page after page of keyboard figurations and of nothing else. In their persistence in figuration to the exclusion of any other musical devices, they are similar to many Venetian toccatas. Actually these pieces seem to be studies of the various possibilities of figuration. Unique are such oddities as subdivision of the unit beat into five and seven notes, a feature which occurs occasionally in Spanish music of the period.

SPANISH ORGAN MUSIC AT MID-CENTURY

The published examples of Spanish organ music written during the middle years of the century reveal the same decline in quality and quantity we observed in England during this period. Perhaps the picture is distorted by the scarcity of available material. It is more likely that the political decline of Spain was paralleled by a general decline in Spanish culture and that this is reflected in the extant music. In any event, between the extensive works of the Aguilera - Coelho - Correa generation and the voluminous keyboard works of Cabanilles (1644-1712) we have only a few scattered

[23] *Ibid.,* II, 107.

pieces by less important composers. The situation in Spain, however, differs from that in England in that the older musical tradition of Spain never broke down completely, nor was it ever replaced with a newer tradition based on foreign models. The English organ style of the last third of the century was completely unlike that of the first third; in Spain there was a continuous tradition from Aguilera through Cabanilles. The types of music written by both composers are more similar than dissimilar, and there is a stylistic continuity throughout the century that is obvious. The minor composers who bridge the gap between Correa and Cabanilles transmitted a tradition; they did not abandon or greatly modify their inheritance.

The five published works of José Jimenez (died 1672), a set of variations, a *tiento,* an insignificant verset, and two compositions entitled *batalla,*[24] reveal nothing strikingly new. The variations are in the tradition of the Cabezon *diferencia* and, in comparison with other variation sets of the period, very restrained in figuration. The *tiento* is likewise restrained in tone. The excessive diversity and length of the Coelho type of *tiento* did not generally appeal to later composers who followed the tradition of Correa in tightening thematic content and development. The two *batallas* introduce us to a type of composition encountered throughout the century. These pieces are *tientos* employing the same techniques we otherwise associate with the form. They use bustling figurations suggestive of the battle scene and certain cliches, such as trumpet calls, which point up the programmatic content of the pieces.

Mus. ex. V-18.
Jimenez: *Batalla de Sexto Tono,* measures 103-106.[25]

[24] The variations are in *Angles A, I* and the *tiento* in *Angles A, II.* The verset and the two *batallas* are in *Anthology of Classical Spanish Organists,* volume i, ed. Felipe Pedrell, reprinted: New York: Associated Music publishers, 1968.

[25] Pedrell, *op. cit.,* 50.

To modern ears there is a certain naivete about compositions such as these which hardly more depict a battle than other pieces not bearing the title.

A *medio registro de dos tiples* of José Perandreu[26] is interesting for its attempts to involve the accompanying voices more distinctly in the contrapuntal development of the piece. The tendency to have such voices merely sustain chords, a tendency noted in Aguilera and Correa, is partially avoided in this example. The composer accomplishes this end by having the two lower voices engage in lengthy duos which are then duplicated canonically when the two solo voices enter. Unfortunately the contrapuntal skill of the composer is limited and the lines have a certain squareness about them atypical of the polished writing we normally expect of the Spaniards.

The five *tientos* of Gabriel Manault (died 1687), one *falsas* and four *de medio registro,*[27] reveal that lesser Spanish composers fell as easily into the pit of extended sequential figuration in the Italian manner as did English composers of the period. All Manault's works employ sequence *ad nauseum.* This coupled with the excessive stylization of the figurations draws all the life from the *medio registro,* a form which demanded from its beginnings skill in contriving solo lines of interest and verve.

By far the most capable composer between Correa and Cabanilles is Pablo Bruno (1611-1679), whose thirteen *tientos* are well conceived and competently written.[28] These compositions show in several ways that the composer was influenced by the Italians. The *Tiento lleno 6° tono*[29] is set in the form of an Italian *canzone* complete with the tri-partite organization, thematic variation, and themes derived stylistically from the French *chanson.* The spirit of the *Tiento de falsas 2° tono*[30] is similar to that of the *ricercari* in Frescobaldi's *Fiori Musicali.* The composition gives little hint of its Spanish origin. The use of thematic material in which two voices set up natural progressions of decorated suspensions is common in such pieces in Frescobaldi's works. The following passages are identical in musical content:

---

[26] *Angles A,* I, number 8.
[27] In *Angles A,* I and II.
[28] In *Angles A,* I, II, III, IV.
[29] *Angles A,* II, number 11.
[30] *Ibid.,* I, number 11.

Mus. ex. V-19.
Frescobaldi: *Altro recercar post il Credo,* measures 24-27.[31]

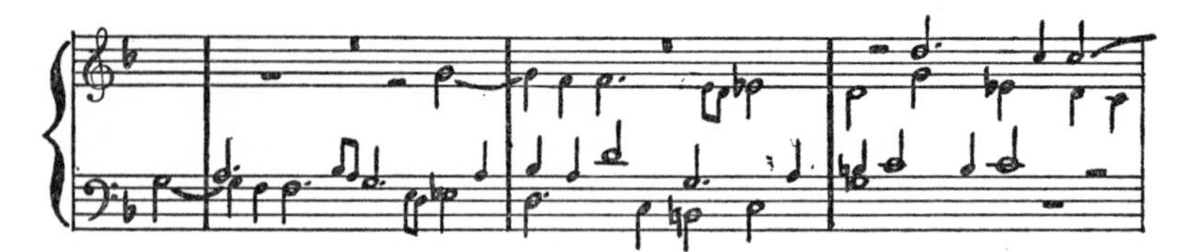

Mus. ex. V-20.
Bruno: *Tiento de falsas,* 2° *tono,* measures 1-4.

In his compositions for solo registers, Bruno falls again into the trap of extended sequential figuration. The novelty of the bland, almost entirely diatonic harmony typical throughout Europe in the middle decades of the seventeenth century led some composers to rely too heavily on the same unimaginative harmonic progressions. The organization of sequential writing based on the descending progression of fifths becomes particularly laborious in the solo compositions of Bruno. Equally persistent is Bruno's habit of repeating a two-measure phrase over such a harmonic sequence:

Mus. ex. V-21.
Bruno: *Tiento de dos tiples* 6° *tono,* measures 34-39.[32]

[31] Frescobaldi, *Fiori Musicali,* ed. Pidoux, V, 39.
[32] *Angles A,* III, 74.

In his large *tientos llenos* Bruno achieves coherence by extensive use of the principle of thematic variation. These pieces show how closely the *tiento* approached the variation form so favored by earlier Spanish composers. One particularly beautiful composition which Bruno entitles *tiento* is in fact a *differencia*.[33] The number and variety of sections in Bruno's works seems unlimited. One composition has nine major sections, each developing the theme in its own unique manner.[34] At times the theme is treated in *ricercar* style; at other times it serves as the basic for the development of short, concise motives; in other situations it is presented as a *cantus planus;* and in one section appears in inversion to the accompaniment of quintuplet figurations. In this manner Bruno unifies a composition as long as any of Coelho's (344 measures) without the thematic chaos of the earlier composer.

The unique feature of Bruno's writing lies in the area of rhythm. Sections in compound time consistently use hemiola, various syncopated figures, and other cross rhythms. In one composition, for instance, the device of hemiola appears at two rhythmic levels in close succession:

Mus. ex. V-22.
Bruno: *Tiento lleno. 5° tono,* measures 141-144.[35]

We have already mentioned the frequent Spanish rhythm of 3 + 2 + 2. In this same *tiento* Bruno employs the rarer pattern 2 + 3 + 3 in a number of places.

[33] *Ibid.,* I, number 13, *Tiento sobre la letania la Virgen.*
[34] *Tiento lleno, 4° tono, Ibid.,* III, number 10.
[35] *Ibid.,* IV, 45.

Mus. ex. V-23.
Measures 187-190.

THE LAST THIRD OF THE CENTURY–THE WORKS OF JUAN CABANILLES

Spanish keyboard music in the last third of the seventeenth century is completely dominated by the prolific works of Juan Cabanilles (1644-1712). Although four volumes of organ works have already been published by Angles,[36] the composer's liturgical work remains completely unavailable. We can, however, obtain a clear picture of Cabanilles' *tientos* from the portion of them that has been published.

By his nature Cabanilles is neither a radical nor a highly individual composer. His works show a continuation of the traditions already described. The *falsas,* the *tiento* for right and left hand solos, and the *tiento lleno* are all represented by well-constructed pieces. To these Cabanilles adds the following novel types: 1) the *tiento de contras* in which lengthy pedal points underlie large rhapsodic constructions, 2) compositions resembling toccatas and preludes of other traditions essentially outside the contrapuntal tradition of the *tiento,* and 3) a few *tientos* based on the styles of Italian song and dance. The Italian influence is also present in certain retrospective pieces reminiscent of Frescobaldi, a well-developed *tiento* on four subjects, and another on the hexachord.

Cabanilles is conservative not only in formal matters but also in musical syntax. Harmonically his idiom represents the tonal vocabulary common elsewhere in the middle of the century, and he avoids harmonic experimentation as completely as his precursors. His bland harmony is rarely relieved by anything more than an occasional secondary dominant, and in overuse of harmonic sequence he is as guilty as Bruno. It is interesting to note in the work of a late seventeenth-century composer the scarcity of such common

[36] Joannis Cabanilles, *Musici Organici,* 4 vols., ed. Angles, Barcelona: Biblioteca Central, 1927 to 1956.

Baroque harmonies as the diminished seventh chord. Not only is his general harmonic style unadventurous, at times it is completely anachronistic. The opening of *Tiento* 35 is an example.[37] Here meandering harmonies lead from the opening D minor to a modally conditioned cadential point in C major. The complete absence of tonal direction suggests the beginning of a sixteenth-century Venetian toccata.

Mus. ex. V-24.
Cabanilles: *Tiento* 35, measures 1-8.

Twelve of the published *tientos* bear the designation *falsas.* That this designation was used for compositions in various styles is evident. They vary from a naively simple and diatonic fugal movement completely devoid of any harmonic peculiarities to compositions which imitate the *durezza e ligature* Italian style. Those *falsas* which are fugal in style generally have subjects which contain either a diminished interval or a simple chromatic progression. While such commonplace features would hardly be noticed outside Spain at this late date, there they still appeared to have merited the term false.

Cabanilles obviously wished to modify the *ricercar* style of the *falsas* in some of his pieces. In one example he interpolated a passage in sixteenth-note motion which seems somewhat out of place.[38] In another composition there is a middle section based on a quarter-note motive between the opening and closing sections built on chains of half-note suspensions.[39]

[37] *Ibid.,* III, 31.
[38] *Ibid.,* I, 1.
[39] *Ibid.,* I, 125.

That by the late seventeenth century the influences of the early Baroque had finally penetrated conservative Spain is evident in another *falsas,*[40] a composition which obviously begins as an attempt to imitate the Frescobaldi toccata for the elevation. The written out trills, the descending chromatic bass, and the augmented triad in first inversion used as an appogiatura are certain trademarks of the Neopolitans. After a very convincing beginning, Cabanilles could hardly sustain a style as intense as this and the composition degenerates into harmonic progressions of banal simplicity. Throughout the century there is evidence that the Spanish composers attempted to employ the musical language of the Baroque in their musical environment which lacked sufficient intensity, conciseness, and emotional fervor. The result is often incongruity.

The *tiento de contras,* an apparent invention of Cabanilles, derives its inspiration from the pedal toccatas of Frescobaldi and the occasional *point d'orgue* in the French repertory. These *tientos* are made up of short sections of motivically oriented material strung together over a pedal point. There is no attempt to relate one motivic section to the next. When the ear can no longer tolerate a given pedal note, the composer moves to a related note and transposes the entire string of snippets to that pitch. The result is inordinate length, little structural cohesiveness, and inevitable boredom. One inexplicable feature of these compositions is their use of passages which seem unmistakably North-German in spirit. What connection there was between Cabanilles and the Buxtehude school we cannot know. In any event the opening of *Tiento* 38[41] could be the beginning of a North-German *praeambulum.* As in his imitation of Frescobaldi, Cabanilles cannot sustain the mood of his opening measures.

[40] *Ibid.,* III, 196.
[41] *Ibid.,* III, 63.

Mus. ex. V-25.
Cabanilles: *Tiento* 38, measures 1-5.

In his *tientos* for single manual, designated variously as *lleno, pleno,* and *de todas manos,* Cabanilles uses two distinct types: 1) the traditional contrapuntal type based on a single theme which is developed in variation technique and 2) a type which in other countries would be classed as a toccata. In the more traditional type the composer adds little to the material we have already described. These pieces begin in conservative, *ricercar* style and progress through variations in more active rhythmic styles. Cabanilles does little to discipline the excessive length of these compositions, yet the fertility of his musical ideas hardly exceeds those of his precursors. His *tiento* on the hexachord,[42] even though it may exaggerate the procedures, is none the less typical of them. An outline of this composition follows:

[42] *Ibid.,* III, 147.

Measures	
1 - 62	*Ricercar* presentation of the theme in whole-note motion with figurations of tied notes and suspensions
63 - 80	Imitative treatment of the theme in quarter-note motion
81 - 100	Theme in half-note motion with embellishment by sixteenth-note running figures
101 - 117	Theme in half-note motion and in retrograde accompanied by suspensions
118 - 156	Section in 6/4 meter, theme in dotted half notes
157 - 178	Return to duple meter. Theme in half notes accompanied again by scale passages
179 - 241	3/2 meter. Fugal theme derived from the hexachord. This section contains extensive figurative passages in which the theme is absent
242 - 285	Again in duple meter. Theme in half-and quarter-note motion decorated by numerous sequential figurative ideas
285 - 301	Toccata-like coda.

Even the undertaking of so extensive and serious a hexachord composition this late in the century is evidence of the retrospective nature of Spanish music. The musical style of this composition further confirms this thesis. Particularly conservative is Cabanilles' presentation of his theme solely on C and G. No exploration of its transposition to other key areas occurs. The constant shift from one idea to another is more characteristic of early than late seventeenth-century musical styles. Cabanilles here as elsewhere reflects stylistic features typical of other traditions in the decades from 1620 to 1640.

Throughout the earlier part of the century no compositions exclusively in toccata style exist in the Iberian repertory. Although so much of the interest of the music we have been discussing lies in figurative writing, none of it seems to have been directed solely to that end. Prior to Cabanilles, figurative development was always bound, if at times rather loosely, to fugal and variation techniques. Perhaps the severe Spanish mentality of the century resisted display for display's sake and preferred it partially clothed by the threads of contrapuntal elaboration. Cabanilles, however, left some *tientos* which are essentially toccatas. The compositions rely on two techniques: short segments each based on sequential treatment of a motivic figure and the repetition of a more extended phrase at another pitch level. The first technique results in compositions made up of unrelated short sections. These are similar to pieces of the Italian composer Rossi. They lack, however, the latter composer's imaginative sense of modulation. Cabanilles tenaciously sticks close to the home key. The second technique is used in *Tiento 70* entitled *Coreado o de ecos.*[43] The opening three-measure keyboard flourish first appears on D; it is then transposed to G, C, and A. The remainder of the composition is largely made of similar passages. The following is typical:

Mus. ex. V-26.
Cabanilles: *Tiento 70, Coreado o de ecos,* measures 13-19.

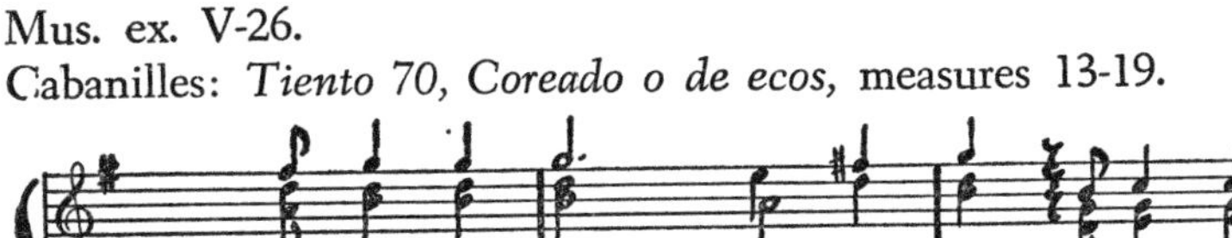

Six published compositions of Cabanilles actually bear the name toccata.[44] The first of these uses the repetition technique we have just described. The second is a *tiento* for left hand solo. Numbers three and four open with passages on pedal points. Since the pedal points are effected by written out trills in one case and rapidly repeated notes in the other, these compositions are probably intended for harpsichord. Both are rather naively constructed. The final two toccatas are actually in the style of the Italian *canzone*. The various dance movements and variation sets contained in the second volume of Angles' edition are most certainly harpsichord music.

The style of Iberian organ music remained peripheral to that of the mainstream of European music for the instrument. The

---

[43] *Ibid.,* IV, 136.
[44] *Ibid.,* II, 153 ff.

heavy borrowings from Italian, English, and Dutch traditions seem never to have been repaid by cross influences. The long, meandering *tientos* of the Iberians had little in common with the more organized tendencies in other traditions. This coupled with a very conservative harmonic outlook and, at times, a sixteenth-century attitude toward keyboard embellishment left the music largely unexportable. If during the entire century there was any cross influence, it lay early in the century in the Sweelinck generation. From Sweelinck to the North-Germans and hence to Bach is a direct line to which we now turn.

CHAPTER VI.

The Netherlands & North Germany.

To combine in the same chapter the study of Dutch organ music of the seventeenth century with that of North Germany demands an initial explanation. The position of Jan Pieterszoon Sweelinck in the history of organ music of the early decades of the century suggests that he must represent the culmination of an extensive previous development in Dutch music. The evidence, however, seems to suggest that the generations before Sweelinck produced hardly any keyboard music, much less organ music, in the Netherlands. Even within his generation Sweelinck stands head and shoulders above his contemporaries both in the quantity and quality of the works he produced. Apel points out[1] that of the seven Dutch and Belgian composers whose works we know, four spent their creative lives outside the Netherlands. Henderick Speuy (c. 1575-1625) has left a not-too-important collection of psalm settings. Pieter Cornet (c. 1560-1626) left only six fantasias, a toccata, and some minor works based on the chant. These are hardly enough to justify Apel's claim that this composer was a serious rival of Sweelinck. Sweelinck's corpus of organ music ranks as an unusual and singular one in seventeenth-century Dutch music. Even in the latter half of the century, the Netherlands produced little of consequence besides the works of Anthoni van Noordt.

Sweelinck's influence, however, was to be felt strongest in the most vibrant of all the many seventeenth-century traditions of organ music, that which developed around the Hanseatic cities of North Germany. The bond which exists between Sweelinck's music and that of the school of Scheidemann, Tunder, Weckmann, Bruhns, Buxtehude, and Lübeck is the closest possible. The principal members of the first generation of North-German composers, Scheidemann and Jacob Praetorius, as well as many of their less important contemporaries, were students of Sweelinck. They brought back to

---

[1] *Apel K.,* 324.

Germany and transformed for their own purposes the musical language of their teacher. So great was the Dutchman's fame as a teacher, that he received within his own day the name, Maker of Organists. It was in Germany and not in the Netherlands that Sweelinck's subsequent influence was to be felt; his many German students took his ideas and style and modified these to produce another stunning means of musical expression.

The ideas which his German students took back with them to Hamburg and to Lübeck were as much English as they were Dutch, and even elements of Spanish musical style can also be observed. Sweelinck therefore must be regarded partly as a transmitter of other national styles to his pupils. His connections with the English virginalists are well known, and his works appear in certain of their manuscript sources. We have already noted the similarities which exist between Sweelinck's music and that of Coelho and Correa. The close political connections which existed between the Netherlands, Spain, and England during the period are reflected in Sweelinck's eclectic musical language; and these traditions he passed on to his students.

There is a close musical and historical connection between Sweelinck, and the North-German school, a connection which justifies their common treatment.

THE WORKS OF SWEELINCK

In the Netherlands, the organ fortunately escaped the wrath of the iconoclasts, a wrath which led to its degradation and destruction in other countries which had adopted the Reformed faith. The Dutch countered the threats to the instrument by an intense civic pride which assured that older instruments would be preserved and that new ones would be built. The Dutch Reformed Church harbored, about use of the organ in the divine service, the same suspicions which led to such dire consequences in Switzerland and later in England. These suspicions, however, were balanced by a very positive attitude toward the organ and its music outside the confines of the service itself. Organists, who in the Netherlands were generally in civic employment and who were, thus, not directly servants of the Church itself, were called upon to provide elaborate music before and after services. These recitals, for they were nothing else, were regarded as merely another adornment to the prosperity of the seventeenth-century Dutch economy, merely another symbol that God shone favorably upon the fruits of Protestant enterprise. There is nothing in the least modest or pious about a fantasia of Sweelinck. This music, as was the type of organ for which it was designed, was a manifestation of the affluence of the new Dutch republic in general and of the wealth and success of Amsterdam in particular. No longer was the organ relegated to filling the incidental moments in the service, as it had been in the Catholic Church. In being freed from his liturgical responsibilities, the organist was at liberty to conceive music for the sake of musical expression itself. The grandeur and majesty of Sweelinck's music reflects this new freedom, a freedom which also became part of the North-German heritage.

The spirit of northern Protestantism breathes in Sweelinck's works. These is hardly a trace of the emotional fervor of the early Italian Baroque. Harmonic experimentation; rhapsodic writing; and rapid changes from one emotional quality to another, all features of Italian music of the period, are shunned in favor of a severe style in which the concept of working out musical material in a thorough and reasonable way is dominant. The figurative devices which Sweelinck borrowed from the virginalists he applied in his own disciplined and mechanistic manner, and the interest of his music lies to a large degree in this figurative process. The ear delights in the constant variety of patterns as they are applied to fantasia themes, psalm tunes, and Lutheran chorales, or used, in and of themselves, in a toccata or echo fantasia. The severity with which the composer applies these patterns is closely related to the mentality of the Dutch culture of the seventeenth century. In a sense, it is the Protestant work ethic expressed in musical terms. The ordered, rational, disciplined attitudes expressed by this culture are similar whether expressed in the political, business, or artistic arenas.

Since none of Sweelinck's organ compositions come down to us in autograph sources or contemporary editions and since the principal sources are copies made largely by his German pupils, the problem of establishing a definitive version of his works has proven most difficult. The original edition (1894) by Max Seiffert was expanded by him in a new edition of 1943. Modern scholarship has solved many more problems of authenticity. Fortunately the results have appeared in an excellent new edition,[2] although the editors freely admit that final resolution of all problems posed by Sweelinck's keyboard works is certainly impossible.

The Fantasias

Leonhardt's edition contains nine compositions entitled "fantasia" and another in similar format entitled *"ricercar."* Of these ten pieces, all but the last, an inconsequential short two-voice piece, are compositions of considerable extent, complexity, and seriousness. It is rare for keyboard compositions of the early seventeenth century both to approach a length of two hundred to three hundred measures and to be cohesively structured. For instance, the *tentos* of Coelho were all of approximately this length; but they are rambling, unstructured works. The fantasias of Sweelinck, however, are tightly, effectively, and rationally organized about a single and easily perceived subject presented initially in the conservative and imitative style of the Italian *ricercar.* The subjects have a simplicity about them which marks their contours in the listener's mind. Their rhythmic organization is of little importance, for they typically move only in whole- and half-note motion. Some obvious melodic feature stands out in each of them:

The outline of the common chord:

The repeated dominant note with a rotation about it:

Chromatic melodic progression from I to V:

Such straightforward themes are the foundation of the entire elaborate structure of these fantasias.

[2] Jan Pieterszoon Sweelinck, *Opera Omnia*, vol. I, fasc. I: Fantasias and Toccatas, ed. Gustav Leonhardt; vol. I, fasc. II: Settings of Sacred Melodies, ed. Alfons Annegarn, Amsterdam: 1968.

The *ricercar*-style of the opening of the fantasies may conclude after a single exposition or it may be continued to other expositions. In the fourth fantasia the initial exposition is followed by two more in the same style, the first juxtaposing a new melodic phrase against the subject in the manner of a true countersubject:

Mus. ex. VI-1.
Sweelinck: *Fantasia* (Leonhardt, number 4), Measures 35-40.

The second is based on a *stretto*:
Mus. ex. VI-2. Measures 67-72.

In these opening sections Sweelinck reveals his inherently conservative nature, for his language here is that of a sixteenth-century contrapuntalist. Even the intrusion of chromatic elements has nothing of the Neopolitan flavor. They exist merely as a graft onto the essentially Renaissance musical style.

At the conclusion of the *ricercar* section, usually approximately one-third the length of the total composition, the composer effects a radical change in musical structure. From this point on, the theme serves as the foundation for what may best be described as free variation. The musical interest lies almost entirely in an integration of the devices of English virginal variation and the older techniques of *cantus firmus* writing. There are certain stock devices upon which the composer relies. One is the texture of the *bicinium* in which the theme appears in one hand while the figurations appear in the other. In the following example the theme appears in diminution, a typical practice of Sweelinck:

O

Mus. ex. VI-3.
Chromatic Fantasia, measures 149-150.

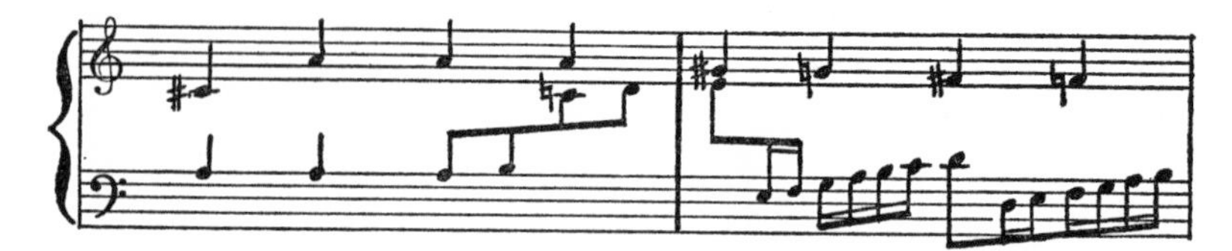

Augmentation is just as commonly used as diminution. Sweelinck employs Andrea Gabrieli's technique of using the theme as a whole-note *cantus planus* and often follows this by use of the theme in double whole notes. Few of these fantasias lack passages of such augmentation. There are even examples in which the figurative material added to the augmented theme is itself derivative from a diminution of the theme:

Mus. ex VI-4.
Fantasia (Leonhardt, number 3), measures 163-168 (Thematic notes: d, f, g, a, b-flat, a).

Use of the melodic contours of the main theme as a source of figurative patterns is passed on by Sweelinck to his North-German pupils. It reappears commonly in the chorale fantasy. The following passage from Sweelinck's *ricercar* could have been drawn from such a piece:

Mus. ex. VI-5.
Ricercar (Leonhardt, number 7), measures 256-260.

The hand of the master improvisator no doubt underlies these fantasias. The stable, unchanging theme provides a ready-made unity, and the constant, almost rhapsodic change of the figurative ideas provides endless interest and fascination. There are no subsequent Dutch pieces which pretend to be similar. The organization, essentially the same techniques, as well as the grandiose scale of these compositions reappears among Scheidemann and his followers in the chorale fantasia.

The Echo Fantasias

Of all Sweelinck's compositions, those typically associated with his name are the echo fantasias. Among the six in the Seiffert edition, Leonhardt doubts the authenticity of two. The occasional use of echo dates from the early sixteenth century, although there were few efforts to employ it thoroughly within a composition. The attempts to explain Sweelinck's preoccupation with echo by citing sixteenth-century vocal practice, particularly that of the Venetians, are weak. The explanation lies, without doubt, in the potential for dialogue between the *Hoofdwerk* and *Rugwerk,* a potential that must have been realized in improvisation long before the origin of these pieces. Perhaps it was a feature of the music of some unknown predecessor of Sweelinck.

There is no pattern with which Sweelinck opened echo fantasias. Number 12 in the Leonhardt edition starts as a *ricercar* and number 14, with fugal treatment of a *canzone*-like subject. The most rich and complex of these pieces begins with the echo of a three and one-half measure phrase. Sweelinck rarely echoed blocks of material of this size:

Mus. ex. VI-6.
Echo Fantasia (Leonhardt, number 13), measures 1-7.

Canon plays an important part in these pieces. It occurs naturally when the characteristic interchange of motives between voices becomes so structured that no rests intervent:

Mus. ex. VI-7.
Echo Fantasia (Leonhardt, Number 12), measures 54-59.

That canon is more than an accidental occurrence and that it plays an important part in the composer's musical thoughts is revealed by the lengthy introduction to number 11 in Leonhardt's edition. This introduction is structured around one canonic passage after another.

The characteristic texture of the echo fantasia, however, is homophonic, and not polyphonic, a texture in which certain figurative motives are used in dialogue in one hand while the other hand sustains rudimentary chordal harmonies. From an infinite repertory of possible motives Sweelinck actually selected a limited number. Most common are the following, which are used either in the form given below or in very simple modifications:

Mus. ex. VI-8.

Sequence is the means by which these motives are expanded into significant blocks of musical material. In organization of the harmonies which underlie his sequences, Sweelinck was generally conservative. The most common type of sequence simply moves harmonies up or down the interval of a second without further concern for harmonic propriety. An equally conservative sound results from the composer's preference for ascending sequences whose harmonies first move downward a third and then upward a fourth:

Mus. ex. VI-9.
Echo Fantasia (Leonhardt, Number 13), measures 93-96.

Although Sweelinck occasionally employed ascending sequences in which the bass moves chromatically and which involve secondary dominants in the process, these suggestions of modern tonality are few. The rarity of sequences built on harmonies moving in descending fifths is particularly obvious. Such progressions suggest a harmonic modernity foreign to Sweelinck's style. Sweelinck at other times employed the same static harmonic basis used in the Venetian toccatas. For instance, a segment of one echo fantasia (Leonhardt, number 13, measures 190-211) is made up of eight measures on the triad of C, five measures on the triad of F, another two on C, and a final seven measures on G. Harmony serves the composer not in the dynamic manner of the early Italian Baroque, but as the sturdy unyielding structures of the late Renaissance.

The Toccatas

The Leonhardt edition contains twelve compositions entitled toccatas (Numbers 15-26). These compositions vary in length from as little as thirty measures to as many as one hundred thirty-eight. They vary even more in internal content, for beyond the statement that all exploit keyboard figurations as ends in themselves, few statements can be made that apply to them all. In some respects these toccatas are companion pieces to the echo fantasias. They employ many of the same techniques, such as serious introductions, relatively static harmony, exploitation of the same figurative ideas, and the use of sequential writing. The following passage could have been drawn from a composition of either type:

Mus. ex. VI-10.
Toccata (Leonhardt, number 19), measures 79-82.

These compositions reveal again that Sweelinck was influenced by the late Renaissance Venetian toccatas. Three toccatas contain sections in *ricercar* style, sections which serve to break up the otherwise endless keyboard figurations. Constant infatuation with running scale passages is another feature these toccatas have in common with those of Merulo and others of his school. Sweelinck's toccatas, however, differ markedly from those of the Italians in the wealth and variety of figurative patterns. Sweelinck moved constantly from one such pattern to the next and rarely did he employ a single motive for long at a time. There is little doubt that he relied heavily on the novelty of these patterns to sustain interest in compositions which lack other perceptible elements of organization. The modernity of his borrowings from the English must have been ample to have excited the imaginations of the Dutch burghers. The following passage demonstrates the rapidity with which he changed motivic patterns:

Mus. ex. VI-11.
Toccata (Leonhardt, number 20), measures 70-75.

Sweelinck left one prelude in *durezza* style available in two versions (Leonhardt, numbers 27 and 27a). The second version, marked *Pedaliter* in its manuscript, is hardly by Sweelinck. In the first place, he possessed no pedal organ sufficient to support the manual *plenum* upon which such a piece would certainly have been played; and, in the second place, the rewriting is hardly the work of a competent composer.

WORKS BASED UPON CHORALE MELODIES AND PSALM TUNES

There is little indication that the Church fathers limited or censored the type of music Sweelinck chose for his recitals. No doubt some of his secular variations, which lie beyond the scope of this book, must have on occasion been played at the organ. We know that it was a duty of the organist to make before the service a prelude upon the psalm tune of the day. The use of melodies derived from sources other than the Reformed tradition, Gregorian hymns and Lutheran chorales, seems to have been completely natural to Sweelinck. Of the thirteen variation sets in the Annegarn edition, two are based on Gregorian tunes, three on psalm tunes of Louis Bourgeois, and the remainder on Lutheran chorales. Although some of these German hymns were used in Dutch translations as alternatives to the Genevan psalms, other melodies had only German versions. No doubt Sweelinck came to know these tunes from his contacts with his German students. It is also possible that the extant compositions of Sweelinck actually do not fairly represent his original work. German copyists no doubt favored German melodies, and tended to ignore others.

The influence of Sweelinck in later history of organ music is strongest in the works based on the chorale. He was the first major composer to direct a large part of his attention to such settings, and, although earlier examples exist, they are all the work of lesser figures. Sweelinck's concern for works based on sacred *canti fermi* is paralleled in his day only in the works of Titelouze. Sweelinck established the types of settings to be used by succeeding German composers:

1) The *Bicinium* — a two-voiced texture with the chorale melody in whole or half notes in one hand with mechanistic figurations in the other. Occasionally the voice carrying the hymn tune may participate in the motivic play:

Mus. ex. VI-12.
Allein zu dir, Herr Jesu Christ (Annegarn, number 2), measures 114-118.

Sweelinck favored the *bicinium* texture as the opening of a set of variations and he used it in this fashion in six of his thirteen sets.
2) The *Tricinium* – a three-voice expansion of the *bicinium* in which the two free voices are mechanistically figured. Sweelinck prefered to place the hymn melody in the inner voice and to allow the outer ones to be figurative. Occasionally a two-voiced movement moves directly into *tricinium* style variation without break. Both movements employ the same figuration at the point of juncture:

Mus. ex. VI-13.
Ick heb den heer lief (Annegarn, number 11), measures 32-34.

3) The Chorale Motet – In this setting the texture is normally four contrapuntal voices and is much less florid and instrumentally conceived than that of 1 and 2. One voice, in Sweelinck usually the soprano, bears the melody in half-note motion embellished occasionally with short figurative patterns. The other voices are structured on points of imitation, the themes of which are derived from the *cantus firmus*:

Mus. ex. VI-14.
Onse Vader in hemelrijck (Annegarn, number 9), measures 1-5.

Sweelinck seemed to reserve this type of treatment, which he no doubt regarded as a most conservative one, for the more serious chorales. It appears, for instance, as the opening movement of *Wir glauben all'*, the chorale used as the German *credo*, and for all three extant movements of his cycle on Luther's famous hymn *Vater unser im Himmelreich*.
4) The Ornamented Chorale – Here the chorale melody, which Sweelinck always placed in the soprano, serves as the foundation for extended melodic embellishment. The other voices are almost completely supportive, although they may enter with snatches of pre-imitation. Although none of the sources suggests this disposition, certainly the chorale was intended for one manual and the other voices for another. The chorale is often subject to a degree of ornamentation which renders it beyond recognition:

Mus. ex. VI-15.
Ick heb den heer lief, soprano, measures 115-122.

The constant flux of the figurations of the composer's free compositions is also characteristic of his chorale settings. In movements such as the *bicinia* which depend so much upon mechanistic figuration, he moves rapidly from one idea to another. Tusler has attempted to suggest that the selection of figurations is based on the emotional quality of the particular line of the hymn.[3] There is no evidence that this is true. Beyond selection of a particular style for a given variation, Sweelinck never seems to concern himself with connecting music with word. Even the order of movements as they appear in the sets which have come down to us may not be the composer's. There is evidence that German compilers arranged the variations to suit their own needs. They may well have retained movements which reflected German sensitivity to the hymn text and left uncopied those that did not. For instance, the absence of lighter textures, *bicinia* and *tricinia,* in *Vater unser* may be the result of the copyist's tastes and not that of the composer.

OTHER COMPOSERS FROM THE NETHERLANDS

The remaining extant music from the Netherlands hardly attests to a thriving tradition of organ composition. No composer left a body of music to compete with that of Sweelinck. One gets the impression that as the century progressed, psalm settings continued to be written, but the more serious fantasia became anachronistic. The echo fantasia seems to have been the sole property of Sweelinck himself. No other Dutch examples of it exist and its techniques were absorbed into North-German tradition. Of the composers of Sweelinck's generation Henderick Speuy (c. 1570-1625) and Pieter Cornet (c. 1560-1626) left significant works for the organ. Speuy's edition of 1610 contains twenty-four psalm tunes set in *bicinium* style.[4] The melodies appear in the unadorned and somewhat sterile rhythms in which they were sung. The *cantus* may appear in either the right or the left hand or it may "migrate" from one to the other. The elaborating voice is made up entirely of the figurative patterns we have so often discussed. These compositions offer nothing beyond that which we have already seen in Sweelinck.

The individuality of Cornet is another matter. His works[5] consist of four elaborate and complete fantasias, plus another unfinished one on the hexachord; a composition in the style of an Italian *canzone*; a toccata; and single settings of *Salve Regina* and *Tantum*

[3] Robert Tusler, *The Organ Music of Jan Pieterszoon Sweelinck,* Bilthoven: A. B. Creyghton, 1958, 79.

[4] Henderick Speuy, *Psalm Tunes,* ed. Noske, Amsterdam: Heuwekemeijer, 1962.

[5] Pieter Cornet, *Collected Keyboard Works,* ed. Apel, *CEKM* XXVI.

ergo, settings which reveal the composer's Catholic background. The fantasias are at least superficially similar to those of Sweelinck. However, Cornet's pieces are more clearly allied to Renaissance style in that none of them exploits the monothematic principle. In some of Cornet's fantasias the initial theme is not necessarily the most important one; a theme introduced later may override it completely.

Cornet made use of augmentation and diminution of thematic material as did Sweelinck, but he employed the techniques incidentally and not in a thorough manner. English keyboard figurations are naturally employed, but they too occur more as ornamentation to the essentially polyphonic structure than as an end in themselves. Cornet used fewer figurative patterns than did Sweelinck and had a particular penchant for [rhythmic figure] and [rhythmic figure], which appear in nearly every piece. The fantasias of Cornet are similar to those of Coelho in that neither composer shows an inclination toward tight, cohesive musical organization such as we have seen in Sweelinck's fantasias.

That Cornet reflects eclectic influences is further borne out by his *canzone,* which is essentially Italian in style, and his toccata, which is very much like those in the English virginal repertory. Both pieces are among the most successful in the limited number of works by Cornet. The two settings of Gregorian melodies are both competently written. They, however, hardly add anything new to the tradition of liturgical organ works. Before we leave Cornet's works we should mention a peculiar cadential mannerism used no less than five times in this small group of pieces. This mannerism approaches the dominant degree of the final chord by a half-step leading tone:

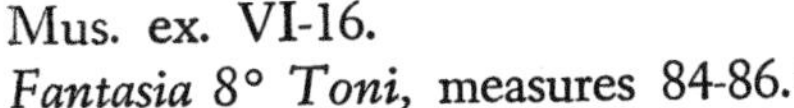
Mus. ex. VI-16.
Fantasia 8° Toni, measures 84-86.[6]

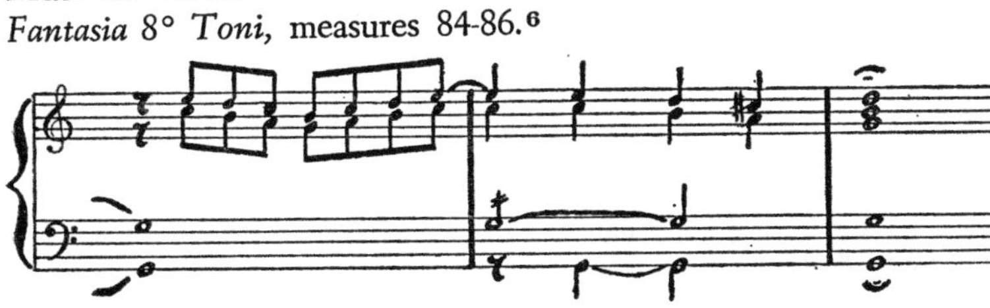

[6] *Ibid.,* 48.

It is interesting to observe that this sound reappears with some frequency in later North-German works.

By far the most interesting figure in Dutch music of the latter half of the century is Anthoni van Noordt, whose tablature of 1659 contains psalm settings and a number of fugal compositions entitled *fantasia.*[7] Beyond the fact that these fantasias are mono-thematic and that they are multisectional, they bear no connection to those of Sweelinck. They are, as Apel suggests, truly Baroque fugues. Gone are the *ricercar*-like subjects treated in such Renaissance grandeur. Carefully crafted themes are no longer used in the manner of *canti firmi* around which the polyphony moves. Contained in these subjects are the major figurative motives of the musical texture. No longer is figuration used to oppose a theme or largely to decorate it. Instead, figuration grows out of the theme itself in an organic way. In the second of these fantasias the most persistent motive is , which is taken directly from the first measure of the theme. This motive and its expansion appear in almost every measure of the piece. Van Noordt, like so many of his contemporaries, had a love of countersubjects based on the descending, chromatic fourth. Often they were reserved for a later section in one of these fugues. In the second fantasia the subject and its countersubject appear as follows:

Mus. ex. VI-17.
Fantasia II, measures 58-61.[8]

[7] Anthoni van Noordt, *Tabulatuur — Boeck van Psalmen en Fantasyen,* ed. Seiffert, Amsterdam: Alsbach en Co. 1957.
[8] *Ibid.,* 61.

Other technical devices used to organize the later sections of his pieces are *stretto* and diminution. In the following example only the first three notes appear in diminution as the theme is presented in *stretto*:

Mus. ex. VI-18.
Fantasia VI, measures 82-86.[9]

There is nothing to indicate that these fantasias are inherently organ compositions; but, on the other hand, Apel's assertion that they work best on the harpsichord is equally indefensible. There is nothing in these pieces of the facile style which is characteristic of writing for the harpsichord.

In his variation sets on sacred melodies van Noordt used only the tunes of the Genevan psalter, and he did not employ either Gregorian hymns or Lutheran chorales. He made a special effort to keep the *cantus firmus* free of ornamentation. Thus he normally presented it in the simple and pristine rhythm in which it was sung. Also in an effort to keep the melody obvious, the composer favored the more transparent textures of the *bicinium* and *tricinium*. When one compares these works to the similar works of Sweelinck, the most obvious difference is the direction of the figurative process by force of mid-century tonality. The following passage is typical of many others:

[9] *Ibid.*, 74.

Mus. ex. VI-19.
Psalm 119, Verse 1, measures 10-16.[10]

Van Noordt often interchanged a motive between two ornamenting voices, writing in much the same manner that one finds in the trio sonatas of the same period. The voices participate in a dialogue which confirms the individuality of each. This technique is typical of trio-style chorale preludes of Middle-German composers of the latter part of the century.

Mus. ex. VI-20.
Psalm VII, Verse 3, measures 45-51.[11]

10 *Ibid.,* 40.
11 *Ibid.,* 15.

The *obbligato* use of pedal, unknown in Sweelinck's and Cornet's works, connects van Noordt to the North-German tradition. The pedal is often restricted to merely bearing the psalm tune in the tenor voices on a four-foot stop or in the bass voice at written pitch. More sophisticated use of pedal requiring at least a minimum facility is to be found in other pieces where the *cantus* is borne by the right hand, two voices are carried by the left, and the pedal is allotted the bass. This texture is perhaps the most common one in North-German chorale settings.

Mus. ex. VI-21.
Psalm XXIV, Verse 1, measures 20-23.[12]

Throughout van Noordt's tablature are works not always of modest dimensions, very competently written, well constructed, and eminently suited to the sonorities of the organ. These compositions deserve more attention than they have thus far received.

NORTH GERMANY

In German organ music of the seventeenth century, there are three largely distinct traditions: the South-German (associated with the Roman Catholic liturgy and centered in such cities as Vienna and Salzburg); the Middle-German tradition of the Lutheran small town culture of Saxony and Thuringia; and the North-German school which developed around the old and thriving cities around

[12] *Ibid.*, 51.

the Baltic Sea.[13] Of these cities, Hamburg and Lübeck were the most important, with lesser centers being Lüneburg, Bremen, and Danzig. The civic pride of the Dutch was an even more potent force in these cities, which vied amongst themselves for as great an opulence in their organs as in the church buildings which contained them. The spirit of Gothic architecture reached this portion of Europe at a late date. During the fifteenth and sixteenth centuries a style of simplified Gothic based on brick and not stone construction was developed in these cities. Not enough has been said about the relationships of architecture to musical style, and yet there can be no doubt that the soaring interiors of such structures as the Marienkirche in Lübeck contributed to the flamboyant style of organbuilding there. The North-German art of organ building reached its zenith in the works of the Hamburg builder Arp Schnitger (1648-1719). Hamburg itself possessed no less than five of his instruments, and others were scattered throughout the area. These instruments, as well as those by other fine builders in this tradition, stood as much on their architectural as on their musical merits. The question of whether the musical style of North Germany gave rise to the instrument or the instrument gave rise to the musical style is the old one of the chicken and the egg. But what can be asserted is that there hardly could have been a more fortuitous combination of expansive architectural space, the genius of the master organ builder, and imaginative composers than occurred in these years in North Germany.

If the Gothic spirit lived into the sixteenth century in North-German architecture, it lived into the seventeenth century in its music. Webster defines "Gothic", when not used as a term of derision, as signifying "rugged grandeur, of the blended effects of vivid imagery with the appeal to the mysterious and infinite." A more concise phrase could hardly be written to describe the nature of the North-German style. The imagery is, of course, tonal, not visual, and is associated with the effects of sound developing in large resonant spaces. Block chords, startling silences, rambling pedal solos, soaring and never-ending melodies, echo effects, unusual

[13] Much of the following material originally appeared in my article "North-German Organ Music," in *Music, The A.G.O. and R.C.C.O. Magazine,* in September 1969, (copyright 1969). I am grateful for permission from the editors to reuse it.

harmonic progressions, juxtaposition of thick and thin textures, inventive keyboard figurations, and rhythmic structures varying from the mechanical to the rhapsodic all contribute to this goal of tonal imagery.

The North Germans developed open-ended musical structures, the *praeambulum* (*praeludium*),[14] the chorale variation, and the chorale fantasy, in which these effects could be made vital and meaningful. The limitations of the small chorale prelude, the restrained toccatas, and the simple preludes and fugues of Middle- and South-German composers contrast strikingly with the rhapsodic and improvisational structures of their northern colleagues. Improvisation, that time-honored art of all great organ traditions, is of the nature of North-German art. The temporal organization of music is left, at least to a degree, unbound and open; a large composition is based on a number of disparate short sections. Its effect is less dependent upon formal, logical relationships than upon the contrasting nature of the various sections.

Improvisational order is closely bound to a new organ virtuosity. This is certainly not to suggest that in the previous history of the instrument virtuoso playing had not existed. But in North Germany, there is for the first time in association with the organ the use of technical display as an end in itself.

No introductory discussion of North-German music would be complete without the mention of the unique *obbligato* pedal which is a feature of this style, and this style only, in the seventeenth century. The pedal had been used in other traditions, if it was used at all, to bear slow moving *canti firmi* and to play the simplest of bass lines. Even in the early decades of the century, the North Germans achieved a pedal dexterity comparable to that of manual playing. Only in North Germany was the pedal organ a fully developed instrument, an instrument exploited by the composers in solos for pedals alone; writing for double pedal; and fully developed, florid fugal lines intended for pedal.

There are three generations of seventeenth-century North-Ger-

[14] The two terms are simply equal to the English term *prelude*. Rather arbitrarily I have chosen to use the term *praeambulum* in the following discussion. Stylistically there is no difference between a North-German toccata and a *Praeambulum*. The terms are intermixed very frequently. In any event the designation prelude and fugue used in many editions of these works is inappropriate.

man composers: the first represented by Heinrich Scheidemann and Jacob Praetorius (the younger); the second by Franz Tunder, Matthias Weckmann, and Adam Reincken; and the last by Dietrich Buxtehude, Georg Böhm, Nicolas Bruhns, and Vincent Lübeck, whose long life extended well into the eighteenth century.

The First Generation — The Works of Scheidemann and Praetorius

Both Heinrich Scheidemann (c. 1597 - 1663) and Jacob Praetorius (1586 - 1651) had been students of Sweelinck in the early decades of the seventeenth century. They returned to Hamburg to make that city the center of German organ music in the period from about 1620 to 1645. As we have already suggested, these composers transmitted Sweelinck's techniques to the setting of German chorales In the process of transmission, however, they altered and adapted their teacher's methods to suit their own purposes. Settings of the chorale, then, are the most important compositions of both composers. In comparison to the chorales, the *praeambula* of Scheidemann's day are far less pretentious and hardly suggest anything of the late North-German *praeambulum.*

The Chorale Settings

The remarkable development of the organ in Lutheran churches during the seventeenth century has, very naturally, a theological basis. The organ existed to allow further exposition of and elaboration upon the melodies of German hymnody. In turn the hymns served as a means to effect a corporate exposition of the Gospel, to act as a type of congregational sermon. Certain chorales became almost canonically connected to certain days of the church year, and this hymn of the day became the musical focal point of the Lutheran service. The organists were expected to extemporize on that chorale before and after the service and to introduce its singing by a short prelude.[15] Evidence exists that the organ participated in the alternation practice in which various verses of the chorale might be sung in unison by the congregation, others polyphonically by the choir, and yet others in organ settings. Only later did the organ

[15] The English term *chorale prelude* often is misused to refer loosely to any chorale setting. It should apply only to shorter works of the type used to introduce chorale singing. It is so used below.

actually accompany congregational singing. Not only was the natively Lutheran use of the organ so important, but the musical inheritance from Roman Catholicism did not suffer in German hands. The functions of the organ in the older Roman Catholic tradition were continued in the Reformed faith. Hence the organ participated in the performance of the *Magnificat* at Vespers, the *Te Deum* at Matins, and retained in the Mass the alternation function at least in the *Kyrie*. The two traditions combined to provide the richest type of environment for the flowering of organ and organists.

The entire works of Scheidemann and the works on chorales by Praetorius are available in excellent modern editions.[16] In his generation, Scheidemann is rivaled only by Samuel Scheidt in extensive treatment of chorales, and his settings of the *Magnificat* are matched only by Titelouze. Although the works of Praetorius which have come down to us are fewer than those of Scheidemann, the quality of the work of these composers is equally high. An examination of the works fails to bear out the assertion that Praetorius is the more conservative composer: the style of both composers is essentially the same.

The most conservative form of *cantus firmus* treatment is that of the unadorned *cantus planus* moving in whole-note motion in the bass or tenor voice while the other voices form about it a sedate contrapuntal surrounding. This type of treatment is not natively German, but is essentially international in tone. An example from Scheidemann is indistinguishable from a French *Plein jeu* of the latter part of the century:

[16] Heinrich Scheidemann, *Orgelwerke*, ed. Fock and Breig, Kassel: Bärenreiter, 1967-1971. Vol. I: *Choralbearbeitungen*; vol. II: *Magnificatbearbeitungen*; vol. III: free compositions; Jacob Praetorius, *Choralbearbeitungen*, ed. Breig, Kassel: Bärenreiter, 1974.

Mus. ex. VI-22.
Scheidemann: *Magnificat VIII Toni* (Fock, II, number 8), Measures 1-6.

Very often simple points of imitation relieve the vertical element in the music and anticipate the arrival of the melody in its *cantus planus* form. In longer works of this type the elaborating voices often break into eighth-note motion based on abstract figures which have nothing to do with the *cantus* whatsoever:

Mus. ex. VI-23.
Scheidemann: *Kyrie summum* (Fock, I, number 22), measures 38-41.

This type of severe treatment the North Germans reserve essentially for those melodies inherited from the Roman liturgy: the Gregorian hymns, the *Kyrie* settings, and some movements from the *Magnificat* intonations. Apparently the metrical order of the chorales was felt to be strong enough to work against too severe a treatment in their setting. If several settings of a given Gregorian melody are grouped into a variation set, the first is always the *cantus planus* version. Subsequent settings in the group adopt more modern forms.

Similar in style but more rhythmically pliable in the presentation of the *cantus firmus* are the four-voice settings of chorales themselves. In these the *cantus* often appears in the soprano. It is rare to find any setting in which points of imitation are not interwoven into the fabric of the supporting voices, although it is equally rare to find one in which the technique is used throughout. The same tendency to switch rapidly from one idea to another which appears in the music of Sweelinck is also characteristic of that of Scheidemann and Praetorius. The true chorale motet, in which the entire composition is made up consistently of points of imitation, is not found in the works of either composer. The essentials of the technique, however, were well-known. Why these composers should have avoided its use is difficult to say. The close connection in style of the technique of pre-imitation to the vocal practice of the sixteenth-century motet is revealed in the following most simple and beautiful example:

Mus. ex. VI-24.
Praetorius: *Vater unser im Himmelreich*, verse 7 (Breig, number 6), measures 1-10.

The style of the *bicinium* was taken over by Scheidemann from his teacher, although none of the few extant compositions of Praetorius employ it. The Scheidemann examples are hardly distinguishable from those of Sweelinck, although the former's North-German imagination occasionally shows through in the unusual rhythmic organization of his figurations:

Mus. ex. VI-25.
Jesus Christus, unser Heiland II, Variation 2 (Breig, I, number 17), measures 38-41.

Scheidemann's favorite texture is the *tricinium,* which he normally scores in trio style with the pedal carrying the chorale at either eight- or four-foot pitch. The composer achieved a strikingly modern pliability of the added voices. These reflect a concept of figuration not stylistically dependent upon the development of mechanistic figurative patterns alone but more upon a true sense of contrapuntal integrity.

Mus. ex. VI-26.
Es spricht der Unweisen Mund wohl (Breig I, number 8), measures 1-5.

The forms of the chorale in which the melody is presented unadorned are not, however, the most characteristically North-German settings. It is the ornamented chorale and its extension, the chorale fantasy, which are the real products native to this tradition, products which are rarely found elsewhere in the literature. The ornamented chorale, in which the notes of the hymn support an elaborate coloratura, on the one hand; and the coloratura conceals the notes of the hymn, on the other, must have appealed to the Gothic orientation of the North-German minds. The well-known melody stands mystically hidden in the musical structure which, nonetheless, depends upon it. By a careful selection of the type and extent of melodic embellishment the composer can control the overall expressive character of his composition. The complex, symbolic language which underlies the chorale preludes of the eighteenth century, particularly those by Bach himself, is almost entirely absent from the North-German school. That the meaning of the chorale text is ignored, however, is untrue, for the composer addresses the issue in terms of the emotion of his composition as an entirety. Literal, word-for-word expression, which so entranced writers such as Pirro, rarely exists here. The following examples illustrate the care with which the composers selected a level and quality of embellishment. The plaintive quality of the opening line of verse two of Scheidemann's *Vater unser*[17] contrasts strikingly with the assertive, masculine opening of his *Jesu Christus, unser Heiland.*[18] The chorale notes are encircled.

Mus. ex. VI-27.
Vater unser

[17] Breig I, number 28.
[18] Breig I, number 16.

Mus. ex. VI-28.
Jesus Christus, unser Heiland

While the figurative patterns used by both Praetorius and Scheidemann are of course not new, certain figures occur so frequently that they become trademarks of the style. The most important ones are as follows:
The filling in of an interval between two chorale notes:

Stepwise movement between chorale notes embellished by this figure:

The motive:

The descending scale ending on an accented note:

The ascending scale ending on the final of the mode often appears as a concluding cadence. The absence of a leading tone often gives this pattern a peculiarly anachronistic flavor:

Scheidemann often preserved the original metrical structure of the chorale by placing the chorale note of the embellished line in relatively the same place it occupies in the unornamented line. In more ornate passages he commonly substituted an octave equivalent for the original note of the chorale. Observe the example from *Jesus Christus, unser Heiland* above. By such substitution, the composer can manage to obscure completely the original melody. In the work of both composers there are examples of relatively short settings using the chorale melody once and once only. The ornamented chorale, however, is a basic ingredient of the more expansive chorale fantasy.

Without doubt the compositions most characteristic of the North-German repertory from Scheidemann to Buxtehude are the chorale fantasies. The term "fantasia" might imply that the compositions are whimsically conceived. Actually they show a surprising uniformity of style and technique and throughout the century they were constructed around the following:

1) the ornamented chorale just discussed
2) the *cantus planus* technique
3) the systematic use of echo
4) a developed sense of pre-imitative entrances.

Even the order in which these elements were presented was largely standardized. Most fantasies open with an extensive embellished treatment of the opening lines of the hymn and many of them end with a section in echo. Many omit any sections based on *cantus planus* and many intertwine the techniques of echo and embellishment. Compositions of more than two hundred measures in length are, however, made up entirely of these few elements.

In the chorale fantasy the technique of embellished chorale is often extended to include the appearance of the ornamented line in the tenor voice. In Scheidemann's marvelous fantasy on *Jesus Christus, unser Heiland* the composer treated each line of the chorale first as a soprano- and then as a tenor-ornamented melody. In sections in which a tenor melody is used, the texture is very much like the French *tierce en taille*. In the fantasia on *Lobet den Herren, denn er ist sehr freundlich,*[19] there are two complete ornamented treatments of the chorale, one following upon the other. In the second treatment the ornamentation is more complex and abstract than in the first. The first line of the chorale in each version is given below:

[19] Breig I, number 23.

Mus. ex. VI-29.
Version 1

Mus. ex. VI-30.
Version 2

The echo techniques of North-German composers often exceed the simple motivic echos used by Sweelinck. Motive echo is, of course, often used; but in other cases entire phrases in all voices are echoed. Crossing of hands, a requirement of many such compositions — particularly in the fantasias of the last generation of this school, appears first in Scheidemann's works.

Mus. ex. VI-31.
Scheidemann: *Magnificat VIII Toni* (Fock II, number 9), measures 97-100.

Another technique is to echo an entire passage, than a smaller part of it, then perhaps the final two chords, and then only the final chord. A type of *stretto* applied to echo technique results. The following passage from Praetorius is an extreme example in which the composer first echoes six notes, then four, three, two, and finally a single note. Here the echo device is used within the context of a single ornate voice.

Mus. ex. VI-32.
Durch Adams Fall ist ganz verderbt (Breig, number 2), measures 87-90.

Although there are individual short preludes by both Scheidemann and Praetorius, most shorter settings are grouped in variation sets apparently to be used in alternation practice. Scheidemann's *Magnificats* pose an impediment to understanding their use. He provided only four movements generally in the following order: 1) *cantus planus* chorale, 2) chorale fantasy of embellished chorale, 3) chorale fugue, and 4) *tricinium*. Since it normally takes at least six organ movements to perform a complete *Magnificat* in alternation, Scheidemann's intention is not clear. A suggestion has been made that polyphonic vocal settings were used for the two missing organ movements. The mixture of chant, choral polyphony, and organ settings would have been unusually rich.

The Free Forms

The Scheidemann generation of composers hardly achieved in the free forms of organ composition (those which did not depend upon the chorale) anything of the richness found in the works just discussed. There is barely a suggestion in the music of the path the North-German *praeambulum* was soon to take. It is not that we lack examples of free forms from the two major composers and from others of the same period. A large body of such pieces is to be found in a remarkable set of tablatures in the possession of the library of the city of Lüneburg.[20] These manuscripts contain many

[20] John R. Shannon, *The Free Organ Compositions in the Lüneburg Organ Tablatures*, St. Louis: Concordia, 1958, 2 vols.

examples in free forms by Scheidemann, a few pieces of Praetorius, and many compositions by lesser known and anonymous composers.

The majority of the compositions bear the designation *praeambulum,* which seems to suggest that their original function was to serve as a prelude to something, perhaps the performance of a vocal motet. The short length (about fifty measures) of many of them also suggests this usage. Most of them are scored for a rather straightforward, four-voice texture. They open with a chordally-conditioned passage of some dozen measures. After this passage cadences, there occurs either a short *fughetta* based always upon a simple, non-figurative theme or a passage exploiting the device of sequence to which the Scheidemann generation seems to have been especially attracted. A final short section ends the composition in the chordal style in which it began. An anonymous prelude from one of the tablatures illustrates these features. The opening is based on the principal triads of the tonic key:

Mus. ex. VI-33.
Praeambulum ex g. b moll, measures 1-6.[21]

A short *fughetta* follows, beginning in the following manner (measures 17-20):

Mus. ex. VI-34.

The composition then concludes (measures 30-52) with another chordal section similar to the beginning section.

[21] *Ibid.,* number 12.

There are occasional longer compositions in this repertory and most of these are by Scheidemann himself. An excellent *Toccata in G*[22] is unique in that it attempts to translate the idiom of the chorale fantasia into a composition devoid of *cantus firmus*. It opens with a lengthy section based upon a florid soprano line supported by three manual voices in the left hand. The remainder of the composition is made of fugal episodes and echo sections similar to those in Sweelinck's echo pieces. His teacher's influence is also strong in Scheidemann's *Fantasia in G*.[23] The piece is similar to the Dutchman's toccatas. The influence of the Italian *canzone,* an influence which will be discussed with the free organ compositions of the next generation, initially appears in two of Scheidemann's compositions.[24] The first of these is an overt copy of the form complete with the tri-sectional structure and the thematic variation associated with the *canzone*. The second begins with a *canzone*-style theme but soon dissolves into the texture of an echo fantasia with no connections in style or technique to Italian models.

The Second Generation: Tunder, Weckmann, Reincken

The Free Forms

The strong tradition of chorale settings established by the first generation is continued by the second. All of its major composers, Franz Tunder (1414 - 1667), Matthias Weckmann (1621 - 1674), and Adam Reincken (1623-1722!), left significant works based on the chorale. From the historical point of view, however, it is the free forms of Tunder and Weckmann which demand our consideration, for these works lay the foundations of the mature North-German *praeambulum,* the form used most characteristically by Buxtehude's generation. The Lüneburg tablatures contain four *praeludia* of Tunder which are definitely organ works[25] and fourteen free compositions of Weckmann,[26] most of which were probably harpsichord works. Their implications for the history of organ music are too strong, however, to ignore here.

---

22 Breig III, number 21.

23 *Ibid.*, number 17.

24 *Ibid.*, numbers 18 and 19.

25 Franz Tunder, *Vier Praeludien, Organum IV*, No. 6, ed. Seiffert, Köln: Kistner and Siegel, n.d.

26 Matthias Weckmann, *Vierzehn Praeludien, Fugen und Toccaten, Organum IV*, No. 3, ed. Seiffert, Köln: Kistner and Siegel, n.d.

The four Tunder compositions introduce us to a more developed concept of the *praeambulum.* The rigid chordal sections which opened the earlier examples of compositions of this type have been given up in favor of figurative sections often based on dramatic gestures well adapted to the North-German organ sonority. What had been *fughette* and sequential middle sections now have become fullfledged self-supporting fugal sections. The procedure which sandwiches a fugal section between two figurative ones is standard for the *praeambula* of the middle generation. Later it was expanded into a five-section format by the addition of yet another fugal and another figurative episode. The most interesting sections of Tunder's *praeambula* are the introductory ones. The strict, four-voice texture is given up in favor of pliant textures in which a thinner sound can be contrasted with a thicker one. Particularly the alternation of lighter manual passages with more stern ones involving the pedal and manuals is characteristic:

Mus. ex. VI-35.
Praeludium (Seiffert, number 3), measures 8-10.

Tunder opens three of his four pieces with a single voice flourish, a mannerism imitiated many times in pieces of the last generation of composers:

Mus. ex. VI-36.
Praeludium (Seiffert, number 3), measures 1-3.

Tunder's fugal writing has the same stiff manner of the fugal writing of the earlier generation of composers. His subjects lack elasticity, and as a result there is a certain squareness about a Tunder fugue that acts in contrast to the more florid beginnings and endings of his *praeambula*. This rigidity of writing, however, disappears among the composers of the third generation. Matthias Weckmann's close personal connection to Italian music may be the explanation.

We know that Weckmann enjoyed a close friendship with Froberger, whose Italian-oriented style, as we will see in the next chapter, was a product of his study with Frescobaldi. While it is difficult to speculate how broadly the Weckmann-Froberger friendship was responsible, in any event there is an intrusion of Italian style and emotional content into North-German music at mid-century. Only three of Weckmann's free compositions are definitely organ works. One entitled *fantasia* (Seiffert, number 1) and the other *fuga* (Seiffert, number 2) are both actually *canzoni* and depend upon thematic variation to unify their various sections. The theme and its two variants in the fugue are as follows:

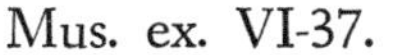
Mus. ex. VI-37.

Only the conclusion of the fantasia with its chords punctuated by rests and its florid coda reveal its North-German origin. The third of these organ works, a *praeambulum,* is closer to the style of Tunder. There are, however, two fugal sections between the opening and closing figurative ones and these fugal sections are also bound to one another by thematic variation.

Weckmann's five *canzoni* for manuals alone were most likely created for the harpsichord. They are obvious and at times not-too-original imitations of their southern models. A light, facile keyboard style showing little of the mechanistic severity of Sweelinck and his school is evident throughout these pieces. No doubt this Italian style did much to soften and lighten the musical language of the North Germans. Thematic variation naturally underlies these compositions as it did the works we just mentioned. In one case Weckmann transformed his initial theme into one in *gigue* rhythm. Such *gigues* were particular favorites of Buxtehude.

Mus. ex. VI-38.
Canzon (Seiffert, number 6), themes.

A new type of fugal theme appears in Weckmann's works. This type has none of the square and stodgy shape of those by Tunder and his predecessors. Instead it has a light, percussive quality and depends for its shape on the outlines of rudimentary harmonic motion. The following example has many relatives in the *praeambula* of the next generation:

Mus. ex. VI-39.
Canzon (Seiffert, number 4), initial theme.

The toccatas in Seiffert's collection are definitely harpsichord works and reflect the influence of both Frescobaldi and Froberger.

The Chorale Settings

The patterns of composition based on the chorale developed by the first generation of composers are continued by the second. It was in chorale settings that Tunder, Weckmann, and Reincken conceived their strongest works, works in almost all cases large in design and serious in content. The seven extant works of this type by Tunder[27] indicate his highly individual musical mind much more than do his *praeambula*. *Herr Gott, dich loben wir, Was kann uns kommen, In dich hab' ich gehoffet*, and *Komm Heiliger Geist* are traditional chorale fantasies combining the ornamented chorale, *cantus firmus* chorale, and echo. To these conventional techniques, Tunder adds canonic writing, which abounds in *Komm Heiliger Geist*:

Mus. ex. VI-40.
Komm Heiliger Geist (Walter, number 3), measures 19-22.

Jesus Christus, unser Heiland is a three-movement set of chorale variations of considerable technical difficulty. The opening variation is set for five voices with double pedal. This movement is the certain model for Bach's *Clavierübung* setting of *Aus tiefer Not* in which the upper of the two pedal voices bears the *cantus firmus* (BWV 686). The final variation of this set is unusual for the angularity of its figuration.

Mus. ex. VI-41.
Jesus Christus, unser Heiland (Walter, number 4), measures 22-24.

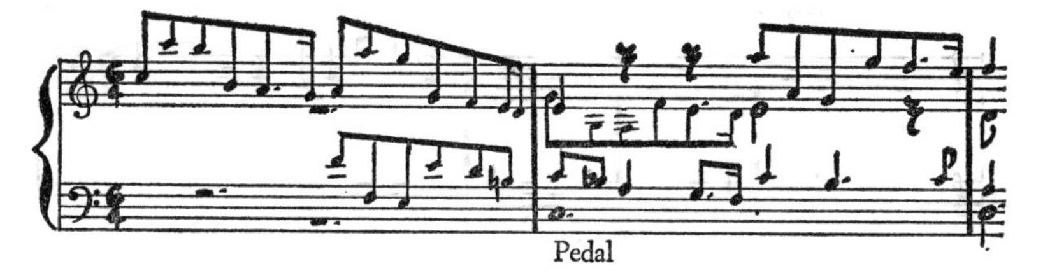

The most conservative technique used in these seven compositions is that of the chorale motet in the setting of *Jesus Christus, wahr' Gottes Sohn*. No more thorough and complete example of this form

[27] Franz Tunder, *Sämtliche Choralbearbeitungen*, ed. Walter, Mainz: Edition Schott, 1956.

occurs anywhere in the literature. Tunder carefully selects his musical material to mirror the changing quality of the text. The piece begins almost in Renaissance serenity and concludes in Baroque grandeur. The remaining composition in this set, *Auf meiner lieben Gott,* for manuals alone, is a particular unusual combination of chorale fantasia and choral variation. The tri-sectional work is played without break; and each section treats the chorale in its entirety:

Section 1 (measures 1-15): Chorale ornamented in the soprano
Section 2 (measures 16-35): *Cantus firmus* chorale in the soprano
Section 3 (measures 36-145): A completely developed chorale motet which incorporates echo into its texture!

Weckmann has left us seven sets of chorale variations[28] which in every way are the equal of these works of Tunder. Weckmann's sets vary from as few as two movements (*Gott sei gelobet*) to as many as six (*O Lux beata Trinitas*). In all cases the opening movement is some type of serious *cantus firmus* setting, several times for more than four voices. The second movement is invariably an embellished chorale or an extended chorale fantasy based on that technique. Weckmann seemed to prefer thick, solid textures. He concluded two variation sets, the *Magnificat* and *Es ist das Heil,* with movements for six voices. Even in the embellished chorales he was dissatisfied with the three accompanying voices. In *Es ist das Heil* he added a fourth and he frequently allowed the ornamented voice to lie within the harmonies which surround it:

Mus. ex. VI-42.
Es ist das Heil, verse 6, measures 24-28.[29]

[28] Matthias Weckmann, *Gesammelte Werke,* ed. Ilgner, *Das Erbe deutscher Musik,* Zweite Reihe, IV, Leipzig: Henry Litolff, 1942.

[29] *Ibid.,* 55.

In this and in other compositions Weckmann's embellishments take on a truly Gothic complexity. Each line of the chorale in the movement from which the above example is drawn is embellished a number of times. Each time the embellishments become more and more ornate, the hymn tune less and less obvious, and the final result is figuration which the ear hears as only dimly related to the chorale. The following example is merely one of the variations of the first line of this setting:

Mus. ex. VI-43.
Soprano, measures 46-55.

Weckmann also approached the lighter textures of the *tricinium* from a more serious point of view. He appears to be one of the first composers to require of himself canonic relationship of the ornamenting voices. He was skilled in his use of traditional figurative patterns within the context of canonic writing:

Mus. ex. VI-44.
O Lux beata Trinitas, Canon in *Hypodiapason post Semiminimam,* measures 13-15.[30]

There are also a few times when the composer stretched the norms of figuration. Baroque chromaticism generally occurs at a relatively

[30] *Ibid.,* 89.

slow speed as a function of harmonic rhythm. Weckmann used sixteenth-note chromatic scales as a figuration in and of themselves.[31]

It would be inappropriate to leave the study of this generation of composers without the mention of the esteemed Adam Reincken. His ninety-nine year life spanned the period from his student days with Scheidemann to the famous visit (in the last year of his life) of the young Bach, whose improvisation he so praised. Two gigantic chorale fantasias are his only extant organ works, although his reputation certainly suggests that he was the author of many more. His other keyboard pieces contained in the complete edition[32] are certainly not organ works, nor are they of the same quality as the fantasias. C. P. E. Bach recounts how his father improvised for half an hour on *An Wasserflüssen Babylon* in the presence of the aged Reincken the year before the latter's death.[33] These two pieces seem to be written-out examples of this tradition of improvisation. Each treats each line of the melody in the traditional way; what is unusual is the length. It is certainly interesting to note that the chorale tune *An Wasserflüssen Babylon* is particularly mentioned by C. P. E. Bach and that that fantasy is one of the two preserved today. It is a pity that more of Reincken's works are not extant. Were there free compositions of equal extent and quality?

The Third Generation: Buxtehude, Bruhns, Böhm, Lübeck[34]

The principal interest of the last generation of North-German composers changed from works based on the chorale to free compositions. Of the four major composers of the generation, only Buxtehude himself left any large number of works which continued the tradition of Tunder and Weckmann's chorales. Bruhns left only a single fantasy and Lübeck only one fantasy and an unfinished

---

31 See *Nun freut euch, ibid.,* 125.

32 Adam Reincken, *Collected Keyboard Works,* ed. Apel, *CEKM XVI.*

33 See: Hans T. David and Arthur Mendel, *The Bach Reader,* New York: W. W. Norton, 1945, 219.

34 The editions used below are:
Dietrich Buxtehude, *Sämtliche Orgelwerke,* 4 vols., ed. Hedar, Copenhagen: Hansen, 1952.
Georg Böhm, *Sämtliche Werke,* 2 vols., ed. Wolgast, Wiesbaden: Breitkopf und Härtel, n.d.
Nicolaus Bruhns, *Orgelwerke,* ed. Stein, Frankfurt: C. F. Peters, 1939.
Vincent Lübeck, *Orgelwerke,* ed. Keller, New York: C. F. Peters, 1940.

set of variations. Böhm's works on the chorale, although certainly more numerous, have an orientation that points away from his native land. The grandiose development of a single hymn tune in a composition ten or more minutes in duration must have become less and less palatable to the congregations of Hamburg and Lübeck at a time in which French and Italian styles were running rampant throughout the European musical world. It is possible that the decline of the chorale fantasy as we see it in the extant music may reflect the copyist's interest and not the interests of the composers themselves. Throughout the study of North-European organ music there runs the problem of the lack of autograph manuscripts. Compilers, many of whom were Middle-German, may have copied the works to which they were particularly attracted. In any event, in the literature as we know it, we can see a definite decline of works of large scale based on the chorale and a simultaneous increase in large scale works in free form.

The Mature North-German Praeambulum

The mature North-German *praeambulum* is a collage of many disparate musical elements. It maintains interest by the relationship which a single element has to the environment which surrounds it. A single section of music is contrasted with others around it in such a way that the whole composition is the sum of its very different parts. No single section ever attains a dominance over the work as a whole; each single section contributes its small share to the overall result. Although there are some attempts thematically to unite one section with another, generally by the processes of the variation *canzone* technique, these efforts provide only a minimum level of organization. The rhapsodic element, which, as we have seen, runs throughout the entire tradition, remains prevalent in the *praeambulum.* A single section may or may not be tightly structured; an entire composition never is. A premium is placed on the elements of rapid change, flux, and surprise. No single effect is developed extensively; and there is rapid change from one musical effect to the next.

The *praeambulum* is often confused with the Middle-German prelude and fugue. Hedar's edition of the works of Buxtehude, for instance, improperly uses this designation throughout. The prelude-and-fugue differs from the *praeambulum* in that its two movements (and there are only two) are independent of one another. The prelude may be isolated successfully from the fugue and either can stand musically alone. Although there are a few works in the North-German tradition which meet these criteria, most do not. Any single section of a *praeambulum* is insufficient to stand alone and can properly be understood only as part of an entire composition. To divorce one section from the whole is to dismember the work entirely.

The various elements which make up the *praeambulum* are:

1) sections based on figuration now conditioned by tonal harmony
2) the virtuoso pedal solo
3) the use of mechanistic rhythmic patterns
4) fugal sections that are simple, direct, and rather short
5) the use of variation technique to bind one fugal section to another
6) dialogue passages juxtaposing pedals alone with the manuals
7) the use of double pedal
8) the use of echo
9) dramatic gestures such as unaccompanied scale and arpeggiated passages
10) The dramatic use of silence
11) transitional sections based on unusual harmonies derived from the *durezza* tradition of the Italians
12) the use of certain *ostinato* effects
13) the use of dissonance as an end in itself.

Of course, these devices are not mutually exclusive. Many may occur in a single given section. There was a tendency to follow a format which alternates figurative and fugal sections. The five-section form is the most common: figurative – fugal – figurative – fugal – figurative. There are, however, many exceptions to this. There are examples, for instance, of compositions which place one fugal movement directly after another.

By the late seventeenth century tonal harmony is the conditioning factor of keyboard figuration. Such sections can be reduced to strong, chordal progressions against which the figurative patterns move.

Mus. ex. VI-45.
Buxtehude: *Praeambulum in A* (Hedar II, number 4), measures 5-7.

Not only is the figuration of multi-voiced textures so conditioned, but also the direction of single lines, either in the manuals or in the pedals, is determined by an implied harmony. The matured tonal sense of the late seventeenth century allows solo lines to make musical sense and to move with musical logic. It is an interesting musical exercise to work out the implicit bass of one of these lines:

Mus. ex. VI-46.
Bruhns: *Praeludium in E Minor* (Stein, number 2) soprano, measures 1-3 (bass hypothetical).

The motive force behind sections of mechanistic figurations, favored particularly by Buxtehude, is this same harmonic logic. Many of the fugal subjects of all the composers are conditioned by this mechanistic style, and the fugues they generate tend to be driven by the persistence of one or two motivic ideas:

Mus. ex. VI-47.
Buxtehude: *Praeludium in D* (Hedar II, number 11), measures 25-28.

There is as much interest in such fugal movements in development of motive as there is in contrapuntal interplay. One can say that a complex level of fugal writing is foreign to the North-German style. Even in those fugal sections based on the more sedate, *ricercar*-type subject there is a general absence of *stretto,* augmentation, diminution, etc. The fugal sections are generally short; a length of even fifty measures is unusual. Very often one of these sections is divisible into two parts, the second adding a new countersubject to the old subject. Various fugal sections are often bound to one another by the process of thematic variation. At other times fugal sections within a given composition bear no thematic similarities. Rhythmic structures characteristic of the dance appear in many places. For the more restrained fugues, the *courante,* with its implicit 3/2 against 6/4 meter is favored. For lively movements the *gigue* rhythm is preferred.

The importance of pedal writing in North-German style has been mentioned already several times. The pedal often acts in contradistinction to the manuals. The interchange of a motive between the pedal and the manuals is a particularly characteristic texture:

Mus. ex. VI-48.
Buxtehude: *Praeludium in D* (Hedar II, number 11), measures 14-15.

The use of the double pedal seems to have been dictated as much on the grounds of technical display as upon musical necessity. The pedal often carries two voices of a *ricercar*-style fugue:

Mus. ex. VI-49.
Lübeck: *Praeludium in G Minor* (Keller, number 4), measures 34-37.

Several of the elements under discussion are used primarily for their dramatic effect. So frequently do those elements occur that they become trademarks of the style. Most depend upon some type of textural structure for their effect. One of the most common is a single voice flourish usually contrasted immediately with block chords. Two of the most common types of flourishes are the fanfare and the ascending scale or arpeggiated passage dropping to a single pedal note of unusual harmonic import:

Mus. ex. VI-50.
Buxtehude: *Toccata in D Minor* (Hedar II, number 20), 104-105.

Mus. ex. VI-51.
Lübeck: *Praeludium in G Minor* (Keller, number 4), measure 10.

The North Germans were masters of the use of dramatic silences. Sudden, unexpected rests in all voices were no doubt a stunning effect in the resonant buildings in which this literature was originally performed. The concluding fugue of the greater of Bruhns' e minor *praeludia* is a study in silence. Its halting subject gives rise to a number of such passages and its conclusion with an entirely empty measure is most effective:

Mus. ex. VI-52.
Bruhns: *Praeludium in E Minor* (Stein, number 2), measures 152-155.

Silences often introduce the *durezza*-style transitions which frequently occur between sections based on mechanical pulsation. *Durezza* sections also conclude many *praeambula*, particularly those in which there has been a fast moving *gigue* as the last major section. Often these *durezza* sections appear in the unadorned shape they normally have in Italian music. At other times the harmonic progressions are used as the basis for subtle melodic ornamentation. One particularly beautiful passage drawn from Buxtehude gives decidedly the same effect as in Frescobaldi and the Italian Baroque:

Mus. ex. VI-53.
Buxtehude: *Praeludium in E Minor* (Hedar II, number 9), measures 104-113.

In many instances dissonance and unusual harmonic progressions occur for their own dramatic value. Sudden harmonic shifts, particularly at the conclusion of a figurative section, are common. There are also occasions in which conventional controls of dissonance are suspended in order to obtain a dramatic effect. In the following passage the stepwise progression in contrary motion of the voices produces sharp clashes which are otherwise inexplicable:

Mus. ex. VI-54.
Buxtehude: *Praeludium in A Minor* (Hedar II, number 4), measures 111-112.

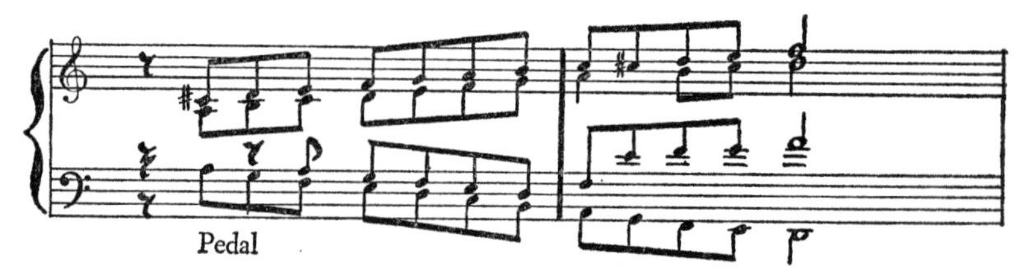

Finally, only Buxtehude introduced (as a means of organizing figuration) several pedal *ostinato* effects into his *praeludia.* An excellent example is the last section of the *Praeludium in* C (Hedar II, number 1). There are others: the opening of the *Praeludium in G Minor* (Hedar II, number 24) and the conclusion of another in the same key (Hedar II, number 22).

The Canzoni and Chaconnes of Buxtehude

In the manuscripts there are nine compositions by Buxtehude entitled either *cantzon, canzonet,* or simply *fuga.* These pieces continue the tradition of the Weckmann *canzoni.* There is a subtle difference, however, between the texture of Buxtehude's pieces and those of his predecessor. The harpsichord orientation of the Weckmann examples is evident in the many arpeggiated figurations, broken chord passages, etc. These are missing in the *canzoni* of Buxtehude. His works were no doubt designed to be played on the lighter divisions of the North-German organs.

While the influence of the Italian tradition on Buxtehude is certainly obvious in this type of composition, he nonetheless departed from the stylized type of themes traditionally associated with it. His themes tend to be made of long, spun-out, sixteenth-note motion emphasizing some particular figurative turn:

Mus. ex. VI-55.
Canzona (Hedar I, number 4), measures 1-4.

The fugal writing is facile and unforced. Two- and three-voice texture is most common. When the theme is in one voice, the others tend to provide only slightly embellished harmonic support. Many long passages in two voices move in consecutive sixteenth-note motion in thirds and sixths. All is delightfully unpretentious and there are few evidences of dramatic, North-German style. The tri-partite form of the *canzone* is followed in four of these compositions. Others are in a single section and still others in two. The technique of thematic variation is employed but perhaps in a more flexible way than in native Italian practice. Buxtehude is particularly fond of the rhythm of the *gigue* in his derivation of the final subjects in his *canzoni.*

Due to the unusual popularity of the Bach *Passacaglia,* it is often assumed that there must be a lengthy history of similar organ pieces in the seventeenth century. Despite the fact that ground bass forms adapt well to the organ, the occurrence of them in the literature of the century is rare. The most important examples of the *chaconne/passacaglia* form — the terms denote the same thing and no attempt to differentiate one from the other has ever been satisfactory — are the *F-Major Chaconne* of Pachelbel and three by Buxtehude. The Buxtehude examples are in no way unusual. Each employs a four-measure bass, and that in e minor is even more conventional in that the bass line is a slightly modified descending line from the tonic to the dominant. The North-German quality of these pieces is evident in a texture thicker than that found in similar pieces of Southern origin, in a decidedly greater emphasis on vertical structures, and finally in the pedal solos used in some of the variations. The *D-Minor Chaconne* presents the bass first in the tonic, then in the relative major, then in the dominant, and finally again in the tonic.

Chorale Settings

It is typical of cultural processes that by the time a certain movement, trend, or school has reached its height there are already evidences of the beginning of its decline. Chorale settings had been the center of North-German organ practice in the first and second generations of composers and the chorale fantasy had been the most characteristic mode of expression. This serious Lutheran and Baroque practice, however, soon became outmoded in the face of thriving French and Italian tastes. A North Germany that espoused Italian opera in the first decade of the eighteenth century would hardly have found the chorale fantasy palatable in the latter years of the seventeenth. The extant works of the four major composers of the last generation confirm this view, for Böhm left no chorale fantasies; and Bruhns and Lübeck, only one each. Buxtehude himself left five pieces which qualify as fantasies. His most characteristic works, however, are doubtless the shorter, less complex chorale preludes.

Buxtehude's chorale settings consist of twenty-five of these lesser preludes; the fantasies just mentioned; a chorale motet; and several sets of variations, sets which pose problems both of text and intent. He also left a *Magnificat* and a *Te Deum* which do not fit conventional formats. In his chorale settings Buxtehude appears to have two contradictory goals: 1) the desire to restrain the excesses of ornamentation in the embellished chorales, and 2) the wish to introduce into large settings elements derived from the *praeambulum.* It appears that the composer intended to set out the chorale as clearly as possible and yet preserve the importance of dramatic organ style as expressed in the *praeambulum.*

The most obvious element introduced into the chorale fantasy from the *praeambulum* is the *fughetta. Fughetta* subjects, often introduced as a foil to the notes of the chorale, have the same snappy, percussive style discussed above.

Mus. ex. VI-56.
Buxtehude: *Nun freut euch lieben Christen g'mein* (Hedar III, number 6), measures 13-17.

The ornate codas which end several of Buxtehude's fantasies are yet another element derived from the *praeambulum.* These toccata-style endings have no apparent connection to the chorale itself but are made instead of the same free material used in similar situations in the composer's *praeambula.*

The *Magnificat Primi Toni* (Hedar III, number 5) is nothing more than a large *praeambulum* eight sections in length. Many of the sections are short *fughette.* One hunts in vain for any connection between the original psalm tune and the fugal subjects. There appears to be none. The setting of the *Te Deum* (Hedar III, number 7) does quote from the chant; however, the style is still that of a free composition. Even in a section in which the pedal carries a *cantus planus,* the *Te martyrum,* the bass begins with a flourish characteristic of the pedal solos we have discussed.

In his fantasias Buxtehude introduces few new technical devices; he relies almost entirely on his inheritance. Nevertheless, he tends to use simultaneously devices such as *cantus firmus* and ornamented chorale. At the first entrance of the solo voice in the fantasy on *Gelobet seist du* the chorale is to be found in the pedal. The soprano does not bear a paraphrase of the hymn, but instead a freely constructed melody. The fantasy on *Nun freut euch* stands, along with those of Reincken, as one of the most extensive treatments of a single chorale (256 measures). Despite its great length, it remains an exceedingly cohesive composition. This cohesion is partly effected by a thorough working out of one single idea before another is taken up. The tendency to skip quickly from one idea to the next, a tendency characteristic of earlier composers, is not to be found in this or in other works of Buxtehude.

The popular fantasy on *Wie schön leuchtet der Morgenstern* (Hedar III, number 8) is unusual in that it makes no use of the ornamented technique and that it lacks a pedal part. The very clear and restrained *cantus firmus* used in the opening sections is evidence that the earlier tendency toward opaqueness in North-German music has given way to a more lucid style of writing. The fugue, which concludes the composition, is in *gigue* style, which, as we have already pointed out, is a favourite with Buxtehude. Similar *gigues* are also found in the fantasies on *Gelobet seist du* and *Nun freut euch* and in the *Magnificat Primi Toni.*

The forced contrapuntal lines of the chorale motet on *Ich dank dir schön durch deinen Sohn* (Hedar III, number 3) indicate that the form was not native to Buxtehude. Less contrived, but still hardly of the same quality as the composer's other works, is the fantasy *Ich dank dir, lieber Herre* in which Buxtehude's attempts to blend the elements of four-voice block harmony, sequential passages based on suspension dissonances, canon, and *courante* rhythm into a single composition. There is no other like it in the literature.

The shorter chorale preludes of Buxtehude are among his most beautiful compositions. The form of the embellished chorale is adhered to in all these works; however, the embellishment is applied with restraint. Some chorale lines actually are presented unornamented and others receive only modest ornaments:

Mus. ex. VI-57.
Buxtehude: *Herr Jesu Christ, ich weiss gar wohl* (Hedar IV, number 12), measures 1-11, soprano.

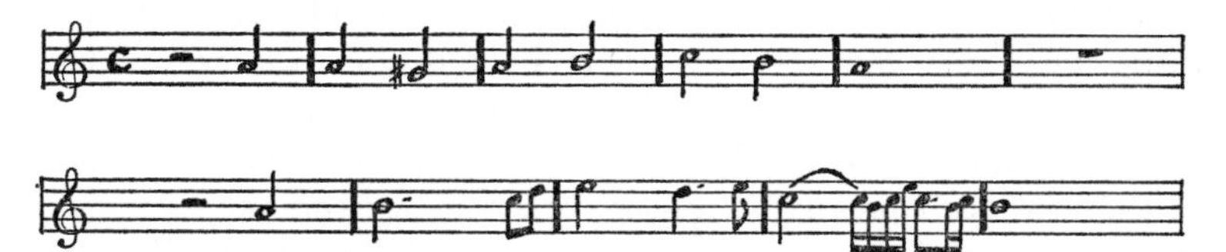

The three voices which support the chorale are as often harmonically as contrapuntally conceived and many passages are no more than thinly elaborated four-voice harmonizations:

Mus. ex. VI-58.
Komm heiliger Geist (Hedar IV, number 15a), measures 1-5.

Frequently short points of imitation precede some lines, although the technique is rarely used consistently throughout a given composition. The goal of a simple and concise presentation of the hymn would make this technique cumbersome. There are occasional examples of tone-painting. The obvious descent in the opening measures of *Durch Adams Fall* (Hedar III, number 4) as well as the chromaticism throughout the piece can hardly be missed. Such examples, however, are rare. The subtle selection of material for the embellished line, as well as the amount of the ornamentation, is directly related to the overall meaning of the chorale text. The student is invited to compare the assertive beginning of *Erhalt uns Herr bei deinem Wort* (Hedar III, number 6) with the plaintive opening of *Nun bitten wir* (number 19b).

Trying to see the group of compositions published in part one of Hedar's volume III as a continuation of the North-German tradition of chorale variation poses problems. It is doubtful that the form of any of these sets is as Buxtehude left it. For instance the order of movements, (*tricinium, bicinium,* embellished chorale, *bicinium*) of the setting of *Vater unser im Himmelreich* (Hedar III, number 6) is not an order any composer of this school would have condoned. Since all these compositions occur in miscellaneous manuscripts which are collections of chorale preludes by many composers, it appears likely that only movements which appealed to the compiler's tastes have been preserved. These variation sets contain less that is natively North-German than other works of Buxtehude. The frequency with which one encounters the *tricinium* texture and the omission of the favourite texture of the North Germans, the embellished chorale, is particularly bothersome. At times the three-voiced compositions seem strikingly like those of Pachelbel and his school. Why the composer in his variations should have relied so heavily on the *tricinium* is unclear. In any respect, these variations are not of the same quality established in the variation tradition of Tunder and Weckmann.

Both the fantasies of Bruhns on *Nun komm' der Heiden Heiland* and Lübeck on *Ich ruf' zu dir* are large and powerful works. It is difficult to resist the temptation to name Bruhns' composition the most glorious of all North-German fantasies. Each of the four lines of the chorale is set to an individual section of music that is a complete movement unto itself. Each section is concluded with an elaborate final cadence and each is stylistically different, in some respect or another, from the other sections. The four sections are concluded with a coda in flamboyant, North-German style. All the old elements are present but they are used in remarkably controlled fashion. This composition also marks the first appearance of the vocabulary of French *agréments* in German organ literature.

The Lübeck fantasy continues the tradition of Buxtehude in that it further blends elements of the *praeambulum* into chorale settings. The chorale is often so hidden and there is so much material that has only tangential relationship to it that the line of demarcation between the two forms is very nearly obscured. There is no longer any trace of the *cantus firmus* chorale and the use of echo is kept to a minimum. The fugal episodes, which we saw in the fantasies of Buxtehude, are even more important and extensive in the Lübeck fantasy. When we consider the advanced style of this piece as well as the fact that the composer lived well into the eighteenth century, we are led to believe that this may be the last composition in a great tradition.

The chorales of Böhm are in style and emotional content hardly North-German at all. The eclecticism of this composer leads him to a fondness for imitating French, Italian, and Middle-German styles and his organ music is pervaded by his love of the harpsichord. Many of his works in the complete edition obviously are not for organ. The manual variations on the chorale, which carry in German practice the name *partita,* were as often associated with chamber as church performance, and many works of this type in the Middle-German tradition seem much more in the idiom of the harpsichord than in the idiom of the organ. Böhm's variations on *Ach wie nichtig* (Wolgast, II, number 1) are decidedly for harpsichord. Not only do the free voice leading of the opening chorale and the facile, broken style of the variations suggest this, but the composer writes a low A, available only on that instrument. It is likely that other sets do not belong to the organ: *Freu dich sehr o meine Seele* (number 8), *Gelobet seist du* (number 9-1), and *Wer nur den lieben Gott lässt walten* (number 14). Even in those *partitas* in which the pedal plays a prominent role and in which trio style is more suggestive of organ performance, the light, open harpsichord style is still evident.

More evidence of the Middle-German sympathies of Böhm is his use of the chorale motet fashioned not in the complex form of Tunder but in the very clear, transparent type of writing in which each line of the soprano melody is preceded by a short and uncomplicated point of imitation. Within this limited format a composition such as *Christ lag in Todesbanden* (number 6-1) is a masterpiece.

The only chorales of Böhm which betray his origin are a handful of examples of the short, embellished chorale precisely in the style of those of Buxtehude. One of his embellished chorales, *Vater unser im Himmelreich,* deserves special consideration (number 12-2). This composition transforms the ornamented chorale into an Italian arioso. The homophonic construction of the lower voices represents a written-out continuo over which the very plastic, ornamented chorale flows. Such a piece undoubtedly had a profound influence on the style of the young Bach:

Mus. ex. VI-59.
Vater unser im Himmelreich (Wolgast, number 12-2), measures 7-9.

CHAPTER VII.

Middle & South Germany.

The resolution of the religious conflicts of the sixteenth century left Germany clearly divided along sectarian lines. The Lutheran faith had sprung up in the small-town, semi-rural culture of Saxony and had spread rapidly northward into the Baltic and Scandinavian areas. Southern Germany, on the other hand, had remained loyally Roman Catholic; and in the early seventeenth century it was closely allied to Italian traditions in liturgical and aesthetic matters. In the organ literature of the century however, there is little stylistic demarcation between that which was Middle-German and that which was Southern. It is true that the Saxon and Thuringian organists found in the chorale a focal point for their art which their Southern colleagues lacked. But beyond this important element, the interaction between these two schools, if indeed this is what they should be called, was nearly complete. Pachelbel, who was by far the best and most representative composer of Middle-German music, probably spent some time in Vienna in Roman Catholic service. In any event the large number of his Magnificat fugues gives credence to this assertion. His musical style remained unaffected no matter which religious tradition he served.

Neither the Southern- nor the Middle-German schools can be traced in the early years of the century. While composers such as Hassler and Erbach carried the sixteenth-century Venetian tradition into Germany, their work concluded an old practice rather than initiating a new one. Froberger's study with Frescobaldi and his subsequent introduction of elements of that composer's style into German keyboard music is the actual beginning of the Southern tradition. Froberger remains its chief exponent around whom other composers seem pale. The origin of Middle-German music is largely obscure. The decidedly provincial nature of the school, which served to produce many competent local artisans but no splendid artists, very naturally evolved without leaving an obvious line of development. Although a few names are known to us from the early years of the century — names such as Christian Michael of Leipzig and Johann Klemm of Dresden — the music they left is so scanty that it could not safely be termed representative. The first major work of Middle-German music is Erasmus Kindermann's *Harmonica organica* of 1645. However, printed music was uncharacteristic in the region, and no well-defined manuscript tradition follows this one publication. Only when we arrive at the last quarter of the century is there any abundance of music, and most of this is associated with Pachelbel and his close associates.

A comparison must be drawn between North-German music, and South- and Middle-German music. The Southern traditions had about them none of the Gothic flamboyance of the North. As our study has revealed, the organ was largely relegated in the Roman Catholic service to alternation performances and occasional musical interludes. Hence the South-Germans had no liturgical motivation to indulge in North-German virtuosity. The small-town culture of Thuringia and Saxony placed a premium on musical craftsmanship, modesty, simplicity, and directness. Here there was little motivation to produce works of any complexity or technical display, a fact that undoubtedly caused the young Bach many headaches upon his return from his Northern training.

Before we begin to discuss the Froberger and Pachelbel schools, we must, however, deal with the problem posed by the works of Samuel Scheidt, a composer who produced an unexcelled body of organ literature in the early decades of the century but whose subsequent influence in the development of German organ styles was unfortunately almost non-existent.

THE WORKS OF SAMUEL SCHEIDT

Without question the publication in 1624 of Samuel Scheidt's *Tabulatura Nova* was one of the landmarks in German organ music. What is peculiar about it, however, is that a work as monumental as this should have exerted so little influence in the further development of literature for the instrument. No similar publications or developed manuscript tradition followed this publication, and there is no evidence that Scheidt had about him a circle of disciples and pupils. Scheidt (1587-1654) had been from 1607 to 1608 another of Sweelinck's German pupils. Apel's treatment of Scheidt[1]

---

[1] *Apel K.*, pp. 356 ff.

places him in the midst of the Dutchman's North-German pupils. To suggest, however, that Scheidt is merely a displaced North-German is misleading. The Italian notation he employed, his general avoidance of the ornamented chorale, his conservative fantasias, and the general discipline which underlies his mode of musical expression place him decidedly outside the North-German circle. Although there are certainly elements of Sweelinck's style in the *Tabulatura Nova,* Scheidt is far more cosmopolitan than his fellow pupils. English and Italian elements, for example, are particularly strong in his work.

The first two parts of this three-part collection have a haphazard structure.[2] Secular works, most certainly intended for the harpsichord, are freely intermixed with the fantasias and the variations on chorales. A set of twenty-four canons, which have nothing to do with the keyboard at all, is even included at the conclusion of Part I. Part III of the *Tabulatura* is based on the conservative elements from the Catholic liturgy, elements which were the inheritance of early Lutheran musicians. The opening two compositions in this part constitute the *Kyrie* and the *Gloria* of a *missa brevis.* In his edition, Mahrenholz rearranges Scheidt's order so that the *Credo* on *Wir glauben all' in einem Gott* and the Communion on *Jesus Christus, unser Heiland* follow this *Kyrie/Gloria.* It is doubtful, however, that Scheidt had in mind such an expanded organ mass. The other works in this part are a complete set of *Magnificat* settings, a set of selected hymns for the Church year, and two compositions for six voices with double pedal, compositions obviously designed to conclude a service of worship.

A clue to the nature of Scheidt's musical style is to be found in the notation in which he set out his publication. The title *Tabulatura nova* refers to a type of musical notation (Italian keyboard *partitura*) new only to Germans, in which each voice is allotted its own staff in open score. This conservative type of keyboard notation best expresses a conservative musical texture in which the polyphonic integrity of each of the voices is normally maintained. It is less useful as a means of notating textures which rely on a freer concept of voice leading. Scheidt's style is particularly conservative in just this

[2] The only complete edition is: Samuel Scheidt, *Werke,* ed. Mahrenholz, Hamburg: Ugrino Verlag, 1953 and 1964, Band XI/1 (Part I) and Band VI/2 (Parts II and III). Further citations refer to this edition. There is also an anthology of Scheidt's works available in Peters Edition.

matter of texture. However much he may borrow from the freer, more open style of the English virginalists, he never sacrifices an almost sixteenth-century adherence to the concept of voices. In this respect Scheidt's music is similar to that of his French contemporary Titelouze.

The Fantasias

Four of Scheidt's five fantasias (some are entitled *fuga*) are very similar to those of Sweelinck. The opening *ricercar* sections, the *cantus planus* treatment in the middle sections, the use of *bicinium* and echo textures, and the final contrapuntal working out of the theme exist much the same as they are found in his teacher's works. Two personal features of the younger composer's works are obvious: 1) his use of multiple subjects in both the fantasia on the Palestrina madrigal *Io son ferito lasso* (Part I, number 2) and in the *Fuga Contraria* (Part II, number 1), and 2) an expansion of the *cantus planus* technique beyond that normally employed by Sweelinck. In the fantasia on the madrigal, four subjects are initially presented and treated in contrapuntal opposition in the manner originally worked out by the Neapolitan school. These four subjects, however, are so contrived that together they form the four phrases of one very acceptable melody, a melody which becomes the *cantus firmus* for the lengthy middle section in this composition:

Mus. ex. VII-1.

A similar procedure is followed in the *Fuga Contraria,* where the original subject and its inversion are used in an identical manner.

Scheidt's expansion of the *cantus planus* technique is associated with carefully indicated registration changes. In all cases he set the long-note melody in the pedal, first at two-foot pitch, then at four-foot, and finally at eight-foot. Thus each presentation of the melody assumes another voice in the texture and new variation material is introduced in the other voices.

One of Scheidt's fantasias is for three voices (Part II, number 6), a texture unusual in a piece of such dimension. It is interesting to note that its principal theme is a transposition of the initial theme of Sweelinck's hexachord fantasia. Scheidt's own composition on the hexachord (Part I, number 4) is unlike his other fantasias. It is merely a lengthy set of variations on the ascending and descending theme, a set which begins with two-voice and proceeds to three- and four-voice variations. The composition depends upon excessive sequential progressions. The great length of the piece, three hundred eighty-three measures, plus reliance solely on sequence, produces a composition which could fairly be termed dull. The composer seems to have felt compelled to undertake this traditional task, but he carried it out in an uninspired and mechanistic manner.

The influence of Sweelinck is also to be seen in an echo fantasia (Part II, number 2) and in the toccata *In te Domine speravi.* The echo fantasia is divisible into two sections, each independent of the other. Section A is chordally structured and the echo involves the entire texture, a procedure rare in pieces by Sweelinck himself:

Mus. ex. VII-2.
Scheidt: *Echo ad manuale duplex,* measures 15-18.

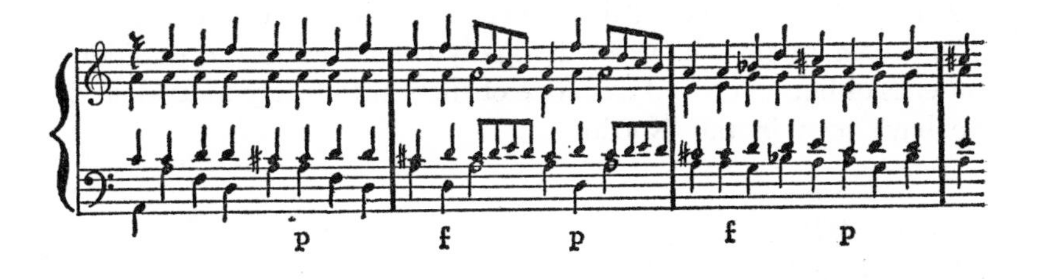

Section B of the fantasia uses echo of the traditional motivic figurations. The toccata is based on a melody which does not appear in the *Liber usualis.* Since this melody was again employed by Scheidt as the basis for one of his canons (Part I, number 10), it must have been a well-known chant which has now fallen into disuse. While at the beginning of the piece, the motive arises from this melody, the latter section of the toccata appears to be freely constructed.

Settings of Chorales and Gregorian Melodies

The settings of chorales and Gregorian hymns in the *Tabulatura Nova* are treated in identical fashion. In these compositions, Scheidt's style is characteristically conservative and bound more tightly to the past than is that of his North-German contemporaries. He maintained a purity of contrapuntal line which rivals that of his sixteenth-century precursors. The chorale melody, which stood as a point of departure for rhapsodic development in the North, stands throughout Scheidt's work as a *cantus firmus* which remains unchanged and unadorned from one variation movement to the next. The ornamental lines move about the *cantus* with a polished security suggestive of high-Renaissance style. Although the composer borrowed freely from the repertory of figurative devices passed to him by Sweelinck from the English virginalists, this borrowing is always controlled by a conservative, contrapuntal environment.

The majority of Scheidt's chorales are variation sets of considerable extent probably intended for an elaborate *alternatim* practice. Although there is great flexibility in the order of movements, most sets begin with an opening chorale motet followed by a *bicinium*. There follows a series of trio movements in which the pedal bears the hymn in various voices. The final movement almost invariably places the *cantus firmus* in the bass voice, occasionally in the tenor echoed phrase by phrase in the bass. The rarity of movements in which the chorale is treated in ornamented fashion is obvious. Occasionally Scheidt included a movement with a "colored" *cantus*. The ornamentation, however, is rigidly connected to the traditional patterns of figuration and has none of the spirit of fiery individualism we have seen in the North:

Mus. ex. VII-3.
Warum betrübst du dich, mein Herz, verse 12, measures 1-5[3]

[3] Scheidt, *Werke,* Part I, number 5, p. 57.

It is surprising to find the *bicinium* to be Scheidt's most inventive texture. Two new types are to be found in the *Tabulatura.* In the first of these, each line of the chorale is presented twice, first in the soprano and then in the bass. The same counterpoint is used as inversion at the fifth or the octave for each of the presentations:

Mus. ex. VII-4.
Christe, qui lux es et dies, verse 7, measures 1-9.[4]

The other novel type of *bicinium* depends upon the derivation from the chorale melody of characteristic motives which then are developed to form the essence of the variation. The melody is not presented in its entirety; the successive motives instead suggest the progress of the hymn tune. In one particularly ornate example, that from the variations on *Christ lag in Todesbanden,*[5] both of these techniques are used in the same variation. Each line is treated in both ways to form an unusually long two-voice movement. The following example illustrates the technique of fragmentation:

[4] *Ibid.,* Part II, number 7, p. 52.
[5] *Ibid.,* Part II, number 5, p. 31.

Mus. ex. VII-5.
Christ lag in Todesbanden, verse 3, measures 55-61.

Such fragmentation is also an important element in the chorale motets which open most of Scheidt's variations. After the initial fugal opening line, the composer may give up imitative writing and instead resort to sections based on motives derived from the chorale. In these sections it is not uncommon to find the long-note melody temporarily omitted.

Although trio settings are the most common type to be found in the *Tabulatura Nova,* there is to be found in them little unusual in the composer's technique. Short points of imitation, figurative patterns common to Anglo-Dutch keyboard music, counterpoint in consecutive thirds and sixths, and motivic interchange characterize the ornamenting voices. Everything is handled with grace and precision, but if we look for innovations, none are to be found in the *tricinia.* Before we leave Scheidt's chorale settings, we should mention one elaborate composition, the fantasia on *Ich ruf' zu dir* (Part I, number 13). This is without doubt the longest chorale motet on record, two hundred fifty-one measures, but yet it is also one of the most nearly perfect. Each line of the chorale is first subjected to a well-developed point of imitation. Then the chorale appears in long-note values first in the soprano voice, then in the tenor, and finally the bass. While such treatment of each line produces a lengthy structure which one might think redundant, Scheidt's remarkable control of contrapuntal line maintains one's interest from the beginning to the end.

One might hope that the high quality of the *Tabulatura Nova* would have been reflected in other Middle-German music of the period, but this does not seem to have been the case. The one hundred four-part harmonizations of chorales which constitute Scheidt's other keyboard publication, the so-called *Görlitz Tablature* (1650) are certainly not on the same level. These pieces are of particular interest to the organist in studying the evolution of chorale harmonizations, and they form a foil to the Bach harmonizations, settings which have often been cited erroneously as the best possible four-voice settings of German hymn tunes.

THE SOUTH-GERMAN SCHOOL

The Works of Froberger

The personality of Johann Froberger (1616-1667) dominated the South-German school of organ composition. Not only is he the school's most prolific and competent composer, but his works provided a model which other composers imitated and copied. His activity in Vienna made that city the center of South-German keyboard composition. Such composers as Kerll, Poglietti, and Georg Muffat were in some way or other attached to the musical life of that city. We have already mentioned the close connection between the music of this school and that of Italy. As a matter of course, many German composers went South for their education. Unmistakable is Frescobaldi's influence on Froberger, with whom the latter studied in Rome from 1637 to 1641. Froberger's works, however, suggest that the Neapolitan intensity of his teacher remained a foreign influence only partially adopted and assimilated. Froberger's style has more in common with post-Frescobaldi Italians, composers who imitated the outward form but not the inward content of Frescobaldi. By the middle of the century the emotional fervor of the early Italian Baroque seems mostly to have died out even in works by composers who in their youth came directly within his sphere of influence. Froberger's works are characterized by a clarity of counterpoint, a direct manner of musical expression, use of formal procedures of lucid quality, and a limited emphasis on either harmonic and contrapuntal complexity or technical virtuosity. The forms of organ music which Froberger used, the toccata, the *canzone,* and the *ricercar,* are the forms of Frescobaldi. Their musical content, however, has little in common with that composer's intense manner of musical expression. Of all seventeenth-century composers, Froberger appears to have travelled the most, and a study of his life reveals him as a cosmopolitan and urbane man. French influence, which plays so great a part in his harpsichord suites, however, plays no visible part in his organ works save in the introduction of the *agréments* into some of his organ works.

The editorial problems associated with the music of so many composers who left their works in unpublished form luckily do not exist in respect to Froberger. His organ works exist in several opulent and carefully edited manuscript editions prepared for his patrons. Thus we have no questions of textual authenticity and few of musical intent. In dealing with the music of any Italian or South-German composer of the period, the question of organ versus harpsichord performance must be examined. The preference for the harpsichord in Italian musical practice, as well as Froberger's standing as a composer of French style suites, makes assigning his works to the organ somewhat difficult. On the grounds of musical style, *ricercari* always seem to fit the organ best; and we can reasonably assume that the thirteen compositions of this type are for organ. The twenty-four toccatas, the six *canzoni* and their companion pieces, and the eighteen *capricci*, are not as easy to assign. The title of one important manuscript (Wiener Hofbibliothek 16550) says very clearly: *VIII Toccate, V Capricci, e Canzone per l'Organo.* Thus there seems to be no doubt that these types fall within the composer's organ works. The only complete edition of Froberger's works remains the excellent one in the *Denkmäler der Tonkunst in Osterreich,* the edition to which the following citations refer.[6]

The Toccatas

We have already mentioned the relationship between the toccatas of Froberger and the North-German *praeambulum.* Both types of compositions share the same format. A typical toccata begins with a rhapsodic introduction characterized by almost improvisational freedom. One or more fugal episodes follow, concluding normally with a coda in freer style. The rhythmic plasticity of the opening sections is the most significant similarity in Froberger's music to the

[6] Johann Jakob Froberger, *Orgel und Klavierwerke,* ed. Guido Adler, *DTO,* Band 8 and Band 21. Reprint, Graz: Akademische Druck und Verlagsanstalt, 1959. An anthology of pieces is also available: Froberger, *Toccaten, Fantasien, Ricercari, Canzonen und Capricci,* ed. Walter, Altötting: Verlag Alfred Coppenrath, 1967.

spirit of Frescobaldi's toccatas. Certain characteristic melodic and harmonic figures, all of Neopolitan origin, are used repeatedly in these quasi-recitative openings: 1) the rapidly ascending scale dropping into a note or chord (generally a secondary dominant in first inversion) of harmonic importance:

Mus. ex. VII-6.
Toccata XIV, measures 6-7.[7]

2) the melodic motive , which is a particular favorite of Froberger and a cliché of the Neopolitan school, and 3) the use of halting, broken scale passages which seem only circuitously to reach their mark:

Mus. ex. VII-7.
Toccata VIII, measures 6-8.[8]

The fugal sections of the toccatas are invariably built on the simplest of themes, often no more than the shortest rhythmic motive treated imitatively. In these sections fugal writing and motivic figuration become sides of the same coin. The most common texture places the theme in one voice and its harmonic support in the others:

---

[7] *DTO,* Band 21, 4.
[8] *DTO,* Band 8, 21.

Mus. ex. VII-8.
Toccata III, measures 22-24.[9]

This simple texture is a dominant one throughout the fugal writing in both Southern and Middle-German styles. Froberger places a premium on concise fugal snippets; and he makes no attempt to work out lengthy, more complicated contrapuntal interplay. The goal here, as elsewhere in the composer's works, is a directness attained by simplicity and lucidity. One fugal section is bound to the next by the all-pervasive device of thematic variation, a device upon which every Italian-oriented composer of the century relied as a matter of course. Froberger is particularly fond of the 12/8 *gigue* meter for his final fugal section, and at times he uses it with cleverly contrived syncopated rhythm:

Mus. ex. VII-9.
Toccata II, measures 41-43.[10]

Three toccatas, numbers five, six, and nine, fall into a special category. These are more extensively developed examples of the Elevation-style toccata of Frescobaldi and other Italians. These through-composed pieces maintain the recitative style throughout, and they therefore contain no fugal sections. For the most part Froberger's harmony is characterized by the unadventuresome vocabulary that was normal in mid-seventeenth-century music. In these Elevations, however, he continued the early Baroque tradition of

[9] *DTO,* Band 8, 9.
[10] *DTO,* Band 8, 7.

harmonic experimentation which led ultimately to the complexities of Bach. In the initial phrase of *Toccata XI,* a piece in an e-minor tonality, he moved principally by the use of secondary dominants to the unlikely chords of e-flat major and c minor:

Mus. ex. VII-10.
Toccata XI, measures 1-9 (harmonic outline only).

The Ricercari and the Fantasias

No essential difference is to be found between the compositions Froberger entitled *ricercari* and those he entitled fantasias.[11] It would be interesting to know if he himself had some distinction in mind that is no longer obvious. The tendency to simplify the older forms, a tendency observable in the toccatas, certainly continues in the *ricercar*-style compositions. Gone are the learned, complex, multi-thematic interworkings of the Trabaci and Frescobaldi type of *ricercar.* Froberger's examples are completely monothematic and his texture, crystal clear. The majority of these pieces are multi-sectional works in which a single theme is treated successively in different ways. *Ricercar V*[12] is typical; it is a five-section work organized in the following manner:

Section 1: The theme is presented fugally.

Section 2: The melodic contours of the theme are retained but the note values are reduced to quarter and eighth notes. This theme is treated in a fugal exposition.

[11] A selection of the fantasias and *ricercari* is available: Froberger, *Ausgewählte Orgelwerke,* ed. Matthaei, Kassel: Bärenreiter, 1965.

[12] *DTO,* Band 8, 109.

Section 3: A thematic variation in triple meter is developed.
Section 4: The melodic contours of the theme are used as a whole-note *cantus firmus.*
Section 5: The melodic contours are again reduced to quarter-note motion and the theme is then presented in quasi-stretto form.

The various sections of a Froberger *ricercar*/fantasia are so independent of one another that they might well have been played alone. It is conceivable that various sections were used in this way, either as interludes in a service or even in the practice of alternation with chant. In a manner characteristic of seventeenth-century composers, Froberger relied on individual sections strung together to produce a longer work. Clear thematic variations relate one section to the next. In the interest of clarity Froberger also avoided harmonic complexity. Only in the selection of the keys of f-sharp and c-sharp minor, keys whose use was unusual in the mid-seventeenth century, is Froberger experimental.

Before we leave these compositions, we should mention Froberger's undertaking of the traditional task of writing a hexachord fantasia.[13] This he accomplished in a seven-section movement similar to those we have discussed. Perhaps the only unusual section is one which employs sixteenth-note figurations which are otherwise not to be found in the *ricercari* and fantasias. The theme is also transformed into a *gigue* rhythm and, in other places, treated sequentially in ascending 5-6 progressions. The light and gracious counterpoint which characterizes all Froberger's works makes this piece one of the most delightful hexachord compositions in the entire repertory. Here again it is obvious that the composer cared less for scholarly complexity than for producing readily accessible music.

The Canzoni and Capricci

Just as the *ricercari* and fantasias are essentially the same type of music, so are the six *canzoni* and eighteen *capricci.* No stylistic difference can be found between the two types save that the *capricci* tend to have more than the traditional three sections and are therefore longer and more complex. The same straightforward, unaffected style which characterizes Froberger's other works is to be found here.

[13] Fantasia I, *DTO,* Band 8, 33.

These pieces too prove to be competently written music in which one looks in vain for surprises in form, harmony, or texture. The initial theme serves as the basis for as few as two and as many as seven contrasting sections within a piece. The process of thematic variation naturally binds section to section. The variations are always obvious, and there is no attempt to obscure their relationships as in Frescobaldi. The majority of Froberger's themes outline or stress in some way the interval between the tonic and dominant or that between the dominant and tonic. He frequently introduced chromatic subjects which before his work had been avoided in *canzone* style. The rhythmic motive occurs again and again in the construction of Froberger's themes. These characteristics are all to be found in the theme with its variants from *Capriccio XIV*.[14]

Mus. ex. VII-11.

The writing of extended fugal movements proved a problem for all seventeenth-century composers, who dealt constantly with the necessity for preserving interest in a texture made up largely of continuous presentations of a single theme in one voice after the other. Thus any one fugal section was forced to be short, or dullness would certainly result. Froberger successfully constructed longer sections in his *canzoni* by controlling texture more competently than his predecessors usually did. Short two-voice duets often relieve the four-voice texture. By use of contrasting registers thematic entrances are set off more dramatically than in the past. Froberger also introduced short passages of non-thematic material which serve as foils to the

[14] *DTO*, Band 21, 63.

continuous thematic entrances. In so doing, he became the first composer to suggest the possibility of episodic writing used in opposition to thematically oriented sections. This is not to imply that these short passages (normally no more than two measures in length) are themselves episodes, but only to indicate that here is a germ of textural differentiation which will be developed in the later Baroque fugue. The following bridge passage is typical:

Mus. ex. VII-12.
Capriccio XIV, measures 28-33.[15]

Froberger's works set the standard for both Middle- and South-German music, particularly in these very direct, unassuming fugal movements. In his organ music he imitated neither the emotional fervor of the early Italians nor the intensity and virtuosity of his Northern compatriots. His style is competent, uncomplicated, direct, and technically undemanding. These features were imitated in all the organ literature in the area throughout the remainder of the century.

Other South-German Composers

The remainder of the South-German organ literature exists chiefly in a body of publications which appeared in the last third of the century:

---

[15] *DTO,* Band 21, 64.

Sebastian Scherer (1631 - 1712): *Tabulatura in cymbalo et organo* (1664). Contents: *Liber primus* — four intonations in each of the church tones; *Liber secundus* — eight toccatas.

Alessandro Poglietti (died 1683): *Praeludia, Cadenzen, und Fugen über die acht Choral Ton* (1676).

Johann Kaspar Kerll (1627 - 1693): *Modulatio Organica* (1686). Contents: Verses for the Magnificat in each of the church tones.

Georg Muffat (1653 - 1704): *Apparatus musico-organisticus* (1690). Contents: twelve toccatas, a *chaconne,* and a *passacaglia.*

Johann Speth (1664 - ?): *Ars Magna Consoni et Dissoni* (1693). Contents: ten toccatas, eight *Magnificat* settings, and a set of variations.

Franz Xaver Murschhauser (1663 - 1738): *Octi-Tonium novum organicum* (1696). Contents: a prelude, five *fughette,* and a finale in each of the church tones.
Prototypon Longo-Breve Organicum (1703 and 1707). Contents: several preludes, intonations, and fugues in each of the church tones.

Johann Casper Ferdinand Fischer (c. 1665-1746): *Ariadne Musica* (1702). Contents: twenty preludes and fugues.

These collections have much in common. They were obviously designed to provide a repertory of service music for the Roman Catholic liturgy, since the majority of their contents is made up of short verset-length pieces arranged in the order of the modes. Only the toccatas in the Speth, Scherer, and Muffat collections are compositions of any length. Many of the remaining compositions are so short they could only have been used in the practice of alternation. There is little premium placed on originality of musical style in the works of any of these composers. Instead, the very order of one composer's collection is often borrowed from his predecessors. Only Speth and Muffat made any effort to perfect an individual musical style. Most of their contemporaries were content to borrow that established by Froberger. What is interesting, however, is that they no longer wrote multi-section *ricercari*, toccatas, and *canzoni*. Their collections are for the most part made up of little pieces that would have formed a single section of a larger Froberger composition.

Scherer: Tabulatura in cymbalo et organo.[16]

The first part of this collection consists of compositions the composer entitles *intonations,* an obvious reference to the Italian origin of this material. Four of these pieces are provided in the following order for each mode: 1) a toccata of the pedal-point type, 2) a *fughetta,* 3) a toccata for manuals alone, and 4) another *fughetta.* There is no intent that one composition should follow the other in performance; they merely provide examples to be selected at the discretion of the organist himself for whatever situation he deems them appropriate. The pedal-point toccatas represent diminutive examples of a type which Scherer developed much more thoroughly in part two of his publication. His *fughette* are brief and similar to an individual section from a Froberger *capriccio* or *canzone.* The toccatas for manuals are more influenced by Frescobaldi's style. The use of passages in *durezza* style, the presence of Lombard rhythms, and the serious mood suggestive of the Elevation toccata tie these pieces to him.

The pedal-point toccatas which make up part two of Scherer's collection also have their inspiration in Frescobaldi, who provided models for them in his second book of toccatas. Each of Scherer's pieces is built over pedal notes which outline the principal harmonic relationships of its key. The fifth toccata in C Major has, for instance, successive pedals on C – F – D – G – E – A – F and C. While there is no doubt that the length of these compositions and the persistent use of this particular technique strain acceptance by modern ears, Scherer does deserve attention for the variety of material he introduces into the upper voices. The frequent changes of motivic material which produce this variety is another feature these pieces share with those of Frescobaldi. Perhaps the most interesting passages are those in which the composer simultaneously undertakes fugal and chromatic writing over the sustained bass. The dissonance level the ear must accept is unusual and in a musical style which otherwise is prevailingly bland:

16 Sebastian Anton Scherer, *Livre d'Orgue,* ed. Guilmant, Mainz: Schott's Söhne, reprint 1967.

Mus. ex. VII-13.
Toccata quarta, measures 43-45.[17]

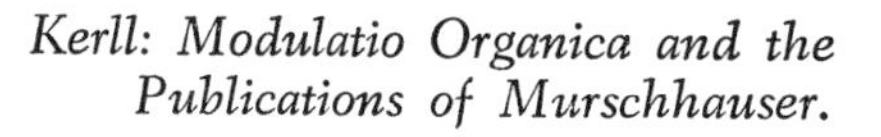

Kerll: Modulatio Organica and the Publications of Murschhauser.

There is considerable similarity between the *Modulatio Organica*[18] of Kerll and the *Octi-Tonium*[19] of Murschhauser. Both are made up of sets of very short pieces in each of the modes. Each set is made up of an opening prelude, a set of *fughette,* and a finale. Although Kerll indicates that his pieces are to serve as intonations for the *Magnificat,* Murschhauser does not. Both collections, however, must have been intended for that usage. These pieces reveal that in Germany as well as France the chant was given up as a basis for *Magnificat* versets, and that free pieces, which might also serve another function, were written instead. The Gregorian intonations occur only in Kerll's pieces in the opening verset of each set where the final notes of the chant are given a rather perfunctory organ setting:

---

[17] *Ibid.,* 71.

[18] Johann Kaspar Kerll, *Modulatio Organica,* ed. Walter, Altötting. Musikverlag Alfred Coppenrath, 1956.

[19] Franz Xaver Anton Murschhauser, *Octi-Tonium novum organicum,* ed. Walter, Altötting: Verlag Alfred Coppenrath, 1969.

Mus. ex. VII-14.
Versus primus, Sexti toni.[20]

There is no evidence of chant in the Murschhauser publication. The preludes in his collection and the finales in both collections are built on short figurative expositions of no outstanding merit. The *fughette* average about a dozen measures in length, but some are as short as five. Their subjects, which naturally receive only a single exposition, are similar to those of Froberger. One type of subject we have not yet mentioned, the repercussive type in which a single note is repeated as a head motive, occurs frequently in both collections:

Mus. ex. VII-15.
Kerll: *Versus secundus, tertii toni.*[21]

The organization of Murschhauser's *Prototypon Longo-Breve Organicum*[22] is similar to that of the two other publications. The compositions it contains, however, are longer and somewhat more complex. Several of the preludes are made up of block chordal progressions, suggestive of the opening of the French overture, most often given in dotted rhythm. The performer is instructed to arpeggiate the chords in performance. This and other evidence of facile keyboard embellishment suggest that the idiom of the harpsichord influenced the writing of many of these preludes. The fugues are often divided into two distinct sections forming in effect two *fughette*. Section B is often based on thematic transformation of the theme of Section A. Fugues in *gigue* style normally invert the sub-

---

20 Kerll, *op. cit.,* 21.

21 *Ibid.,* 11.

22 Murschhauser *Prototypon Longo-Breve Organicum,* ed. Walter, Altötting: Musikverlag Alfred Coppenrath, 1969.

ject in section B. In one fugue, the first one in the third tone,[23] Murschhauser maintained in section B precisely the same order of entrances and pitch levels thereof he had used in section A, even though the theme is subjected to a transformation in meter from $\frac{4}{4}$ to $\frac{6}{8}$ meter.

Poglietti: Praeludia, Cadenzen, und Fugen.

Poglietti, who in his harpsichord works is certainly a composer of consequence, does not surpass Kerll and Murschhauser in his one organ publication.[24] In this publication each mode is represented by a prelude (sometimes called a *toccatina*), a cadenza which is no more than a series of chords probably designed to be embellished in performance, and a *fughetta.* The music has no distinguishing features to separate it from the remainder of the repertory.

Poglietti, however, was also the composer of a set of twelve *ricercari,* which he appears never to have published.[25] These pieces were nonetheless copied repeatedly and appear to have served as instructional examples for the severe type of counterpoint described by Fux. The pieces are monothematic ones in which the subject is presented in two or more expositions, often with newly contrasting material. What is of interest from the technical point of view is that the themes, which on the surface do not appear to differ from the linearly conceived ones of the late sixteenth century, are actually treated more from a harmonic than a contrapuntal standpoint. The themes are constructed to suggest chordal movement, which is actually the motivating force for maintaining musical interest. For instance, the theme of number eight gives rise to such passages as the following, whose thrust is sheerly harmonic:

23 Murschhauser, *op. cit.,* 26.

24 Alessandro Poglietti, *Praeludia, Cadenzen und Fugen,* ed. Walter, Heidelburg: Süddeutscher Musikverlag, 1970.

25 Poglietti, *Zwölf Ricercare,* in *Die Orgel,* Reihe II, 5 and 6, ed. Riedel, Lippstadt: Kistner und Siegel, 1957.

Mus. ex. VII-16.
Poglietti: *Ricercar secundi toni,* measures 15-18.[26]

The outward appearance of these *ricercari,* which are similar to others by such composers as Pachelbel, is like those of the sixteenth century. Their content, however, is motivated by an entirely different force, that of mid-century tonal harmony. Before we leave these pieces, we should note that Bach may have derived the subject of the large E-flat fugue in the *Clavierübung* from the subject of number ten (*quinti toni*) of this set.

Speth: Ars Magna Consoni et Dissoni.

The works of Speth and Muffat are more important than those of the composers just discussed. Not only did Speth and Muffat work in more extended forms than the small verset, but their works have a stamp of individuality lacking in most works of their contemporaries. The ten toccatas which open the *Ars Consoni*[27] are some of the most extensive compositions of the South-German school. The majority consist of an introductory section in toccata style, a fugal section, and a final toccata. The format is often broadened to include transitional chordal passages. The multi-sectional format is given up in the fifth toccata, which is a cohesive example of the late Baroque prelude. After an introduction of five measures, a single motive is taken up and developed throughout the remainder of the piece. Speth's fine sense of harmonic movement directs the development of this motive into a composition of much longer duration than most preludes of this school.

There is evidence of North-German influence in the opening of *Toccata quarta,* particularly in its fully-voiced chords, halting rests, and use of echo. The beginning is given below:

---

26 Poglietti, *op. cit.,* 4.

27 Johann Speth, *Ars Magna Consoni et Dissoni,* ed. Fedtke, Kassel: Bärenreiter, 1973.

Mus. ex. VII-17.
Speth: *Toccata quarta,* measures 1-6.[28]

The serious quality of the Northern style is balanced by ample Italianate elements. The opening of *Toccata sexta,* for instance, is certainly influenced by the pastorale for keyboard instruments which we find occasionally in the harpsichord works of Frescobaldi and others. The pastoral key of F Major, the pedal point, and the two flute-like voices are certainly derived from this idiom:

Mus. ex. VII-18.
Toccata sexta, measures 1-3.[29]

The success of Speth's toccatas lies more in the composer's well-developed sense of the implications of tonal harmony than in any other one element. Not only does the composer facilely manipulate figurative motives within an harmonic framework, he uses harmonic passages for their own unique effects. A new harmonic element, one which became almost a trademark with the young Bach, is the use of the secondary dominant ninth chord with root omitted, the diminished seventh chord. In the following passage, suggestive of many similar ones in the works of Bach, this chord appears several times as a striking harmonic element:

---

28 Speth, *op. cit.,* 14.
29 *Ibid.,* 18.

Mus. ex. VII-19.
Toccata tertia, measures 31-38.[30]

Part II of the *Ars Consoni* is made up of a set of *Magnificat* settings similar in format to those of Kerll.[31] Each set consists of an opening prelude, five versets, and a finale. The style of the fugal versets is no more complex than others we have seen. Occasionally Speth provided versets which give up fugal style in favor of decidedly homophonic textures. The following example suggests that soprano-dominated melody supported by harmonic accompaniment was gradually replacing the contrapuntal orientation of late seventeenth-century music:

Mus. ex. VII-20.
Magnificat sexti toni, versus 5, measures 1-4.[32]

---

30 Speth, *op. cit.,* 13.

31 The *Magnificat* settings are also available in an edition edited by Klaus (Heidelberg: Süddeutscher Musikverlag, 1960).

32 Speth-Fedtke, *op. cit.,* 50.

The preludes and finales from these *Magnificats* add nothing new to our study. They are in many cases small gems of musical composition, very carefully crafted and stylistically perfect. The final section of the *Ars Consoni* is made up of variation sets without doubt designed for the harpsichord.

Muffat: Apparatus musico-organisticus.

The twelve toccatas which make up the bulk of Muffat's *Apparatus*[33] are the longest pieces in the South-German repertory. The seventh toccata reaches the surprising length of two hundred ten measures. These toccatas are reminiscent of those of Frescobaldi in that they are constructed of numerous sections of almost entirely unrelated material. Such an obvious technique as thematic variation, used so successfully by Froberger to integrate longer compositions, is not to be found here. If there is logic used to organize the whole, it is not apparent. Not only did Muffat draw upon every Italian and South-German style, he also included within his toccatas sections which are French in origin. Sections can be found in these toccatas in each of the following styles:

1) scale passages in one hand against static chords in the other, a derivation from the Italian toccata.
2) *canzone*-style *fughette.*
3) *ricercar*-style *fughette.*
4) *durezza*-style passages.
5) sections based on harmonic and sequential development of a single figurative motive.
6) sections in dance rhythms, particularly the gigue and sarabande.
7) sections in the style of the introductory section of a French overture, complete with dotted rhythm and *tirades.*
8) sections in arpeggiated figuration.
9) sections in the intimate style of the Elevation toccata.

The eclectic stylistic repertory upon which Muffat drew as well as his persistence in composing pieces of from five to seven major sections in length, produces in the end a potpourri effect. Muffat was no doubt imitating the rhapsodic style of Frescobaldi.

---

[33] Georg Muffat, *Apparatus musico-organisticus*, ed. Walter, Altötting: Musikverlag Alfred Coppenrath, 1957.

As a composer, Muffat lacked both the emotional intensity of his Italian predecessor or that composer's refined sense of propriety in the selection of musical material.

Perhaps the last half of *Toccata Septima* represents Muffat at his best. Beginning at measure eighty-eight and running to the conclusion of the piece there is a well-contrived fugal movement which transcends others in this tradition. Four well-defined themes appear in the course of the movement:

Mus. ex. VII-21.

Themes one and two are developed separately and then combined; themes three and four are then similarly presented. In the final section all four themes appear in what then turns out to be a quadruple fugue. Such an undertaking is to be found only this once in these toccatas, and, to the author's knowledge, nowhere else in the South-German literature of the century.

A *chaconne* and a *passacaglia* conclude the *Apparatus.* While the first of these pieces is perfunctory, the other is one of Muffat's most successful works. The composition decidedly reveals the French training which the composer apparently had under Lully. It also confirms that the *passacaglia,* as well as the *chaconne,* were not regarded by the French as exclusively ground bass forms. It is true that the initial ascending bass of this *passacaglia* is the subject of several later variations. However, other bass lines suggestive of other harmonic progressions are also introduced. Muffat's symmetrical presentation of the beginning eight measures as strophes six, twelve, eighteen, and twenty-four produces a rondo and not a ground bass form. The eight-measure structure of the dance provided Muffat a framework without the formlessness one often encounters in his toccatas in which his figurative imagination could function. This composition particularly deserves performance.

Fisher: Ariadne Musica.

Fisher's *Ariadne Musica* has been cited and discussed many times as Bach's model for his *Wohltempierte Klavier*. The ordering of preludes and fugues around a progression of keys, the labyrinth of music, as well as certain obvious thematic similarities between Fisher's work and that of Bach, make the connection unmistakable. In his use of keys, Fisher is not particularly remarkable; all keys he employed, save B major, were in use in South Germany in the late seventeenth century. Froberger's *ricercari* in F-sharp minor and C-sharp minor have already been mentioned. The full implication of the modern key system was missed by Fisher, in that he omitted examples in the major keys of F-sharp and C-sharp and in the minor ones of E-flat, B-flat, and G-sharp. The relatively conservative tonal basis of the collection is further confirmed by the existence of three preludes and fugues with a tonality on E, one major, one minor, and one Phrygian. The Phrygian fugue is based on the opening line of the chorale *Aus tiefer Not,* a fact that ties the *Ariadne* to organ performance. The frequent pedal points, impossible of being performed on stringed keyboard instruments, are further evidence that the collection is intended for the organ.

As we have seen, the pairing of a prelude and a fugue is actually rare before Fisher's work. Preludial and fugal sections were often intermixed in various patterns; they rarely stood as two distinct pieces related to one another primarily on the basis of key. This procedure, so readily accepted by Bach, was more closely related to eighteenth-century than to seventeenth-century practice. Fisher sometimes connects the prelude with its fugue in subtle ways. For instance the fugue on *Aus tiefer Not* is linked to its prelude by a common rhythm. A set of fugal entrances over a pedal point concludes the prelude in E-flat major. The theme of this set of entrances is related to the following fugue. Stylistically, Fisher's preludes and fugues are similar in scope and style to individual sections of Froberger's *canzoni, capricci,* and *ricercari.*

THE MIDDLE-GERMAN SCHOOL

The origins of the Middle-German tradition into which Bach was born and in which he grew up are obscured. This tradition produced no one important figure in organ composition until Pachelbel. There was no composer, such as Froberger in the South and Scheidemann and Tunder in the North, who earlier imprinted his stamp on the tradition. The school developed in a provincial atmosphere removed from large city churches with stable musical establishments and long histories of musical performance. It was a small court-and-town church environment which naturally cultivated the musical artisan more than it did the master musician. In contrast to the elaborate and meticulously prepared manuscripts of Froberger and the many carefully edited publications of other South-German composers, the Saxon-Thuringian musicians left scattered manuscript sources. Very few of these composers published any of their works, for they did not regard them as that important. The result is that, although we know many composers by name, we have only a relatively small amount of music.

This is not to imply that the musical culture was not rich. The craft of the cantor-organist was an honored one pursued diligently throughout Lutheran Germany. Middle Germany, from which Luther himself had come, practiced what her reformer had preached, that music was a valid expression of the Gospel, an art to be practiced for the glory of God. The Bach family was only one of several who practiced music from one generation to the next. Since music was seen to be a divine art, it is no accident that the Middle-Germans made the chorale central in their organ style. Middle-German music is essentially a synthesis of Italian and Southern techniques and the Lutheran hymn.

A craft-oriented tradition, which passes its techniques from parent to child, from master to apprentice, normally places a low premium on a high level of individual creation. So it was with Middle-German organ music. These composers took the methods passed on to them by their teachers, continued to practice their art competently on the basis of that instruction, and produced works of utility, simplicity, and native charm. It is no accident that when the young Bach returned home from his student days in Lüneburg, he found his newfangled North-German ideas hardly suited to the needs of townsfolk who were hardly attuned to such forceful virtuosity and invention. Small wonder that he spent his life misunderstood and largely a musical alien among his own kinsmen.

Earlier Composers of the School and Some Members of the Bach Family

The most important document of Middle-German music at mid-century is the *Harmonica organica* (1645) of the Nürnberg organist Eramus Kindermann (1616-1655).[34] Kindermann was the teacher of Georg Kaspar Wecker, who in turn was one of Pachelbel's teachers. The *Harmonica organica* opens with a set of fourteen preludes of intonation length and grouped in the order of the twelve church modes as defined by Glareanus. It is interesting that Kindermann solves the problem of authentic and plagal forms of modes in polyphonic music by simply allowing a single piece to serve for both forms. There are two sets of six preludes each; the second set merely transposes the six tonalities down a fifth. Preludes thirteen and fourteen, in modes eleven/twelve and seven/eight respectively, are transpositions up a major second. Kindermann's preludes are based upon chordal progressions modestly enlivened by short passages of keyboard figuration.

From the historical point of view, the ten fugues which follow are more interesting, for they affirm the importance of the chorale fugue in the early history of Middle-German music. The subjects of six of the ten are drawn from chorales. One of them, number sixteen, blends the opening lines of three Lenten chorales: *Christ lag in Todesbanden*, *Christus der uns selig macht*, and *Da Jesus an dem Kreuze stund*, into a fugal movement no more pretentious than the other modest pieces in this collection. The *Magnificat* setting which concludes the *Harmonica* is perhaps its best music. The opening verset is a short prelude and fugue based on the appropriate Gregorian intonation. Other versets are free fugues, simple *cantus firmus* settings, and for verse four an unusual example of an echo piece. Such a Northern intrusion into Southern practice is rare.

Very little music of this tradition exists in the period from about 1650 to 1680, and it is hence difficult to trace the development with any accuracy. Three available works of the Mülhausen organist Johann Rudolf Ahle, a chorale prelude, a set of chorale veriations,

[34] Erasmus Kindermann, *Harmonica organica*, ed. Walter, Altötting: Musikverlag Alfred Coppenrath, 1970.

and a toccata,[35] reveal a style which is often awkward and at times simply archaic. His music lacks the grace and polish typical of other works of the school. This lack is particularly noticeable in the composer's habit of skipping almost randomly from a passage in one style to one in another. The chorale prelude on *An Wasserflüssen Babylon,* a relatively short setting of only seventy-six measures, mixes in an almost haphazard fashion passages in fugal style, passages in *bicinium* style, and figurative passages built of motives similar to those used by Sweelinck. A similar arbitrary mixture occurs in the rhapsodic toccata, which lacks both the concise quality of South- and Middle-German music and the fire and intensity of Northern free compositions. On the other hand, the four variations on the chorale *Mensch, willst du leben seliglich* apply figurative technique with such mechanistic zeal that only boredom could possibly result:

Mus. ex. VII-22.
Ahle: *Mensch, willst du leben seliglich,* variation 2, measures 1-5.[36]

A set of eight fugues organized in the order of the church tones, as well as another based on the chorale *Dies' sind die Heiligen zehn Gebot',* by Wolfgang Carl Briegel (1626-1712) has been preserved.[37] It is difficult to differentiate Briegel's style from that of other contemporary composers. His subjects are traditional in both conception and treatment. He adheres to the lucid writing typical of fugal movements throughout the literature of this school. As a means to this end, there are many passages in these fugues in two-part counterpoint. Often the composer opens a fugue with a lengthy duo before the initial third voice entrance:

[35] The two chorale works are in: Gotthold Frotscher, *Orgelchoräle um Johann Sebastian Bach, Das Erbe deutscher Musik,* Reihe I, vol. 9, p. 3. The toccata is in: A. G. Ritter, *Zur Geschichte des Orgelspiels,* Leipzig: Max Hesse, 1884, appendix, number 117.

[36] Frotscher, *op. cit.,* 7.

[37] Wolfgang Carl Briegel, *Acht Fugen durch die Kirchentöne,* ed. Krumbach, *Die Orgel,* Reihe II, 19, Lippstadt: Kistner und Siegel, 1963.

Mus. ex. VII-23.
Briegel: *Fuga primi toni,* measures 1-8.

The few extant organ works by earlier members of the Bach family enable us to trace the development of at least one Thuringian musical clan. Two chorale preludes are extant from the pen of Johann Sebastian's great-uncle, Heinrich Bach (1615-1692).[38] Both are in a simple *ricercar* style devoid of any keyboard figuration. The setting of *Erbaum dich mein, o Herre Gott* treats the initial line of the chorale in a modest, yet beautiful way. The consistent use of the ascending chromatic passage

and the motive as counterpoints to the hymn melody is particular effective. Since many of the chorale settings of the Middle Germans were designed as preludes to the singing of the hymn, the chorale fugue is particularly common in the works of this school.

It is just this form that pervades the *44 Chorale zum Präambulieren* of Johann Christoph Bach (1642-1703), the older son of Heinrich Bach.[39] These short compositions, most of which are between twenty-five and thirty-five measures in length, are designed to fulfill this liturgical function. After an initial point of imitation

---

[38] Diethard Hellman (ed.), *Orgelwerke der Familie Bach,* Leipzig: Peters, 1967, 1.

[39] Johann Christoph Bach, *44 Choräle zum Praambulieren,* ed. Fischer, Kassel: Bärenreiter, n.d.

based on the opening line of the chorale, the composer concludes his brief piece by a pedal point above which simple figurative passages in consecutive thirds and sixths move. The counterpoint is characteristically note-against-note. In some of the settings citations of other lines of the chorale are interwoven.

The single prelude and fugue of Johann Christoph[40] is a piece of much greater length and more important musical content than are the chorales. The prelude contains several passages which shift tonality from the E-flat major home key to G major and back again, a shift unusual in a musical style normally lacking harmonic surprise. The fugue is based on the commonly used chromatic descent through the interval of a fourth. The *stretto* of this fugue with its resulting double chromaticism is also more complex than the tonal effects normally undertaken by Middle-German composers:

Mus. ex. VII-24.
Johann Christoph Bach, *Prelude and Fugue in E-flat Major,* measures 62-66.

Only a handful of chorale settings are extant from the pen of Johann Michael Bach (1648 - 1694), the younger brother of Johann Christoph and the father of Johann Sebastian's first wife, Maria Barbara. These are scattered throughout several modern publications.[41] Unlike his brother, Johann Michael preferred to set the entire chorale melody. The three variations on *Wenn wir in höchsten Nöten sein* employ an ornamented chorale for verse one, a simple trio with the *cantus firmus* in the inner voice for verse two, and a *bicinium* for verse three. The ornamented verse has the same unaffected, Italianate melodic quality of the lesser settings of Buxtehude.

40 *Harvard Anthology of Music* II, number 237. Also published in: Hellman, *op. cit.*, 7.

41 Two are in Frotscher, *op cit.*, 20; two in Hellman, *op. cit.*, 18; and three in Karl Geiringer, *Music of the Bach Family*, Cambridge: Harvard University Press, 1955, 56.

The *bicinium* also ornaments the *cantus firmus* by almost continuous sixteenth-note motion. The conclusion of the verse is given below:

Mus. ex. VII-25.

Of the published pieces by Johann Michael, the real jewel is his setting of *Wenn mein Stundlein vorhanden ist.* The *cantus firmus* is presented in its entirety both in the soprano and in the lowest sounding voice, which at times is the tenor and at other times the bass. Again we find the charm of this piece to be elusive, since the best examples of this literature never depend upon technical novelty or display, but upon a perfection of craftsmanship that only the music itself can authenticate. The genius lies in the selection of just the appropriate melodic turns, just the right suggestions of the chorale in the supporting voices, just the proper control of texture—in short, the complete mastery of a simple, yet effective, musical language.

A number of less important composers of Pachelbel's day deserve mention. Their works, while competently written, offer nothing that is unique in the history of this musical style. These are listed below along with some of the works which have come down to us:

George Caspar Wecker (1632 - 1695) — One fugue is available.[42]

Heinrich Michael Keller (1638 - 1710) — There is one large chorale setting of *Gelobet seist du* unique in that each line of the hymn is treated as a complete *fughetta.*[43]

Johann Friedrich Alberti (1642 - 1710) — Five chorale preludes are available.[44]

---

42 In Ritter, *op. cit.,* number 79.

43 Frotscher, *op. cit.,* 51.

44 Two in Frotscher, *op. cit.,* 11; one in Hermann Keller, *Eighty Chorale Preludes,* New York: Peters, 1957, number 40; and one in Karl Straube, *Choralvorspiele alter Meister,* New York: Peters, 1907, number 1.

Gottfried Pestel (1659 - 1732) – A set of twelve durezza style preludes is available.[45]

Christian Witt (c. 1660 - 1716) – Three fugues are available.[46]

Nicolaus Vetter (1666 - 1710) – Seven fugues and seven chorale preludes are available.[47]

Andreas Armsdorf (1670 - 1699) – Five chorale preludes are available.[48]

The Works of Pachelbel

The organ works of Johann Pachelbel (1653 - 1706) are not only the most voluminous of any composer of the Middle-German school, but also the most representative. The three volumes of *Denkmäler* publications done in the early years of this century[49] still constitute the most complete edition of the composer's works. Since that time there has been no effort to provide another complete edition of the organ works, although there are two editions of selected works readily available.[50] Together these two editions, along with one providing a selection of the composer's *Magnificat* fugues,[51] provide ample representation of the works contained in the older editions. The student should be cautioned that both the Matthaei and Fedtke editions are guilty of implying the use of *obbligato* pedal in situations where it was not called for by the composer. The use of the pedal in the entire repertory of Middle- and South-German music was largely at the discretion of the performer, and the situations in which pedal was mandatory were generally specified by the composer. Occasionally compositions of Pachelbel have appeared in other publications grouped into prelude and fugue combinations that imply an

---

45 In John R. Shannon, *Selected Compositions from the Mylau Tabulaturbuch, CEKM*, XXXIX.

46 *Ibid.*

47 The fugues are in Shannon, *Selected Compositions . . . Mylau;* the chorale preludes are in Frotscher, *op. cit.* (five) and in Keller, *op. cit.*, (two).

48 Four are in Frotscher, *op. cit.*; and one in Keller, *op. cit.*

49 *DTB*, volumes 2 and 4 and *DTO*, volume 17 (Jg. VIII/2).

50 Johann Pachelbel, *Ausgewählte Orgelwerke*, ed. Matthaei, Kassel: Bärenreiter, five volumes; and *Orgelwerke*, ed. Fedtke, Frankfort: Peters, 1972, four volumes.

51 Johann Pachelbel, *Magnificat Fugen*, ed. Hübsch, Heidelberg: Süddeutscher Musikverlag, 1954.

intent not actually the composer's. Pachelbel rarely paired preludes and fugues. His practice was to write individual preludes, toccatas, and fugues and to leave further grouping to the discretion of the performer. Pachelbel, like other Middle-German composers, never appeared to be attracted to the multi-sectional *canzone* which rapidly went out of fashion after Froberger. Individual free compositions of Pachelbel, however, almost always resemble movements from the larger formats of the Viennese composer's *canzoni, capricci,* and *ricercari.*

The Preludes, Fantasias and Toccatas

Three types of preludial pieces are to be found among the thirty or so compositions of this type in the composer's output: 1) a type in rhapsodic style similar to a single section in a Frescobaldi toccata and to the opening section of a Froberger *capriccio* or *canzone,* 2) the pedal point toccata, and 3) a new type which reflects late seventeenth-century ensemble instrumental practice and which is always designated by the composer as *fantasia.* The first of these three types is so obvious a borrowing from earlier composers' works as to be indistinguishable from them. The same melodic turns used by Frescobaldi and Froberger appear again and again in Pachelbel. The harmonic language derivative from the *durezza*-style prelude is another obviously borrowed element. Some of these preludes are no more than thinly ornamented *durezza* pieces. One device favored by Pachelbel, but obviously not exclusively his, is the use of a major triad directly followed by the minor triad on that same root. The following passage is illustrative:

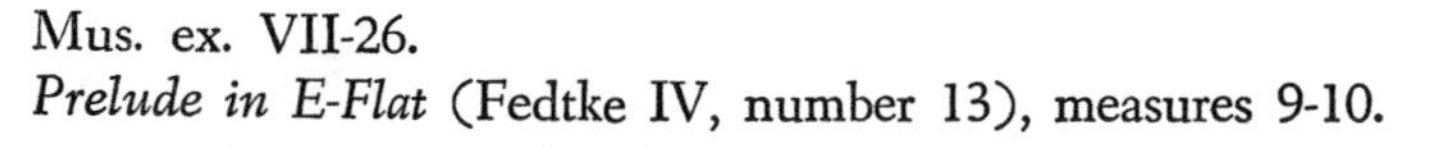

Mus. ex. VII-26.
Prelude in E-Flat (Fedtke IV, number 13), measures 9-10.

The pedal point toccatas are modeled after those of Scherer and others. The extensive length of such pieces is not to be found in

Pachelbel's examples, which remain within reasonable limits. His figurations above the pedal, however, are not original. He is particularly guilty of writing endless passages in which the two florid voices move in continuous thirds and sixths. A figuration which became almost a mannerism of Pachelbel, who used it not only here but also in his *chaconnes* and chorale variations, is one in which two voices together effect what is very close to a single line of sixteenth-note motion. One voice has a continuous line of eighth-notes; the other a series of alternate sixteenth-notes and sixteenth rests.

Mus. ex. VII-27.
Toccata in G Minor (Matthaei I, number 4), measures 9-10.

The Fedtke edition provides the three somewhat novel fantasias (IV, numbers 3, 10, and 26). The pieces are all in 3/2 meter and are basically conceived in a three-voice texture suggestive of the trio sonata:

Mus. ex. VII-28.
Fantasie in a (Fedtke IV, number 26), measures 1-5.

At times the musical ideas seem more native to a schematic for an orchestral score than they do to organ composition:

Mus. ex. VII-29.
Fantasie in c (Fedtke IV, number 3), measures 10-15.

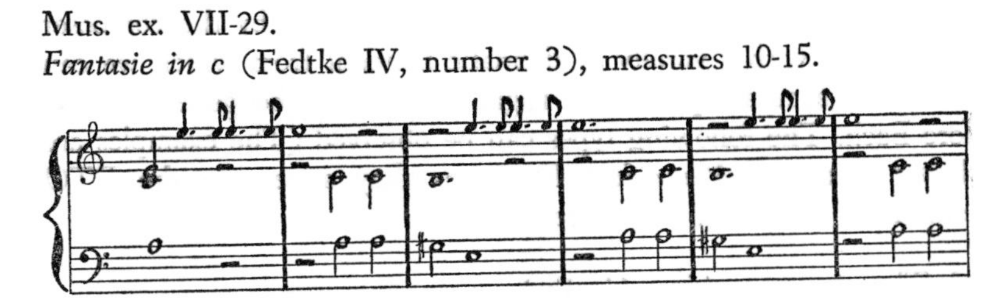

One curious composition in the Pachelbel repertory is the often reprinted *Praeambulum in d* (Matthaei I, number 1). This composition represents the composer's attempt to blend the Northern style *praeambulum* with the Southern style of pedal-point toccata. North-German stylistic traits are obvious in the cascading arpeggios and the Percussive chords, as well as in the two pedal solos. The Northern elements seem an inappropriate intrusion into the static style of the pedal-point toccata, yet the composition lacks the dynamic fire necessary to imitate a Northern toccata. Pachelbel never again appears to have attempted this hybridization; perhaps he sensed the incompatibility of its elements.

Fugues, Ricercari, and Fugues for the Magnificat

The ninety-four fugal movements designed for use in *Magnificat* alternation are similar in style to the other twenty-or-more fugal pieces of Pachelbel. Thus all can be treated simultaneously. A fugue in the composer's repertory is essentially in the same style as a single section of a Froberger *canzone* or *capriccio*. The fugues normally open with what appears to be a four-voice exposition. However, Pachelbel was not overly concerned with integrity of voices, and his normal procedure was to drop one voice before the fourth voice enters. The resulting three-voiced texture is characteristic of the majority of his fugal writing. Occasionally all four voices are present, but only for a measure or two at the conclusion of a composition. The continuous three-voiced texture is relieved by duo passages similar to those in Froberger's works. Most fugues are short; a composition of over fifty measures is rare. Although continuous presentation of the fugal subject is characteristic, Pachelbel made greater use of short bridge passages, which, as we have said, are the germ from which later fugal episodes developed. These bridges, however, are never complex or independent in Pachelbel's fugues.

The large number of fugal compositions left by the composer provides us with a variety of thematic material from which we can derive an accurate picture of fugal subjects in the generation before Bach. The following types can be observed (The examples are drawn from the *Magnificat Fugen* as they appear in the *DTO* edition to which the references refer.):

1) The *ricercar* subject (I. 15.).

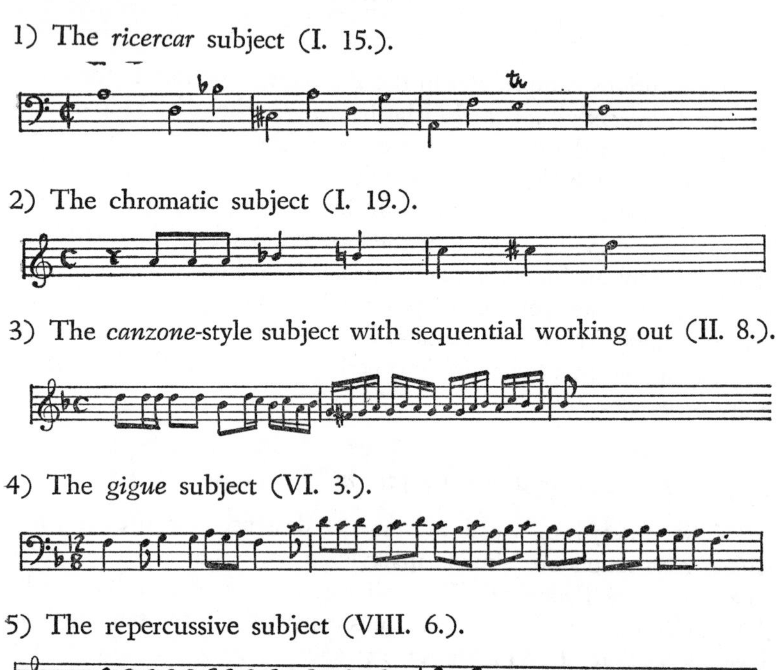

2) The chromatic subject (I. 19.).

3) The *canzone*-style subject with sequential working out (II. 8.).

4) The *gigue* subject (VI. 3.).

5) The repercussive subject (VIII. 6.).

6) The subject built on a specific harmonic movement such as root movements downward by perfect fifths (VIII. 8.).

7) The subject dependent upon a particular keyboard pattern such as a scale (VIII. 13.).

These types are not, of course, mutually independent of one another. A subject exploiting a particular keyboard figuration many times will follow a specific harmonic outline. *Ricercar* subjects are often chromatic, and *gigue* subjects are often repercussive. To a large degree Pachelbel's success in these many fugues lies in his capacity for inventing interesting and lively subjects. Although on the surface it appears the composer was no more individual in this matter than a host of his contemporaries, deeper study reveals that he had a gift for melodic nuance, clever figuration, and appropriate rhythmic balance which set his fugues decidedly apart from others about him.

There are a few fugal movements in Pachelbel's works, some of the *ricercari* and several of the *Magnificat* fugues, which are multi-sectional, double fugues. The opening section is always in rather severe *ricercar* style. The middle section is invariably based on a livelier theme which in the final section is used as a counterpoint to the initial subject. The procedure is borrowed directly from Froberger. One type of composition to be found in Pachelbel's works, the two-voice fugue (of which there are a number of examples in the *Magnificat* versets), does not occur in Froberger's works. Some of these contrast quarter- and half-note subjects with sixteenth-note counterpoint in the fashion of the Sweelinck and Scheidt *bicinia.* Other of the two-voice fugues are more modern in sound. Pachelbel was particularly skillful in suggesting specific harmonic progressions within this skeletal texture, a skill earlier composers had often lacked:

Mus. ex. VII-30.
Magnificat Fugue (II. 3.), measures 21-24.

The *Magnificat* fugues present several problems concerning liturgical practices of the late seventeenth century. There is no doubt that the haphazard order in which these ninety-four pieces are presented in the *Denkmäler* edition is not that intended by Pachelbel.

The mid-nineteenth-century publications of Franz Commer, upon which all subsequent publications of this body of music depend, reflected Pachelbel's intent, and neatly ordered the fugues into two sets of four pieces per mode. Modern editors subsequently grafted on to Commer's sixty-four pieces new *Magnificat* fugues as they were discovered. Thus Pachelbel's original organization was destroyed. Why the composer should have provided only four pieces in each mode when six are required for an *alternatim* performance of a *Magnificat* is not clear. We have already noted the same practice in North Germany. That Pachelbel was not writing merely random pieces casually grouped together for publication is confirmed by the thematic variation which binds many of the fugues together. The following relationships exist between the fugal subjects of pieces in the first mode:

Mus. ex. VII-31.

There are many other similar relationships which indicate that a group of pieces is designed to be played together.

The *Magnificat* fugues also suggest the problem presented by the reconciliation of the old modal system with the new tonality. A number of solutions were provided by composers of the seventeenth century to provide some variety of keys and still to mirror in some fashion the tonality of the psalm tones themselves. In the process the old Gregorian finals were often largely ignored. Pachelbel's original solution is given below:

Tone I — D minor, the conventional procedure.
Tone II — G minor. The intonation was probably also transposed from the C pitch level of the modern *Liber Usualis* to a G pitch level.
Tone III — C major concluding invariably on the dominant to accommodate the chant tones: g a c——a c a g.
Tone IV — A minor concluding invariably on the dominant in order to accommodate the chant: a g a b a——a g a b a f e.
Tone V — F major, the conventional procedure.
Tone VI — F major. (Apparently attempts were finally given up to differentiate between the fifth and sixth tones.)
Tone VII — C minor ending on the dominant. This solution appears unique with Pachelbel. Exactly how the e-natural of the chant tone (c b c d—f e d e) was reconciled with the e-flat of c minor is certainly unclear. Either another intonation was employed, the present one badly bent to make the accommodation, or a harsh musical result occurred.
Tone VIII — G major, the conventional procedure.

Finally we should point out that there appear to be few thematic relationships between Pachelbel's fugues and the intonations themselves. The only obvious use of chant occurs in the first two fugues in the third tone. Otherwise the fugue on a free subject has replaced the *cantus firmus*-based polyphony of earlier *Magnificat* cycles.

Works Based on the Chorale

Pachelbel left seventy-two chorale settings which were first published in the early years of this century in the *Denkmäler der Tonkunst in Bayern,* volume IV/1. All but five of these pieces are available to students in the performance editions of Matthaei (volumes II and III) and Fedtke (volume II). Six sets of chorale variations also exist published by Matthaei as volume IV. Recently another interesting manuscript has appeared containing eighty short chorale fugues each followed by a figured bass harmonization of its hymn melody. The majority of these pieces have been published by Fedtke as his volume I.

The seventy-two individual chorale preludes, which constitute the most important chorale works of Pachelbel, are cast in a very limited number of forms from which the composer rarely departs:

1) the chorale fugue based solely on the initial line of the chorale
2) the *tricinium* with chorale in the soprano for manuals alone
3) the *tricinium* with chorale in the bass (pedal)
4) a composite form in which a chorale fugue opens the composition. The second section is a *cantus firmus* setting with the chorale either in the soprano or bass.

There are also isolated examples of *bicinia* (*DTB* IV/1 numbers 26, 42, and 61), a single ornamented chorale (number 66) and three examples of another combination form which blends the point-of-imitation technique with the *cantus firmus* chorale.

The twelve chorale fugues are all short; none exceeds forty measures in length. Pachelbel makes no effort to ornament or otherwise obscure the basic notes of the chorale subjects. The stark presentation of the notes of the chorale forces these pieces into a serious, *ricercar* style characterized by prevailing quarter-note motion in all voices. Fugal technique is similar to that in the free fugues we have just discussed. The texture again is ostensibly for four voices, but until the concluding measures of a piece only three ever sound simultaneously.

The *tricinia* are all similar. The *cantus firmus* is set out in straight half-note motion against which continual sixteenth-note writing moves in the other voices. Most of this motion is based on the motive , the most pervasive figurative germ in late seventeenth-century keyboard music. Often this motive is used alternatively in the two embellishing voices:

Mus. ex. VII-32.
Wie schön leuchtet der Morgenstern (Matthaei III, number 26), measures 15-17.

Short pre-imitations occur normally at the beginning of the piece before the *cantus firmus* enters and less frequently before later lines of the chorale.

The combination of a fully developed chorale fugue and a completely worked out *cantus firmus* chorale seems to have been an invention of Pachelbel. Despite the fact that it does not occur earlier, it is a great favorite of the composer. He employs it in no less than twenty-five of these chorale preludes. Compositions which have the full chorale in the soprano tend to maintain the quarter-note motion of the chorale fugue throughout. Those which have pedal *canti firmi*, however, break into lively sixteenth-note motion and *tricinium* style when the pedal makes its entrance. Although it is typical for these sections to be in trio style, the left hand is often called upon to double the notes of the pedal *cantus firmus*. The reason for this is unclear. Perhaps the composer assumed his compositions might be played on manuals alone.

So consistently does the composer adhere to these few procedures that any departure from them is readily obvious. One of the *bicinia* (DTB IV/1, number 26) turns out to be a composition of Scheidemann. The archaic style of the other two suggests they too are spuriously attributed to Pachelbel. The only ornamented chorale, a setting of *Wir glauben all' an einen Gott* (Matthaei II, number 1), is rather unimaginatively carried out. The embellishment, which is made up of predominantly continuous sixteenth-notes, has none of the plasticity and individuality of the ornamented chorale in the North. Perhaps the composer realized his inability to deal with such a foreign idiom and chose to stay away from it. The two settings of *Allein zu dir, Herr Jesus Christ* (Matthaei II, numbers 4a and 4b) are among Pachelbel's most lovely pieces. They are no more than slightly elaborated four-voice harmonizations done with a taste for the simple and unaffected which constitutes Middle-German music at its best. The opening line of the second of these is given below:

Mus. ex. VII-33.
Allein zu dir (Matthaei III, 4a), measures 1-7.

No discussion of the chorale prelude is complete without approaching the subject of the relationship between music and the text of the hymn. The stylistic similarity of compositions on chorales of completely dissimilar textual content suggests that this problem was unimportant to Pachelbel. Two chorales as different as *An Wasserflüssen Babylon* (Fedtke II, 3) and *Herr Christ, der einig Gottes Sohn* (Matthaei II, 2) are, for example, musically very similar. There are, however, isolated examples of word painting in some of these compositions. The imitation of shepherd's pipes in the well-known trio on *Vom Himmel hoch* (Matthaei II, 5a) and the occasional use of chromatic writing in the fugal writing on more meditative chorales indicate the composer was aware of the potential of such devices. All in all, he seemed to be largely unconcerned with the matter.

The *Weimar Tabulaturbuch* (1704) contains one hundred sixty chorales, seventy-eight of which are provided with short fugues supposedly by Pachelbel. These *fughette* are all extremely short and consist of a single exposition in three voices of the opening line of the chorale. The compositions are even more diminutive than similar ones of Johann Christoph Bach, and why a composer of Pachelbel's stature should have compiled such a simplistic collection it is difficult to say. Such intonations he certainly could have improvised. The order of the chorales in this collection follows the Church year and bears a remarkable similarity to the order of Bach's original outline for the *Orgelbüchlein*.

Pachelbel has also left seven sets of chorale variations (Matthaei IV). There is certainly a question concerning the intent of these and similar Middle-German sets for organ performance. The fact that chorale melodies serve as the thematic material for this body of music is no reason to assume that it belongs primarily to the organ. A tradition of chamber performance of such variations at the harpsichord certainly existed. In any event there is no stylistic difference between Middle-German variations based on secular melodies and those based on chorales.

For these variation sets there were certain traditionally accepted procedures. The chorale was always initially set forth in a chordal harmonization. Thereafter variations were structured according to the following methods:

1) soprano elaboration of the melody in sixteenth-note motion over a quarter-note harmonization in the left hand.
2) sixteenth-note motion in the left hand with a quarter-note harmonization in the right hand.
3) arpeggiated variation of harmonic structure of the chorale.
4) motivic elaboration of the four-voice harmonic structure.
5) presentation of the chorale in the alto of a trio texture with the outer voices motivically organized.
6) a variation stressing chromatic harmony.
7) a variation based on triplet figurations.
8) a variation stressing thirty-second-note motion in one voice or another.

These procedures are so standardized that they are applied without concern for any textual implications a chorale might have. There is, for instance, little technical difference one can observe between the settings of *Herzlich tut mich verlangen* and *Was Gott tut, das ist wohlgetan.*

The Works of Zachow

The only other Middle-German composer of Pachelbel's generation who left a significant number of chorale settings was Friedrich Wilhelm Zachow, who, among his other accomplishments, was one of Handel's teachers. As one would expect, many of his fifty-three preserved chorales are so similar in style to those of Pachelbel as to be indistinguishable.[52] Twenty of these pieces are fugues on the initial line of the chorale and are in no way extraordinary. The chorale *Jesaja dem Propheten das geschah*[53] has the following structure: prelude — fugue — fugue. The prelude does not seem to be related to the chorale at all. To the author's knowledge no other examples of chorale fugues introduced by preludes exist in this literature, and how such a composition would have been used is unclear.

Four of Zachow's chorales[54] are in the form of the choral motet, a form not employed by Pachelbel or used regularly by other Middle-Germans. The chorale motet results when simple points of imitation, each based on a successive line of the chorale, follow one another. Zachow constructed the clearest and most uncomplicated imitations and concluded each of them with a full cadence. The result is a form in which the chorale is as obvious to the listener as it would be in a *cantus firmus* setting. A typical point of imitation is given below:

Mus. ex. VII-34.
Durch Adams Fall ist ganz verderbt, measures 1-6.[55]

Zachow also left eleven free compositions. The *Fantasia in D*[56] represents a late use of thematic variation. The piece is similar in style to a Froberger *ricercar.* Most of the other fugal movements are hardly unique. One type of prelude we have not yet encountered is made up solely of an extended progression of harmonies presented

[52] Friedrich Wilhelm Zachow, *Gesammelte Werke für Tasteninstrumente,* ed. Lohmann, Wiesbaden: Breitkopf und Härtel, 1966. This is an expanded version of *DDT* XXI-XXII, part iii.

[53] Zachow-Lohmann, *op. cit.,* number 23.

[54] *Ibid.,* numbers 1, 12, 32, 46.

[55] *Ibid.,* number 12.

[56] *Ibid.,* number 61.

throughout in some form of arpeggiated or broken chord figuration. The interest of these pieces must lie almost entirely in the strength and individuality of the harmonies. Unfortunately middle-Baroque harmony, with its limited sense of true modulation, restrained composers such as Zachow. The more developed harmonic language of the eighteenth century and a vastly more complex musical imagination make such pieces in the Bach repertory possible. Those of Zachow seem at best a bit naive.[57]

Buttstedt, Johann Krieger, and Kuhnau

Before we conclude our discussion, three composers deserve brief mention, although their respective works will not change the picture we have already painted. The handful of chorale preludes of Johann Heinrich Buttstedt (1666-1727), one of Pachelbel's many pupils, follow essentially the lines set by his teacher. *Tricinia* and short chorale fugues are the most common types. Buttstedt does show a greater interest in pictorial effects than do other composers of the school. For instance his setting of *Vom Himmel kam der Engle Schaar* opens with a downward passage obviously representative of the descent of the angels:[58]

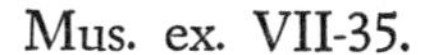
Mus. ex. VII-35.

Frotscher published six very simple chorale *fughette* by Johann Krieger (1652-1735).[59] They in no way differ from others we have seen. His nine free compositions published by Riedel[60] also offer little new. Two *ricercar*-style fugues (numbers 5a and 5b) are bound

[57] Zachow-Lohmann, *op. cit.*, numbers 56 and 57.

[58] Straube, *op. cit.*, number 11.

[59] Frotscher, *op. cit.*, p. 72 ff.

[60] Johann Krieger, *Praeludien und Fugen*, ed. Riedel, *Die Orgel*, Reihe II, number 3, Lippstadt: Kistner und Siegel, 1960.

together by subjects which are inversions of one another. Although its musical value is not great from the historical point of view, the most interesting piece in the collection is Number 8, entitled *Fantasia.* Here there are certain parallels to the late seventeenth-century *concerto grosso* in that the composer employed a *ritornello,* which occurs four times in the piece. Between these *ritornelli* there are episodic passages for two voices alone, passages which are similar to the episodes allotted to the concertino in the concerto. Krieger appears to have fashioned in this piece a modest but very early example of the concerto for organ. Were there other movements of this piece now lost?

Johann Kuhnau (1660-1722) is noted for his many harpsichord works of which the *Biblical Histories* are certainly the most famous. Three compositions edited by Seiffert are his only known organ works.[61] The two preludes and fugues are similar; both open with brief *durezza* passages and have equally brief *ricercar*-style fugues. The third composition, entitled *fantasia,* is another Middle-German attempt to imitate the North-German *praeambulum.* It has many of the clichés of the form: block chordal passages, dramatic unison scale passages, a pedal solo, sudden shifts of mode and movement, a straightforward fugal movement, and a final toccata section. The style was so alien to Kuhnau that his composition is no more successful than other similar attempts.

61 Johann Kuhnau, *Zwei Praeludien mit Fugen und eine Toccata,* ed. Seiffert, *Organum IV*, number 19, Lippstadt: Kistner und Siegel, n.d.

A Selected Bibliography of Editions
of
Seventeenth-Century Organ Literature

The following bibliography of editions of organ literature of the seventeenth century makes no effort to be complete. However, the acquisition of the scores listed here will provide the student with an excellent library of the literature. Absent from the bibliography are a number of anthologies generally well-known to organists. Also absent are certain editions which, because of poor editorial procedures, distort composers' intentions beyond acceptable limits. If multiple editions of the same material are available and one among them seems superior to the others it appears listed with an asterisk (*).

ITALY

Fasola, Giovanni Battista, *Annuale,* ed. Walter. Heidelberg: Süddeutscher Musikverlag, 1965.

The *Annuale* (Venice 1645) contains versets, *ricercari, canzoni,* and fugues.

Frescobaldi, Girolamo. *Orgel und Klavier Werke,* ed. Pidoux, 5 vols. Kassel: Bärenreiter, 1963-1970.

———. *Keyboard Compositions Preserved in Manuscripts,* ed. Shindle, 3 vols., *CEKM* 30.

Jackson, Roland. *Neopolitan Keyboard Compositions (ca. 1600), CEKM* 24.

Mayone, Ascanio, *Secondo Libro di Diversi Capricci,* ed. Kastner, *Orgue et Liturgie* 63 and 65. Paris: Schola Cantorum, 1965.

Pasquini, Ercole. *Collected Keyboard Works,* ed. Shindle, *CEKM* 12.

Pasquini, Bernardo. *Collected Works for Keyboard,* ed. Hayes, 7 vols., *CEKM* 5.

Rossi, Michelangelo. *Works for Keyboard,* ed. White, *CEKM* 15.

Salvatore, Giovanni. *Collected Keyboard Works,* ed. Hudson, *CEKM* 3.

Schierning, Lydia (ed.). *Italienische und süddeutsche Orgelstücke des frühen 17. Jahrhunderts, Die Orgel* II, 9. Lippstadt: Kistner und Siegel.

This publication contains works of Tarquinio Merula and Christian Erbach.

Strozzi, Gregorio. *Capricci da Sonare Cembali et Organi*, ed. Hudson, *CEKM* 11.

Trabaci, Giovanni, *Composizioni per Organo e Cembalo,* ed. Mischiati, *Monumenti de Musica Italiana.* Brescia: Paideia, 1964 and 1969.

Fascicle I: 12 Ricercate dal Libro I, 1603.

Fascicle II: 7 Canzoni francesi, 2 Capricci, 4 Canti Fermi dal Libro I, 1603.

———. *Ricercate* (Il secondo libro), ed. Bonfils, *L'Organiste Liturgique* 54 and 57, Paris: Schola Cantorum.

FRANCE

A basic source for organ music of seventeenth-century France remains *Les Archives des maîtres de l'orgues des XVIe et XVIIe, et XVIIIe siècles,* ed. Guilmant and Pirro, Paris: Durand, 1898-1910. The publication is now available in a reprint (New York: Johnson Reprint Corporation). Various sections are also available in offprint editions (Mainz: Schotts Söhne). The collection is referred to below as simply *Archives.*

Anonymous, *Le Livre d'Orgue de Marguerite Thiéry,* ed. Bonfils, *L'Organiste Liturgique* 25. Paris: Schola Cantorum.

The collection is made up of short settings of the mass, the Magnificat, hymns, and the Te Deum.

Bonfils, Jean, (ed.). *Les Pré-Classiques Français, L'Organiste Liturgique* 18. Paris: Schola Cantorum, 1957.

The majority of the works in this volume are for the harpsichord. Some pieces by Richard and some anonymous chant settings are for the organ.

Boyvin, Jacques. *Premier Livre d'Orgue,* ed. Bonfils. Paris: Les Editions Ouvrières, 1969.

———, *Oeuvres Complètes d'Orgue, Archives* 3.

Chaumont, Lambert, *Pieces d'Orgue sur les huit Tons,* ed. Ferrard. Paris: Heugel, 1970.

Clérambault, Louis Nicolas. *Livre d'Orgue,* ed. Dufourcq. Paris: Schola Cantorum, 1954.

The registrational directions given in this edition are misleading.

———. *Livre d'Orgue, Archives* 3. Available in offprint.

Corrette, Gaspard. *Messe du 8e Ton,* ed. Dufourcq, *Orgue et Liturgie* 50 and 51.

Couperin, François. *Pièces d'Orgue,* ed. Brunold. Monaco: Editions de l'Oiseau-Lyre, 1952.*

_______. *Pièces d'Orgue, Archives* 5. Available in offprint.

Couperin, Louis. *L'Oeuvre d'Orgue,* ed. Dufourcq. Paris: Schola Cantorum, 1954.
The title is misleading. Most of the works contained here are for harpsichord. Only the *Fantasie* (number 15), the *Duo* (number 16), and *Carillon* (number 18) are intended for the organ.

Du Mage, Pierre, *Livre d'Orgue, Archives* 3. Available in offprint.

_______. *Livre D'Orgue,* ed. Raugel. Paris: Schola Cantorum, 1952.
The registrational directions given in this edition are misleading.

De Grigny, Nicolas. *Livre d'Orgue, Archives* 5. Available in offprint.

_______. *Premier Livre d'Orgue,* ed. Dufourcq. Paris: Schola Cantorum, 1953.

Dumont, Henri. *L'Oeuvre pour Clavier,* ed. Bonfils, *L'Organiste Liturgique* 13. Paris: Schola Cantorum, 1956.

Gigault, Nicolas. *Livre de Musique pour l'Orgue, Archives* 4.

Guilain, Jean Adam. *Pièces d'Orgue pour le Magnificat, Archives* 7. Available in offprint.

Howell, Almonte (ed.). *Five French Baroque Masses.* Lexington: University of Kentucky Press, 1961.

Jullien, Gilles. *Premier Livre d'Orgue,* ed. Dufourcq. Paris: Heugel, 1952.

Lebègue, Nicolas. *Oeuvres Complètes d'Orgue, Archives* 9.

_______. *Noëls Variés,* ed. Dufourcq. Paris: Schola Cantorum, 1952.

Marchand, Louis. *Pièces Choisies pour l'Orgue, Archives* 3 and 5. Available in offprint.

Nivers, Guillaume Gabriel. *Deuxième Livre d'Orgue,* ed. Garros, Paris: Schola Cantorum, 1956.

_______. *Livre d'Orgue Contenant la Messe et les Hymnes de l'Eglise,* ed. Dufourcq. Paris: Schola Cantorum, 1956.
The registrational directions given in this edition are misleading.

_______. *Premier Livre d'Orgue Contenant Cent Pièces de Tous les Tons de l'Eglise* (1665), ed. Dufourcq, 2 vols. Paris: Editions Bornemann, 1963.

Racquet, Charles. *Oeuvres Complètes,* ed. Bonfils, *L'Organiste Liturgique* 29-30. Paris: Schola Cantorum.
The volume contains works by other composers. Only Racquet's fantasia is an organ composition.

Raison, André. *Livre d'Orgue,* Archives 2.
———. *Premier Livre d'Orgue,* ed. Dufourcq, *Orgue et Liturgie* 55, 56, 58, 59, 61. Paris: Schola Cantorum.
This volume contains the organ masses.
———. *Second Livre d'Orgue,* ed. Bonfils, *L'Organiste Liturgique* 39-40, 43-44. Paris: Schola Cantorum.
The majority of the volume consists of the noëls.
Richard, Etienne. See Bonfils: *Les Pré-Classiques* above.
Robertday, François. *Fugues et Caprices,* ed. Ferrand. Paris: Heugel, 1972.*
———. *Fugues et Caprices, Archives* 3.
Titelouze, Jean, *Oeuvres Complètes d'Orgue, Archives* 1. Available in offprint.

ENGLAND

Blow, John. *Thirty Voluntaries and Verses for the Organ.* ed. Shaw, London: Schott, 1972.
Bull, John. *Keyboard Music I,* ed. Steel and Cameron, *Musica Britannica* 14. London: Stainer and Bell, 1960.
Gibbons, Christopher. *Keyboard Compositions,* ed. Rayner. *CEKM* 18.
Gibbons, Orlando. *Keyboard Music,* ed. Hendrie, *Musica Britannica* 20. London: Stainer and Bell, 1962.
Locke, Matthew. *Organ Voluntaries,* ed. Dart. London: Stainer and Bell, 1968.
Lugge, John. *Three Voluntaries for Double Organ,* ed. Jeans and Steele. London: Novello, 1956.
Purcell, Henry. *The Organ Works,* ed. McLean. London: Novello, 1967.
Tomkins, Thomas. *Keyboard Music,* ed. Tuttle, *Musica Britannica* 5. London: Stainer and Bell, 1955.
An offprint of nine pieces from this edition is also available from the same publisher.

SPAIN AND PORTUGAL

Angles, Higinio, *Antologia de organistas españoles del siglo XVII,* 4 vols. Barcelona: Diputacion Provincial de Barcelona, 1968.
These volumes constitute the best available anthology of Spanish organ music of the century.
Apel, Willi (ed.), *Spanish Organ Masters after Antonio de Cabezon, CEKM* 14.
Among the contents of this volume are the complete organ works of Aguilera.

Cabanilles, Joannis. *Musica Organici,* 4 vols. ed. Angles. Barcelona: Biblioteca Central, 1927 to 1956.
The published volumes represent only a small part of Cabanilles' organ works.

Coelho, Manuel Rodrigues. *Flores de Musica,* 2 vols., ed. Kastner, *Portugaliae Musica.* Lisbon: Fundacao Calouste Gulbenkian, 1959.

Correa, Francisco de Arauxo, *Libro de Tientos y Discursos de Musica,* 2 vols., ed. Kastner, *Monumentos de la Musica Española.* Barcelona; 1948.

Jimenez, José. *Collected Works for Organ,* ed. Apel, *CEKM* 31.

Pedrell, Felipe. *Antologia de organistas clasicos españoles,* 2 vols., Madrid: 1908, Reprint: New York: Associated Music Publishers, 1968.

THE NETHERLANDS

Cornet, Pieter. *Collected Keyboard Works,* ed. Apel, *CEKM* 24.

Speuy, Henderick, *Psalm Tunes,* ed. Noske. Amsterdam: Heuwekemeijer, 1962.

Sweelinck, Jan Pieterszoon. *Choralbearbeitungen,* ed. Moser and Fedtke. Kassel: Bärenreiter, 1956.
The volume contains selected chorale settings. Some are incomplete and others are unlikely to be by Sweelinck. The edition suffers from an inconsistently applied policy of note value reductions which distorts the intent of the composer.

———.*Opera Omnia,* vol. I, Fascicle 1; *Fantasias and Toccatas,* ed. Leonhardt; vol. I, Fascicle 2; *Settings of Sacred Melodies,* ed. Annegarn. Amsterdam: 1968.*

———. *Werken voor Orgel en Clavicimbel,* ed. Seiffert, *Werken van Jan Pieterszoon Sweelinck* 1. Second edition, Amsterdam: G. Alsbach, 1943.
The edition contains a number of compositions of doubtful authenticity. However, it remains an excellent edition.

Van Noordt, Anthoni, *Tabulatuur-Boeck van Psalmen en Fantasyen,* ed. Seiffert, Amsterdam: Alsbach, 1957.

NORTH GERMANY

Böhm, Georg, *Samtliche Werke,* 2 vols., ed. Wolgast. Wiesbaden: Breitkopf und Härtel.

———. *Fünf Praeludien, Fugen, und Toccaten,* ed. Seiffert, *Organum* IV, 4. Leipzig: Kistner und Siegel.

Bruhn, Nicolaus. *Drei Praeludien und Fugen*, ed. Seiffert, *Organum* IV, 8. Leipzig: Kistner und Siegel, 1925.

———. *Orgelwerke*, ed. Stein. Frankfurt: C. F. Peters, 1939.

———. *Sämtliche Orgelwerke*, ed. Beckmann. Wiesbaden: Breitkopf und Härtel, 1972.*

Buxtehude, Dietrich. *Orgelwerke*, 4 vols., ed. Spitta, revised Seiffert. Leipzig: Breitkopt und Härtel, 1939.

———. *Sämtliche Orgelwerke*, 4 vols., ed. Beckmann. Wiesbaden: Breitkopf und Härtel, 1972.

———. *Sämtliche Orgelwerke*, 4 vols., ed. Hedar. Copenhagen: Hansen, 1952.

Each of these editions is very valuable. The Spitta-Seiffert represents the highest standard of scholarship for its day. The Hedar editions used in conjunction with the editor's study of Buxtehude is excellent in establishing a reliable text, a difficult problem in the study of this composer.

Golos, George and Adam Sutkowski, editors. *Organ Music from Polish Manuscripts, CEKM* 10.

I: *Organ Chorales of Peter Hasse*

II: *Organ Chorales of Heinrich Scheidemann and Franz Tunder*

Lübeck, Vincent. *Orgelwerke*, ed. Keller. New York: C. F. Peters, 1940.

———. *Sämtliche Orgelwerke*, ed. Beckman. Wiesbaden: Breitkopf und Härtel, 1973.*

———. *Vier Praeludien und Fugen*, ed. Seiffert, *Organum* IV, 9. Leipzig: Kistner und Siegel, 1925.

Moser, Hans Joachim and Traugott Fedtke. *Allein Gott in der Höh' sei Ehr*. Kassel. Bärenreiter, 1953.

The volume contains twenty variations on this one chorale by various German pupils of Sweelinck. The edition, while very valuable, suffers from an unfortunate editorial policy in regard to note value reductions, pedal disposition and the like.

———. *Choralbearbeitungen und frei Orgelstücke der deutschen Sweelinck-Schule*. Kassel: Bärenreiter, 1955.

The volume has the same faults as that listed directly above.

Praetorius, Jacob. *Choralbearbeitungen*, ed. Brieg. Kassel: Bärenreiter, 1974.

Reimann, Margarete (ed.). *Lüneburger Orgeltabulatur K.N. 208a, Das Erbe deutscher Musik* 36. Frankfurt: Henry Litolff Verlag, 1957.

A number of passages, allotted in this edition to the pedal, are obviously for the manuals.

Reincken, Adam. *Collected Keyboard Works*, ed. Apel, *CEKM* 16.
________. See also Seiffert, *Organum* IV, 5 below.
Scheidemann, Heinrich. *Fünfzehn Praeludien und Fugen*, ed. Seiffert, *Organum* IV, 1. Leipzig: Kistner und Siegel.
________. *Orgelwerke*, 3 vols., ed. Brieg and Fock, I: Choralbearbeitungen, II: Magnificatbearbeitungen, III: Freikompositionen. Kassel: Bärenreiter, 1967-1971.
________. See also Golos, *CEKM* 10, above.
Seiffert, Max (ed.). *Anonymi der Norddeutschen Schule, Organum* IV, 10. Leipzig: Kistner und Siegel.
________. *Orgelmeister, Organum* IV 2, 5, 7, 21. Leipzig: Kistner und Siegel.
I: J. Praetorius, Schildt, Decker, Olter, and Flor
II: Reincken, Ritter
III: Bruckhorst, Kneller, Leyding
IV: Scheidt, Düben, Aebel, Hasse, Karges
Shannon, John R. (ed.). *The Free Organ Compositions in the Lüneburg Organ Tablatures*, 2 vols. St. Louis: Concordia 1958.
A collection of previously unpublished free compositions from these manuscripts. Most of the compositions are anonymous.
Strunck, Delphin. *Zwei Choralfantasien*, ed. Krumbach, *Die Orgel* II, 12. Leipzig: Kistner und Siegel.
Strunck, Delphin and Peter Mohrhardt. *Keyboard Music*, ed. Apel. *CEKM* 23.
Tunder, Franz. *Sämtliche Choralbearbeitungen*, ed. Walter. Mainz: Schotts Söhne, 1956.
________. *Sämtliche Orgelwerke*, ed. Beckmann. Wiesbaden: Breitkopf und Härtel, 1974.*
________. *Vier Praeludien*, ed. Seiffert, *Organum* IV, 6. Leipzig: Kistner und Siegel.
________. See Golos, *CEKM* 10, above.
Weckman, Matthias. *Gesammelte Werke*, ed. Ilgner, *Das Erbe deutscher Musik*, Zweite Reihe, 4. Leipzig: Henry Litolff, 1942.
________. *Vierzehn Praeludien, Fugen, und Toccaten*, ed. Seiffert, *Organum* IV, 3. Leipzig: Kistner und Siegel.

SOUTH GERMANY

Froberger, Johann Jakob. *Ausgewählte Orgelwerke*, ed. Matthaei. Kassel: Bärenreiter, 1965.
The volume contains selected fantasias and *ricercari*.
________. *Orgel und Klavierwerke*, ed. Adler, *DTO* 8 and 21. Reprint: Granz: Akademische Druck und Verlagsanstalt, 1959.*

Froberger. *Toccaten, Fantasien, Ricercari, Canzonen und Capricci*, ed. Walter. Altötting: Coppenrath, 1967.

———. *Zehn Orgelwerke*, ed. Seiffert, *Organum* IV, 11. Leipzig: Kistner und Siegel, 1929.

Kerll, Johann Kaspar. *Modulatio Organica*, ed. Walter. Altötting: Coppenrath, 1956.

Kindermann, Erasmus. *Harmonica Organica*, ed. Walter. Altötting: Coppenrath, 1970.

Muffat, Georg. *Apparatus Musico Organisticus*, ed. Walter. Altötting: Coppenrath, 1957.

Murschhauser, Franz Xaver. *Octi-Tonium Novum Organicum*, ed. Walter. Altötting: Coppenrath, 1969.

———. *Prototypen Longo-Breve Organicum*, ed. Walter. Altötting: Coppenrath, 1969.

Poglietti, Allessandro. *Praeludia, Cadenzen und Fugen*, ed. Walter. Heidelberg: Süddeutscher Musikverlag, 1970.

———. *Zwölf Ricercare*, ed. Riedel, *Die Orgel* 5 and 6. Leipzig: Kistner und Siegel, 1957.

Scherer, Sebastian Anton. *Livre d'Orgue*, ed. Guilmant, *Archives* 8. Also available in an offprint.
The volume contains both sections of the *Tabulatura in Cymbalo et Organo*, 1664.

Speth, Johann. *Ars Conzoni et Dissoni*, ed. Fedtke. Kassel: Bärenreiter, 1973.

———. *Magnificaten* (from the *Ars Conzoni*), ed. Klaus. Heidelberg: Süddeutscher Musikverlag, 1960.

MIDDLE GERMANY

Bach, Johann Christoph. *44 Choräle zum Präambulieren*, ed. Fischer. Kassel: Bärenreiter.

Briegel, Wolfgang Carl. *Acht Fugen durch die Kirchentöne*, ed. Krumbach, *Die Orgel* II, 19. Leipzig: Kistner und Siegel, 1963.

Frotscher, Gotthold. *Orgelchoräle um J. S. Bach, Das Erbe deutscher Musik*, Reihe I, 9.
An excellent collection of middle-German chorale settings. Many of the pieces, however, date from the 18th century.

Geiringer, Karl. *Music of the Bach Family*. Cambridge: Harvard University Press, 1955.

Hellman, Diethard (ed.). *Orgelwerke der Familie Bach*, Leipzig: Peters, 1967.

Krieger, Johann. *Praeludien und Fugen*, ed. Riedel, *Die Orgel* II, 3. Leipzig: Kistner und Siegel.

Kuhnau, Johann. *Zwei Praeludien mit Fugen und eine Toccata*, ed. Seiffert, *Organum* IV, 19. Leipzig: Kistner und Siegel.

Pachelbel, Johann. *Ausgewählte Orgelwerke,* ed. Matthaei, 5 vols. Kassel: Bärenreiter.
The edition suffers from overediting.
———. *Ciaconen, Fugen, und Ricercari,* ed. Seiffert, *Organum* IV, 14. Leipzig: Kistner und Siegel, 1929.
———. *Fugen über das Magnificat,* ed. Botstiber and Seiffert, *DTO* 17. Reprint Graz: Akademische Druck und Verlaganstalt, 1959.*
———. *Magnificat Fugen,* ed. Hübsch. Heidelberg: Süddeutscher Musikverlag, 1954.
———. *Magnificat Fugen,* ed. Seiffert, *Organum* IV, 14. Leipzig: Kistner und Siegel, 1929.
———. *Orgel und Klavierwerke,* ed. Seiffert, *DDB* 2 and 4 (1901 and 1903). Leipzig: Breitkopf und Härtel.*
———. *Orgelwerke,* ed. Fedtke, 4 vols. Frankfurt: Peters, 1972.
———. *Praeludien, Fantasien und Toccaten,* ed. Seiffert, *Organum* IV, 12. Leipzig: Kistner und Siegel, 1929.
Scheidt, Samuel. *Ausgewählte Werke,* ed. Keller. Leipzig: Peters, 1939.
This edition is somewhat unreliable. Many compositions are shortened by omission and rearrangement of variations.
———. *Görlitz Tabulaturbuch vom Jahre 1650,* ed. Mahrenholz. Leipzig: Peters, 1941.
———. *Tabulatura Nova,* ed. Seiffert, *DDT* 1.
———. *Werke,* ed. Mahrenholz, I: *Tabulaturbuch vom Jahre 1650,* VI: *Tabulatura Nova,* Teil I und II, VII: *Tabulatura Nova,* Teil III. Hamburg: Ugrino Verlag, 1953 and 1964.
Shannon, John R. *Selected Compositions from the Mylau Tabulaturbuch, CEKM* 39 (Forthcoming 1977.)
A collection made up almost entirely of free compositions of middle German composers of the late 17th century.
Zachow, Friedrich Wilhelm. *Drei Fugen für Orgel,* ed. Seiffert, *Organum* IV, 16. Leipzig: Kistner und Siegel, 1930.
———. *Gesammelte Werke für Tasteninstrumente,* ed. Lohmann, Wiesbaden: Breitkopf und Härtel, 1966.
An expanded version of *DDT* 21 and 22, part 3.

Glossary

ALTERNATION, also ALTERNATIM. In masses, canticles and hymns the practice of substituting music for the organ for normally sung sections. The term derives from the procedure of alternating a sung verset and an organ verset.

BASSE DE TROMPETTE and *BASSE DE CROMORNE*. See *RECIT*.

BATALLA. A Spanish *tiento* programatically depicting a battle.

BICINIUM. A two-voice composition, a duo. The term is used almost exclusively in Dutch and North-German practice. Often one voice of a *bicinium* carries a chorale melody in *cantus pianus* fashion.

CANTUS FIRMUS FORMS. Forms based on pre-existing melodies such as the organ hymn and the organ chorale.

CANTUS PLANUS. A *cantus firmus* in unchanging, long-note values.

CANZONE (plural *CANZONI*) or *CANZONA* (plural *CANZONE*). A form of seventeenth-century instrumental composition stylistically derived from the sixteenth-century French *chanson*. Although the term could refer to a transciption of a given *chanson*, its later use almost exclusively refers to an original composition in this lighthearted style. A multi-sectional structure integrated by the process of thematic variation was typical of the form.

CAPRICCIO. The term is generally applied in the seventeenth century to fugal compositions which evidence a greater freedom in matters of style than do the *ricercar* or *canzone*. Froberger's use of the term, however, cannot be distinguished from his use of *canzone*.

CHORALE FANTASIA. The extensive treatment of chorales characteristic of North-German composers. Such compositions are free mixtures of the following techniques: *cantus firmus* settings, ornamented chorale, variation technique, echo, and the chorale motet.

CHORALE FUGUE. A fugal movement based on the initial line of a chorale.

CHORALE MOTET. A setting of a chorale so fashioned that each line of the hymn serves as a theme for a point of imitation. There will be as many points of imitation as there are lines of the hymn. This technique is often used simultaneously with the complete *cantus firmus* in another of the voices.

DIALOGUE. A solo composition in the French repertory exploiting alternately the soprano and bass registers of a single stop or the alternation of two contrasting registers, one in the soprano and the other in the bass.

DIFERENCIA. The Spanish term for variations.

DIMINUTION. The sixteenth-century term refering to a variation process in which a basic melodic fragment is ornamented by the addition of stock figurative patterns.

DISCURSO. A term used by Correa for a *tiento* of more than the usual technical complexity.

DUREZZA. See *TOCCATA DI DUREZZA.*

ECHO FANTASIA also FANTASIA IN ECHO. A composition, associated primarily with the name of Sweelinck, which employs echo devices extensively. The majority of these compositions open in *ricercar*-style before breaking into toccata writing in which echo is predominant.

FANTASIA also FANCY. As the name obviously indicates, a composition free of traditional restraints. In the seventeenth century the term is applied to pieces which may be in toccata style, *ricercar* style, *canzone* style or any combination of these. The term is even applied to certain *cantus firmus* compositions. Any attempt to limit the term more closely is doomed to failure.

FANTASIA FOR DOUBLE ORGAN. An English composition similar in style to the French *récit.* The designation "double organ" (*i.e.* organ with two manuals) refers to the allocation of the solo line to one manual and the accompanimental voices to the other.

FREE COMPOSITION. One which is uninhibited by *cantus firmus,* dance patterns, variation procedures, or other pre-existing musical structures. Under the term fall both fugal compositions and those of the toccata-prelude type.

FUGUE GRAVE. A Franch fugal movement stylistically similar to the *ricercar.*

FUGUE DE MOVEMENT. A French fugal movement stylistically similar to the *canzone.* It is, however, never in multiple sections.

GLOSA. The Spanish term for diminution. It often occurs as the designation for a set of variations.

GRAND JEU. The most flamboyant and extensive type of composition in the seventeenth-century French repertory. It is designed for performance on the ensemble registers of the same name.

HEXACHORD FANTASIA. A composition, generally in *ricercar* and/or variation style based on the six-note scalewise theme of the hexachord. The theme was often used both in ascending and descending motion, and often in the seventeenth century chromatic tones were interpolated within it.

IN NOMINE. Compositions based on the most common English *cantus firmus* of the period.

INTONATION also *INTONAZIONE.* A short toccata designed to provide a choir with its pitch.

MEDIO REGISTRA. Spanish for divided registers. Such compositions were similar in organization to the French *dialogues.*

NOEL. An organ setting of a popular French Christmas song. Most *noëls* are in variation form.

NOTATION. Several types of notation for keyboard music were in use in the late sixteenth and seventeenth centuries. Staff notation was the typical practice in England, France, and South Germany, although there was little standardization in the use of clefs and even in the number of staff lines. The Italians preferred open score (*partitura*) in which each contrapuntal voice was allotted its own staff. The North Germans normally employed a notation known as new German keyboard tablature. In this system a letter notation denotes pitch and a set of vertical and horizontal lines denotes rhythmic values. For a thorough discussion of keyboard notations see: Willi Apel, *The Notation of Polyphonic Music,* Cambridge: The Mediaeval Academy of America, 1953, part I.

OBBLIGATO PEDAL. A voice written for the pedals which cannot be omitted.

OBRA. An alternate name for the Spanish *tiento.*

OFFERTOIRE. A large-scale *grand jeu* designed for performance at that point in the liturgy.

OFFERTORY. A voluntary designed for performance at that point in the liturgy.

ORNAMENTED CHORALE. A type of chorale setting in which the hymn melody is subjected to elaborate melodic ornamentation in the soprano voice.

PARTITA. As used in organ music the term applies to a set of variations generally on a chorale melody.

PLEIN JEU. The most conservative composition in the French repertory, designed to be played on registers of the same name. Characteristic of it is a four- or five-voice etxture and clear harmonic movement. In many ways it is similar to the *toccata di durezza* although it lacks the experimental aspect of that form.

POINT D'ORGUE. A French composition of extensive length built on a pedal point.

PRE-IMITATION. The fugal development of a line of a chorale prior to its complete appearance as a *cantus firmus.*

PRELUDE also *PRAEAMBULUM* and *PRAELUDIUM.* A composition often similar to the toccata and the intonation. The term is more specifically applied to the large preludial and fugal constructions of the North-German school, constructions in which the various sections are mutually dependent upon one another.

PRELUDE AND FUGUE. The pairing of a preludial and a fugal movement. Either movement is constructed so that it can stand as an independent composition.

RECIT. A French composition for solo register. If the solo line lies in the treble, the *récit* is termed *en dessus;* if in the tenor, *en taille.* The bass *récits,* the *basse de trompette* and the *basse de cromorne,* are allegro movements characterized by wide leaps in the melodic lines.

RICERCAR. A form of instrumental composition serious in tone, fugal in texture, and often exploiting such devices as inversion, diminution, and augmentation. A derivative of the sixteenth-century motet, the *ricercar* remained throughout the seventeenth century the format in which composers sought to express their more learned ideas.

TABLATURE. See NOTATION.

TECLA. The Spanish generic term for keyboard; similar to German *Klavier.*

TENTO. Portuguese equivalent for *tiento.*

TIENTO. The term was originally applied to Spanish compositions similar in style to the *ricercar.* Later examples were more extensive compositions combining *ricercar* sections, variation technique, and toccata-style writing. These compositions, then, were more similar to the northern fantasias.

TIENTO DE CONTRAS. The Spanish equivalent for the French *point d'orgue.*

TIENTO DE FALSAS. A *tiento* with a more progressive harmonic idiom than was normally characteristic in seventeenth-century Spain.

TIENTO LLENO also *TIENTO PLENO.* A simple *tiento* similar to a *ricercar.*

TOCCATA. The term has a wider latitude of meaning in the seventeenth century than it later had. It can refer to a meditative composition designed for the Elevation of the Mass, to a rhapsodic composition of many contrasting sections, or to a flamboyant display piece. Many seventeenth-century toccatas combine sections in figurative style with sections in *ricercar* style.

TOCCATA DI DUREZZA E LIGATURE. A type of toccata always in four or more contrapuntal voices which move in prevailing half-note motion. This serious texture is the setting for numerous suspension dissonances, unusual harmonic progressions, and experimental chordal combinations.

THEMATIC VARIATION. The practice of presenting a theme in new rhythmic permutations. Even though a theme may appear in new and contrasting metrical environments, its essential melodic contour is generally retained in recognizable form. Such thematic variations are characteristic of the *canzone* and related forms.

TRICINIUM. An expansion of the *bicinium* into a trio texture. One voice carries the chorale melody generally in *cantus planus* fashion while the other voices are constructed of free counterpoint.

VAJO also *BAIXO.* The Spanish indication for a composition employing a bass solo register.

VERSET also VERSE. In the practice of alternation, a short section of music designed to substitute for a single passage of text.

VOLUNTARY. A free composition in the English repertory normally of modest dimension. Most examples were either entirely fugal or contained fugal sections. Similar pieces were often termed offertory, fancy, or verse.

Index

Italic page number indicates a major reference.